JAZZ PLANET

WITHDRAWN

JAZZ PLANET

Edited by E. Taylor Atkins

University Press of Mississippi / Jackson

www.upress.state.ms.us

The University Press of Mississippi is a member of the Association of
American University Presses.

Copyright © 2003 by University Press of Mississippi
All rights reserved
Manufactured in the United States of America

11 10 09 08 07 06 05 04 03   4 3 2 1
∞
Library of Congress Cataloging-in-Publication Data

Jazz planet / edited by E. Taylor Atkins.
    p. cm.
Includes bibliographical references (p.) and index.
    ISBN 1-57806-608-5 (cloth : alk. paper) — ISBN 1-57806-609-3
(pbk. : alk. paper)
1. Jazz—History and criticism. I. Atkins, E. Taylor, 1967–
ML3506.J47 2003
781.65'09—dc21   2003005322

British Library Cataloging-in-Publication Data available

For my parents,
Bill and Barbara,
and in memory of Connie

TABLE OF CONTENTS

ACKNOWLEDGMENTS

Working on this book has been such a pleasure and privilege. My first word of gratitude goes to the authors who have bestowed upon me the privilege of providing a forum through which to express their experiences and ideas about a music we all cherish. My only regret is that we could not all get together face-to-face to discuss our work collectively.

Seetha Srinivasan of the University Press of Mississippi tracked me down at the 2000 American Studies Association conference and convinced me that a book on transnational jazz was worth pursuing. Her initiative, patience, and guidance have made *Jazz Planet* possible and I thank her for entrusting me with this project. The ASA was perhaps a strange place to hook up with a historian of Japan, but I was there due to the prodding of Raúl Fernández, who heard the earliest draft of my thoughts on "multicultural jazz" and offered staunch encouragement for continuing on this path. It is thus fitting that Raúl's passionate and tireless efforts to document the history of Latin jazz are represented in an essay here. Muchas gracias, mi amigo.

I benefitted enormously from probing questions and helpful suggestions obtained at the Society for Ethnomusicology and American Studies Association conferences, the Reischauer Institute of Japanese Studies at Harvard University, the School of Music Colloquium Series at the University of Wisconsin-Madison, and the Cultural History Series at Indiana University-Bloomington. I am most grateful for advice I received from Nancy Wingfield, Heide Fehrenbach, and Ingrid Monson, all of whom helped me refine and sharpen points made in the introduction, and from Mississippi's anonymous reviewer, whose comments contributed enormously to the flow and consistency of the volume. Karl Neuenfeldt of Central Queensland University, Bundaberg, Australia, provided information on important scholars in the field of international jazz studies. Students in my seminar on "The Jazz Revolution"—Todd Casey, Nathan Van Gelder, Daniel Kirschner, and Omar Lozano—contributed insights and infectious enthusiasm that encouraged me in the planning stages. Reneé Kerwin, with characteristic patience, good humor, and attention to detail, fielded and formatted each chapter, and Karen Blaser saved me hours of labor by scanning previously published essays into workable formats. And finally, a shout-out to Eric Mogren for rescuing me from a predicament of a digital nature.

As always, my wife Zabrina has been a model of patience and emotional support, without which I could accomplish nothing of substance in work or life. May all of my labors as an educator and scholar facilitate the kind of cross-cultural understanding that will make life for my daughters Ella Rose and Annabelle a more pleasant adventure.

TOWARD A GLOBAL
HISTORY OF JAZZ

—*E. Taylor Atkins*

The January 2001 broadcast of Ken Burns's documentary film *Jazz* on public television dramatically elevated the profile of jazz music. Dedicated jazz aficionados hailed the program for bringing a long-neglected and underappreciated art form to the attention of a general audience. Amazon.com reported that sales of jazz recordings spiked immediately following the first episode, suggesting that Burns's caché as "America's storyteller" had generated interest in the music among viewers. Reviews of the film were, nonetheless, almost universally scathing. Many jazz scholars, critics, and artists found Burns's relatively tidy narrative flawed beyond redemption. Reviewers pummelled the filmmaker for devoting three episodes to the 1930s but only one to developments since 1960. Many objected to his gushing hagiographies of Louis Armstrong and Duke Ellington, which deprived other worthy artists of screen time. Most importantly, detractors charged, Burns effaced the contested nature of the jazz idiom itself, by relying too heavily on the ultra-conservative "[Stanley] Crouch- [Wynton] Marsalis line" on canonical figures and developments. However, few of Burns's American critics objected to the filmmaker's decision to omit virtually all mention of relevant developments in other countries: the setting of the jazz history narrative exclusively within the borders of the United States and the personal experiences of American musicians obviously struck most critics as natural and unproblematic.

Although jazz studies has often been criticized for hagiographic excesses and contextual myopia, seldom have its parochial parameters and implicit nationalism been questioned. This is partly a result of a general lack of serious scholarly attention to and artistic respect for jazz until quite late in the twentieth century. Most authors invariably presumed they had something to prove: that jazz (lauded as "the Sound of Surprise" by Whitney Balliett) was Serious Art. All other potential points of entry or lines of inquiry were subordinate to this agenda. The primary purpose of jazz history was to identify significant figures and works, thus facilitating the construction of a canon, and establishing standards of taste for judging future works. The resulting narratives detailed a natural stylistic evolution, guided by a select handful of "geniuses" who captivated the world with the sounds they produced (cf. DeVeaux 1991; Gennari 1991). Such approaches have undoubtedly succeeded in conferring aesthetic respectability and a sense of national accomplishment on the idiom, but too often at the expense of the rich social experiences and cultural crises that concurrently shaped and were shaped by the music.

Only a few rogues within academia—most notably Eric Hobsbawm, William Bruce Cameron, Alan Merriam, and Raymond Mack—deemed jazz worthy of scholarly scrutiny. Their respective studies in the mid-twentieth century hinted at how much could be learned simply by focusing on jazz audiences and no-name musicians instead of "geniuses," or by contextualizing jazz within the broader processes of modernism and cultural "massification." But it was arguably Amiri Baraka's stinging indictment in his 1961 essay "Jazz and the White Critic" that had the greatest impact on reforming the ways that people thought and wrote about jazz. Baraka passionately rebuked previous writers for artificially extricating jazz from the racialized contexts in which it had actually been created. The music could not possibly be gloriously autonomous of racial and class politics, Baraka contended, because those very struggles had in fact given birth to the music and sustained its ensuing development. Exceptional studies have followed, teaching us much about the social receptions of jazz, musical communities, cultural and musical hybridity, gender issues, the improvisational process, and mutual influences between jazz and other arts.[1]

Yet, with a handful of exceptions, American jazz historiography has consistently failed to look overseas for jams of consequence (Dean 1992, vii, xix–xx). Numerous histories—especially the Burns documentary—have convinced us that jazz is a conspicuous thread intricately woven into the fabric of American history. In an essay tellingly titled "The Inevitability of Jazz in America," James Lincoln Collier (1993) declares, "Jazz happened in America, and it could have happened only here" (3). It was the musical expression of national preoccupations and struggles with race, class, individualism, spontaneity, sexuality, national identity, progressive modernity, and the democratization of cultural production; it was also the result of a process of racial and cultural intermingling that defined the American experience. Jazz, we are told, encapsulates and embodies uniquely American national characteristics: the improviser publicly and extemporaneously probing the limits of the music and personal capacity exemplifies the quintessential rugged individualist testing the boundaries of the frontier or risking all for entrepreneurial glory. Moreover, jazz, though originally the subaltern musical idiom of an oppressed social caste whose status was defined by even minute traces of "African blood," ascended to become the nation's most conspicuous, inclusive, and celebrated cultural capital. Many nineteenth-century Americans despaired of ever making a significant national contribution to world culture, but their twentieth-first-century descendants are assured that the music represents a unique gift to the world.[2]

Practically all jazz discourse rests on the premise of American exceptionalism, the dogmatic conviction that "democracy, individualism, and social mobility, civil society, free enterprise, ingenuity and inventiveness, and material well-being" are peculiarly American traits. Rather than viewing frontier expansion, settler colonialism, slavery, immigration, industrialization, and cultural hybridization as transnational processes, many assume they are uniquely American, denying possible analogies to Australia, Brazil, Russia, and elsewhere (Adas 2001, 1695, 1698, 1720). Jazz, though certainly born on U.S. soil, was both product and instigator of early-twentieth-century processes and trends that were global in scope: the mass manufacture of culture, urbanization, the leisure revolution, and primitivism. It is this fact—combined with the sheer, and early, ubiquity of the music—that leads us to conclude that, practically from its inception, jazz was a harbinger of what we now call "globalization." In no one's mind have the music's ties to its country of origin been severed, yet the historical record proves that it has for some time had global significance, if not necessarily for the commonly accepted, purely aesthetic reasons. Jazz exists in our collective imagination as both a *national* and *postnational* music, but is studied almost exclusively in the former incarnation. Our purpose here is to recuperate its career as a transgressor of the idea of the nation, as an agent of globalization.

In the early twentieth century, innovations in communication technologies, radio broadcasting, mass print media, and sound recording
coincided with the height of colonialism and a new ethos of cooperative
diplomacy emerging after the First World War, making it virtually impossible to contain jazz music, its performance techniques, and its ethos of
personal liberation within the borders of one country. The communication and transportation infrastructures and financial networks that enabled
far-flung empires and multinational corporations, and made the new
League of Nations a credible institution, ensured that virtually from its
inception jazz would have a global audience. Moreover, the tumultuous
social and cultural conditions that, in Collier's estimation, made Americans "ready for jazz"—the rise of mass media and a show business infrastructure, the willingness to question prior social and gender values—were
simultaneously in place (albeit to varying degrees) throughout much of
the world. Jazz, in fact, represented nothing more profoundly than the
coevalness of modern time: as they listened and danced to jazz, people
imagined that they were experiencing modernity simultaneously with
their counterparts in distant lands.

In 1922, a mere five years after the first jazz recordings were pressed, it
was already possible for the *New York Times*'s Burnet Hershey to conclude
an account of a world tour with this: "I set out on a tour of the world with
the wanderer's lure of adventure, strange lands and quaint customs. My
trail led along curious rough byways, but all along the route, yawping after
me, ululating along with me, blatantly greeting me, was the inevitable jazz.
No sooner had I shaken off the dust of some city and slipped almost out
of earshot of its jazz bands than zump-zump-zump, toodle-oodle-doo,
right into another I went. Never was there a cessation of this universal
potpourri of jazz. Each time I would discover it at a different stage of
metamorphosis and sometimes hard to recognize, but unmistakably it
was an attempt at jazz" (quoted in Walser 1999, 25–26).

Jazz's global journeys were accomplished with astonishing speed, a
consequence both of expanding American influence in the wake of World
War I, and of the emergence of the recording industry, which "from its
inception" was "transnational in character" (Jones 2001, 54; Gronow and
Saunio 1998, 11–12). The southward expansion of U.S. economic interests
and military muscle, into Cuba, Panama, Puerto Rico, Haiti, and Mexico,

guaranteed that the music would venture into the Caribbean and Latin America. U.S. intervention in the Great War coincided precisely with the explosion of jazz onto the national consciousness, and the new music accompanied the Doughboys on their journeys "over there." James Reese Europe's "Hell Fighters" and Will Marion Cook's Southern Syncopated Orchestra entertained war-weary audiences in the U.K. and France (cf. Shack 2001); Cook's clarinetist—a "black, fat boy with white teeth and narrow forehead" of considerable talent named Sidney Bechet—so enraptured Swiss conductor Ernst Ansermet that he was moved to compose a musicologically astute tribute in *Revue Romande* (Walser 1999, 9–11). Within two years of waxing the first jazz records, the Original Dixieland Jazz Band was jamming for King George V in London and "rocking the Hammersmith Palais de Danse" (Oliver 1975, 141; Goddard 1979; Gronow and Saunio 1998, 29).

By that time, jazz was making waves in the Pacific and Indian Oceans as well as the Atlantic. American, Filipino, Russian, British, and Japanese dance bands traversed a circuit extending from Kōbe, Shanghai, Manila, Singapore, and Hong Kong to Kuala Lumpur, Bangkok, Colombo, Bombay, and Johannesburg, entertaining expatriate communities and native colonial elites in hotel ballrooms and aboard luxury liners. Sidney Bechet and Buck Clayton preached with their horns in the Soviet Union and Shanghai, respectively, while pianist Teddy Weatherford wandered the Dutch and British colonies of Southeast and South Asia, at each stop teaching musicians of various nationalities about the blues. By the mid-1920s, Filipinos— colonial subjects of the United States—had earned a reputation as the ablest jazz musicians in the Pacific Rim. Performing in hotel ballrooms in Kōbe and Ōsaka, Filipinos set the performance standard that inspired Japan's first jazz musicians; their reputation was such that they commanded the highest salaries among non-Americans in the myriad dance halls and cabarets that so enlivened nightlife in interwar Shanghai.

Lest we assume, however, that the world's peoples were either universally seduced by jazz, or hapless in the face of a cultural imperialist onslaught, we must remember that seldom did the music's encroachment go uncontested. As several of the essays in this collection demonstrate, critics of every conceivable political persuasion, from Ireland to Japan, China to the Netherlands, the Soviet Union to South Africa, were simply horrified by jazz's significance and omnipresence. Whereas, as Ballantine contends, in Africa jazz could become an emblem of racial pride, in other parts of the world its black pedigree was cause for alarm. Its proliferation among the decadent bourgeoisie in North America, East Asia, and Western Europe made it detestable to leftist and rightist critics alike. Some attributed to jazz powers to induce Pavlovian responses, such as uncontrollable libidinal surges or suspension of rational thought. Others feared that jazz portended no less than the extinction of recently crafted and thus fragile notions of national self, as fashioned by fascist regimes and anticolonial movements. In the era between the World Wars jazz was virtually the exclusive possession of self-styled urban modernites and *nouveaux riches*, signifying their break with the *ancien régime* and their essential difference from sodbusting bumpkins and hidebound moralists. Jazz indeed jeopardized national unity and aggravated existing social tensions by sharpening awareness of the "unevenness" of modernity (Harootunian 2000, 3), the unequal distribution of its technologies and opportunities. Knowledge of these types of responses should chasten those who contend that jazz is a "universal music" (Bourne 1980).

Nor did the music itself remain unaltered by its overseas encounters. What Hershey heard as "versions" and "attempts at jazz" might more properly be regarded as early ventures by musicians in various locales to adapt jazz to the social circumstances and musical standards with which they were more familiar (cf. Nettl 1985). By the 1930s and '40s, fully conceived efforts to indigenize or nationalize jazz were underway in the Soviet Union, Japan, Republican China, South Africa, and Nazi Germany. By using indigenous folk repertoire, melodic scales, rhythmic patterns, or instrumentation, or by simply substituting ideologically palatable, patriotic content for standard romantic fare, musicians (and, in many cases, their political overlords) sought to neutralize the (African) American pedigree of jazz, thereby reinscribing those national identities to which jazz posed such an ominous threat. Standard histories credit American jazz musicians such as Dizzy Gillespie, John Coltrane, and Randy Weston with initiating musical cross-pollinations, but precedents for what Ted Gioia (1997) calls "world fusion" were in fact set before World War II, in Li Jinhui's "yellow music," Barnabas von Géczy and Oskar Joost's "German jazz," Hattori Ryôichi and Sugii Kôichi's "Japanese jazz," South African *marabi* and *mbaqanga*, and

Sovetskii Dzhaz (see Jones 2001, 73–104; Kater 1989, 21–22; Atkins 2001, 132–39; Pope 1998; Ballantine 1993; and Starr 1994, 175).

The expansion of U.S. security and economic commitments throughout much of the globe after World War II ensured an even wider presence for jazz. Native musicians in Pacific Asia and Western Europe were hired to perform for the increasing numbers of U.S. armed forces personnel stationed in their lands, thus laying the groundwork for the nurturing of indigenous jazz talent. Moreover, a number of important American jazz artists (e.g., Joe Henderson, Hampton Hawes, and Frank Foster) served in the Armed Forces overseas, frequently jamming with their native counterparts. At the height of the Cold War, a belief in the music's inherent democratizing potential motivated the State Department to deputize jazz musicians as counterrevolutionary agents and cultural ambassadors to non-aligned or decolonizing countries. Few of the nascent nation-states wading through the muck of decolonization, and weighing the respective merits of capitalism and communism, were exempt from such attention. Jazz was America's "Secret Sonic Weapon" in the war against communism, a famous *New York Times* headline proclaimed in 1955. To counter Soviet propaganda about segregation and racial injustice in the United States, the U.S. government paraded African American musicians before myriad peoples, hoping to convince global audiences of its racial tolerance and inclusiveness (see for example Davenport 1999). On these State Department tours the music was jammin' but the message was dead serious: if you choose communism, kiss this sweet music goodbye. Jazz was emblematic of the radical differences in human liberty between the "free world" and the communist realm,[3] perhaps for none more poignantly than those who lived within that latter domain. Czech writer Josef Škvorecky (1988) characterized jazz as "a sharp thorn in the sides of the power-hungry men, from Hitler to Brezhnev, who successively ruled my native land."

[N]o matter what LeRoi Jones says to the contrary, the essence of this music, this "way of making music," is not simply protest. Its essence is something far more elemental: an *élan vital*, a forceful vitality, an explosive creative energy as breathtaking as that of any true art, that may be felt even in the saddest of blues. Its effect is cathartic.

But of course, when the lives of individuals and communities are controlled by powers that themselves remain uncontrolled—slavers, czars, führers, first secretaries, marshals, generals and generalissimos, ideologists of dictatorships at either end of the spectrum—then creative energy becomes a protest. . . . Popular mass art, like jazz, becomes mass protest. That's why the ideological guns and sometimes even the police guns of all dictatorships are aimed at the men with the horns. (83–84; see also Jarab 1993)

Reports seeped from under the Iron Curtain that some thirty to eighty million people put their lives on hold for two hours every night to listen to Willis Conover's jazz program *Music U.S.A.* on Voice of America. The Cold War campaign's apparent success rendered jazz's assumed universality into a self-fulfilling prophecy, solidifying a sense that jazz was America's inimitable gift to the world.

Precisely because it had originated among an oppressed group in the United States, however, jazz was a double-edged sword when brandished in postcolonial contexts and ideological skirmishes. So versatile was its symbolic utility that jazz frequently expressed indignation at overbearing American arrogance. As the music of a tormented people, many argued, jazz was the perfect vehicle for expressing the "Third World solidarity" articulated at the 1955 Bandung Conference (Abdulgani 1981). It provided opportunities for peoples of color around the world to build alliances and to envision alternative, "Afro-Asian" transnationalisms that rejected exploitative empires and the zero-sum consequences of Cold War alignments. Trumpeter-cum-Cold Warrior Dizzy Gillespie (who had been under FBI surveillance for alleged subversive activities) chose to ignore prepared statements and rather "told Greeks, Turks, Pakistanis, and Brazilians 'the truth' about American race relations" (Peretti 1997, 115). Several high-profile African American musicians converted to Islam or explored Zen, flagrantly rejecting philosophical and aesthetic systems tainted by "Western colonialism." Moreover, they incorporated West African, Caribbean, Arabic, South American, and South Asian elements into their music as a gesture of respect for artistic heritages dismissed as "savage" in the colonial era (Budds 1990; Weinstein 1992). Their counterparts in places such as Nigeria, Japan, South Africa, Cuba, India, and Brazil likewise evinced renewed interest in creating jazz infused with indigenous aesthetic principles and timbral attributes. The result was a considerable expansion of jazz's sonic palette and expressive potential, and a multilateral, truly global exchange of musical ideas, inspiration, and influence.

The eminent Japanese jazz writer Yui Shôichi (1918–1998) dubbed this phenomenon "jazz nationalism." According to his theory (first articulated in the late 1960s), jazz, rather than sweeping away the diversity of global cultures, provides a mechanism for rediscovering indigenous traditions. Yui argued that as ethnic pride and liberation movements swept the globe in the postcolonial era, peoples of color drew on their respective heritages to create original music that was both part of a universal language called *jazz* and a singular expression of national or ethnic identity. "The movement for 'national independence' [*minzoku jiritsu*] that surged through each country [in the sixties]," Yui wrote, "became the motive power for what must be called 'jazz nationalism' [*jazu nashonarizumu*], 'to be free of America' [*Amerika banare*]" (Atkins 2001, 246–47). The U.S. State Department may have hoped jazz would irrevocably bind other nations to its vision of a capitalistic and democratic "Free World." Instead, artists and audiences around the world reconceptualized jazz to represent liberation from (white) American hegemony.

The evolution of jazz from local subaltern expression to cosmopolitan art form has typically been explained as purely a result of the music's intrinsic charm, and displayed as evidence in a triumphal narrative of benign American cultural achievement. Of course, many did indeed find the music appealing, liberating, and refreshing, for a variety of reasons that are by no means mysterious to those of us who love it ourselves. But this supposed aesthetic detachment from base politics has too often obscured the relationship between jazz's ubiquity, colonialism, nationalist politics, and American military, economic, and cultural hegemony. We must therefore acknowledge that jazz's march to global prominence was facilitated in the interwar period by the conditions of "colonial modernity" (Barlow 1997, 6; Jones 2001), which inexorably linked the economies, political systems, and cultural lives of the world's peoples in an exploitative global framework, and in the post–World War II era by strategic realignments and upheavals associated with decolonization and the Cold War. We must also recognize the ways in which various nations' jazz cultures deployed the music to assert a defiant transnational imaginary that refused to concede to (white) American dominance.

In the face of such evidence, we may take to task not only jazz scholars for their neglect of these matters, but also those ethnographers and theoreticians of globalization who have so undervalued jazz's role as a crucial agent in that very process. We expect that readers of *Jazz Planet* will be persuaded that our understanding of jazz, both as a sociocultural force and as a musical idiom, is significantly impaired by construing it as a narrowly *national* art, expressive of uniquely American experiences and characteristics, and splendidly autonomous from considerations of global politics, cultural power, and national identity. Collectively the essays demonstrate the rewards of expanding the geo-cultural setting of the jazz historical narrative, which can fundamentally reshape our notions of what jazz music is, who creates it, and what it means. But we also view this as an opportunity to test existing theories of globalization, and particularly to critique their overwhelmingly presentist biases.

Generally speaking, the essays here illustrate the inadequacy of "cultural imperialist" notions of globalization as a unidirectional outflow of ideas and cultural commodities from a hypothetical center, resulting in cultural atrophy at a hypothetical periphery. An emerging consensus rather emphasizes the "local" consumption of "global" cultural commodities—indeed asserting the inextricable linkage of globalism and localism—but also depicts this consumption as fraught with tension. In other words, globalization simultaneously subverts and solidifies older forms of identification (nationality, gender, race, locality, etc.). The "local" thereby reasserts itself in relation (or opposition) to the "global"; they are indeed mutually constitutive categories in that each depends on the other for its discursive coherence (see Wilson and Dissanayake 1996, 2–3; Ching 2000).

While no one here takes lightly the serious issues of asymmetry and "cultural imperialism" raised by the ubiquity of jazz and its association with U.S. economic and military hegemony, the essays in this volume also demonstrate that peoples around the world have been actively constructing their own systems for performing, understanding, evaluating, and discussing jazz. Though for many it was emblematic of the annihilation of indigenous social, cultural, and aesthetic value systems, jazz has for others enabled a rediscovery, redefinition, or renewed appreciation of local traditions, which then were marshalled to broaden and transform the music's expressive capacities (see Ballantine 1993, 23; Atkins 2001, 248–55). In jazz we thus find evidence to support a notion of "global/local synergy" (Wilson and Dissanayake 1996; Robertson 1992, 177–78; Fehrenbach and Poiger 2000, xiv); but we also find evidence to support Frederic Jameson's contention that globalization "intensifies binary relations" (center-periphery, local-global, native-foreign) that are rife with "tension or antagonism" (Jameson and Miyoshi 1998, xii).

However, the essays here diverge from most depictions of globalization as a very recent (late-twentieth-century) phenomenon. In an incisive critique of Arjun Appadurai's (1996) influential ideas on globalization, Andrew Jones takes exception with the assumption that global flows of capital and culture are "historically nonpareil." While the intensity and pace of globalizing processes in the late twentieth century are undeniable, Jones posits, "it is important to keep the continuities that bind us to earlier 'transnationalisms' firmly in mind, if only because they serve to remind us of linkages between colonial power and capital that are by no means irrelevant to our current situation" (Jones 2001, 57–58). A focus on jazz—not as a *national* art but as an early *postnational* art—enables us to locate the "prehistory of globalization" (Shami 2000) in the age of colonial modernity, and to examine a cultural form that expressed the energies and anxieties of many of the planet's denizens for most of the last century.

The preceding narrative account of jazz's journeys, though sketchy, offers some proof that a transnational entertainment infrastructure was well established in the early 1900s, and helped shape a burgeoning *global consciousness* that coexisted, if uneasily, with the rampant nationalisms that made that century so violent. That is to say, jazz provided moments and spaces in which it was possible for peoples around the world to imagine they were participating in a cultural movement and a historical trajectory that transcended national boundaries (i.e., modernism, the "Free World" crusade against communism, or anticolonial "Afro-Asian" concord). Of course such global consciousness could only occasionally and temporarily dislodge other, more primary affiliations based on notions of nation, region, gender, ideology, or class, but it remained viable nonetheless, in no small part due to the seemingly universal power of jazz.

A fundamental purpose of the present volume is to address these deficiencies in the respective literatures on jazz and on globalization—and indeed to convince the reader that those literatures cannot really be detached from one another. The handful of books and articles on jazz outside of the United States, superb as several of them are, are simply too scattered to accomplish a systematic reform of parochial jazz studies method, let alone to reinsert jazz within the narrative of globalization. *Jazz Planet's* mission is to gather between two covers important studies that point not only to the global impact of jazz music but also to the variety of local responses it elicited and the significant alterations to which it has been subjected overseas. The authors are less concerned with presenting purely descriptive, narrative histories of jazz in various locales, than with using jazz to explore in depth particular social, cultural, aesthetic, and musical problems in their local manifestations. They offer powerful testimony to the intellectual and aesthetic benefits of scrutinizing jazz beyond the borders of the United States. We maintain that such scrutiny detracts neither from the artistic accomplishments of the great jazz artists, nor from our enjoyment of the music. Rather, it enhances our understanding of this music's capacity to unify and divide, include and exclude, thrill and shock, entertain and enlighten, and otherwise enliven our existence.

Essays in the "Local Heroes" section share a common purpose of spotlighting the innovative contributions of non-Americans to the jazz idiom. With very few exceptions (e.g., Django Reinhardt, Akiyoshi Toshiko, Josef Zawinul, or Antonio Carlos Jobim) non-Americans are systematically slighted in descriptions of the music's artistic development. Scholars and teachers of jazz history with whom I have discussed these matters attribute the absence of non-Americans from the pantheon (and thus the curriculum) less to parochial tendencies than to the issue of "influence." Webs of influence are what hold the jazz master narrative together. If foreign local heroes were *innovative* yet *influenced no one*, they ask, why should we include them? This emphasis on genealogies of influence strikes me as one of the major problems with jazz historiography. Whom, and how many, must one influence to merit inclusion? A favorite Zen *kôan* asks, "If a tree falls in the woods and no one is there to hear it, does it make a sound?" One might similarly ask, "If a jazz musician somewhere in the world takes a revolutionary musical step, and no *Americans* are there to hear it, does it count as a jazz innovation?" It is clear that reedist Joe Harriott (U.K.), guitarist Takayanagi Masayuki (Japan), and baritone saxophonist Christopher Ngcukana (South Africa), for instance, influenced their colleagues significantly; but asymmetries in the international distribution of recordings guaranteed that their meager recorded outputs would practically never reach U.S. shores. If their influence remained "local" does it not count as influence? If they did not influence *American* artists, is their exclusion from the jazz chronicle justified? It seems clear that if we are to expand the boundaries of jazz history we need also to expand our notions of what counts as "influential," or abrogate our obsession with "influence" altogether, for current evaluations of "influence" merely reinforce the parochial tendencies here under attack.

Contributors in the "Local Heroes" section shed long overdue light on those non-American artists who heeded the jazz aesthetic's demand to constantly "innovate" and transform the music, those musicians who became leaders within their communities and nations, who approached jazz performance in original ways by transcending the hegemonic "influence" of America's jazz titans. Collectively, they challenge us to consider how the existence of such figures might affect common assumptions of an American monopoly on creative initiative in jazz. Awareness of these local heroes and their music should force future historians of jazz to reconfigure or diversify the jazz pantheon. At the very least, it is important that they acknowledge that the evolution of jazz as an art did not occur solely within the borders of the United States, but rather in a global context in which musicians from a variety of musical traditions exchanged information and inspiration.

We should also put to rest narratives depicting an ever-resilient jazz absorbing or appropriating from other musics (Taylor [1986]) while retaining its essential core untransformed by the process (in what might plausibly be read as a neo-colonialist act). Might we not alternately conceive of indigenous musics as adaptive yet resilient enough to absorb jazz? The observations of Denis Crowdy and Michael Goddard (1999) suggest just that. They contend that in Papua New Guinea jazz neither overwhelms nor absorbs indigenous musical forms, but rather constitutes little more than a "tool" for local popular music production: "the importance of learning jazz for local players lies in its potential for application as a technical and performance resource in the pursuit of contemporary local music projects rather than as an idiom in itself" (59, 62).

The resilience and adaptability of indigenous musical forms, and the concomitant expansion of jazz's sonic and expressive palette, are common themes of the "Local Heroes" essays. Linda Williams, for instance, demon-strates that the "triplet-rhythmic motif" basic to earlier native musical forms remains a foundational aspect of jazz performance in Zimbabwe. Raúl Fernández likewise contends that Cuban innovations in jazz have maintained solid, identifiable roots in indigenous Afro-Caribbean rhyth-mic traditions such as *habanera* and *son*. Benjamin Givan argues that gui-tarist Django Reinhardt created a viable subgenre (*jazz manouche*, or "Gypsy jazz"), which drew on and expanded on existing Roma guitar techniques and repertoire. Warren Pinckney documents a long history of thriving exchange between jazz and South Asian musics. Through the use of Carnatic singing styles and raga-based improvisations in identifiably jazzy contexts, an "Indo-jazz" subgenre emerges which demonstrates the "elective affinities" of rhythm and improvisation between the two tradi-tions. Christopher Bakriges describes how European jazz artists, though clearly now enveloped in an African musical diaspora, labored to root their "creative improvisational music" in their own respective localities. This process is further documented in Stefano Zenni's analysis of Gian-luigi Trovesi's oeuvre. European jazz "is nourished by an open dialogue with different traditions," Zenni maintains: in Trovesi's compositions Renaissance-era Italian music dances with Balkan folk and African Amer-ican jazz elements, resulting in a music whose "nationality" may be open to question but whose "individuality" is not. National musical identity is a key concern among the Brazilian artists whose *música instrumental* is the subject of Acacio Tadeu de C. Piedade's essay. Sensitive to the potentially humiliating effects of cultural imperialism, Brazilian jazz musicians strive "to avoid contamination from the *bebop* paradigm and to seek an expres-sion that is more rooted in Brazil," by drawing on purportedly more "authentic," indigenous musicalities such as *chorinho*.

Another, related theme revolves around the search for individual musi-cal identities, a basic expectation of all jazz artists whether they are stylis-tic innovators or not. The challenge for non-American musicians has been to accomplish this in a field in which Americans were virtually guar-anteed to garner more exposure and recognition, even in their own respective native lands (see Atkins 2001, 33). The authors here describe multiple ways in which artists in various locales have struggled with the presumption of American creative initiative in jazz, and the crafting of collective and/or personal musical identities. More importantly, they do so without reifying the concept of "national dialects" of jazz based on spurious notions of "national character." Instead, they carefully describe how artists make conscious use of their historical and social circumstances, thus allowing for portrayals of individual imaginative achievement that are not essentially culture-bound. Our collective aim in presenting such evidence, of course, is to globalize narratives of jazz's musical and aesthetic development, and to prick the consciences of those who have either presumed that nothing of substance in jazz could occur outside of the United States, or who have, at best, ghettoized such developments as mere exotica tangential to the "mainstream."

Chapters in "Local Politics" section challenge the triumphal assumption of jazz's "universal" appeal by examining the ways that jazz has been perceived, discussed, debated, and integrated into local contests over identity, power, aesthetics, and status. What role has jazz played in the construction of national, ethnic, gender, and class identities? How has jazz healed or exacerbated social cleavages? How has jazz figured in subaltern revolts, or been used to contrive social cohesion? How does jazz affect discussions of globalization, modernization, urbanization, and indigenous cultural atrophy? How has it been understood in terms of indigenous or imported aesthetic hierarchies and standards of taste? These are some of the questions addressed under the rubric of "Local Politics."

An assortment of overlapping themes appear in these studies. The most basic is that *jazz matters*: it was hardly of peripheral interest to the various ideologues, bureaucrats, artists, law enforcement officials, dictators, writers, politicians, educators, psychologists, activists, scholars, and common folk whose opinions pepper these pages. Rather, they believed that jazz lie at the very heart of the vexing social ills, political problems, and cultural fluctuations they faced. It is, quite frankly, amazing how many discussions, on any number of seemingly unrelated issues, in which jazz is prominent. Given jazz's dual reputation as an American national music and a global art, it is perhaps not surprising that it should figure into debates on the integrity of national identity. Considering that early jazz accompanied some rather breathtakingly athletic, even suggestive, dance steps, neither is it any wonder that jazz featured prominently in discourses on gendered norms of behavior and sexual conduct (see for instance Poiger 2000, 128). Less obvious, however, is the relevance of jazz to class antagonisms, liberal or revolutionary ideologies, intranational regional rivalries, modernization efforts, adolescent psychology, and racial "self-improvement" campaigns.

Multiple themes of ideology, statecraft, public morality, and cultural integrity emerge here. Johan Fornäs navigates the complexities of Swedish responses to jazz in the interwar period, analyzing the ways in which Swedes used jazz, the "ultimate expression" of modernity, to comprehend dizzying transformations in prevailing notions of racial and aesthetic hierarchy, modernity and primitivism, masculinity and femininity. Andrew Jones offers a similarly kaleidoscopic depiction of Chinese reactions to jazz in the same chronological period, arguing that jazz—"an overlapping set of distinctly modern ways of making and consuming music"—signified both "a stylish emblem of China's participation in the culture of global modernity, and a means of critiquing the colonial exploitation upon which that system feeds." Michael Molasky takes us into the postwar era to examine the influence of jazz on Japanese literature: in the fiction of writers such as Itsuki Hiroyuki, jazz was a vehicle enabling an empowering role reversal, which assigned roles of authority and virility to Japanese protagonists and thus assuaged the humiliation of American occupation and domination.

Jazz's ambiguous status as both the genuine, heartfelt folk expression of an oppressed people and the mass-produced, soulless soundtrack of bourgeois frivolity made it either attractive or repellent to leftist intellectuals and activists at the height of the international communist movement (cf. Adorno 1981). In recounting how jazz fared one of several ideological sea-changes in Soviet politics, Frederick Starr writes that Communist party officials bounced between characterizing jazz as the legitimate proletarian music of a suppressed racial group, and as the product of bourgeois decadence and Jewish capital. Bruce Johnson depicts the establishment of the Australian Jazz Convention (the world's oldest annual jazz festival) as ripe with political significance, signifying an "internationally emergent social consciousness" among political progressives in Australia.

Considering jazz's African roots, it is perhaps not surprising that its political implications in Africa would be significantly different than in Europe, Asia, and Oceania: there were at least some Africans who were willing to welcome jazz "back" as their own, as the product of exiled black brethren who had further developed musical raw materials originating in Africa. As its global popularity spread, jazz thus had potential political importance, for it demonstrated black creative genius at a time when peoples of African descent perennially occupied the bottom rung of colonial racial hierarchies. Indeed, jazz presaged the imminent "Africanization" of global culture (an omen not lost on observers in Japan, Germany, the United States, and elsewhere), a potential counterweight to the "Westernization" occurring under the colonial euphemism *mission civilisatrice*. Christopher Ballantine demonstrates these singular features of African political discourses concerning jazz, by outlining the divergent strategies adopted by liberal and radical black organizations in South Africa to deploy musical performance in their broader battle to secure self-respect and racial justice.

While the essays reflect the diversity of their respective authors and cultural settings, together these chapters testify not only to the global reach and transformative powers and adaptive capabilities of jazz, but also to the mediating powers of indigenous cultural values and practices in the consumption of "global" culture. While some readers may come away from the volume further convinced of jazz's universality, others may find more striking the transformation of the music itself as it encounters resilient, malleable native practices and aesthetics. These findings must then be reconciled with the popular and rarely contested notion that jazz is an easily definable artistic idiom, the product and reflection of a uniquely American national experience.

LOCAL HEROES

"SI NO TIENE SWING NO VAYA' A LA RUMBA"

Cuban Musicians and Jazz

—*Raúl A. Fernández*

For many in the world of jazz, the history of jazz in Cuba dates to the recent appearance on the scene of brilliant musicians such as Chucho Valdés and Paquito D'Rivera. Others regard the history of Afro-Cuban or Latin jazz as one branch of the U.S.-centered development of jazz itself, a branch that developed almost exclusively in the United States (see Roberts 1999; Hasse 2000; and Ward and Burns 2000).

In this paper I argue that there is a long history of jazz in Cuba, nearly as long as the history of jazz in the United States itself. Cuban musicians developed a separate and independent jazz tradition in the twentieth century. In the pages that follow I explore the history of Cuban musicians in jazz, a story that has been obscured by the manner and conditions in which it was developed by musicians inside and outside the island. Inside Cuba, jazz-oriented musicians plied their trade in a nearly subterranean manner, as the powerful and complex local dance music occupied center-stage for most of the century. Inside the United States, expatriate Cuban musicians became submerged in the world of jazz as the music grew and developed. Together, Cuban jazz musicians inside and outside the island lay the foundations for a new hybrid of hybrids, a mixture of jazz and Afro-Cuban music, that became a most exciting genre all of its own under the name of Latin jazz. Of course, just as jazz was not created and transformed only in the United States by U.S. musicians, the development of Latin jazz was not limited to Cuban musicians, but included artists from Puerto Rico, the Dominican Republic, the United States and many other countries. In this essay I excavate and bring together, as a single story, the musical travails of Cuban jazz musicians in the nineteenth and twentieth century inside and outside of Cuba, and the contributions they made to Latin jazz, and therefore, to jazz as a world art form.

IN THE BEGINNING

Cuban musicians, and Cuban music, were participants in the birth of jazz in New Orleans. The musics of Cuba and the United States came together for the first time in New Orleans and Havana in the mid-nineteenth century.[1] Throughout the nineteenth century there were active trade links between Havana, the capital of the major Spanish island colony in the Caribbean, and the Crescent City. Musicians, too, traveled back and forth between Havana and New Orleans. For example, in 1836, an opera company based in Havana relocated to New Orleans. The opera's Italian conductor, Luigi Gabici, became an important New Orleans music teacher. He tutored Cuban-Mexican clarinetist Thomas Tio, an event which would have important consequences in the birth and development of jazz. Thomas's son, Lorenzo Tio, Sr., also became a clarinetist and teacher, and his grandson, Lorenzo Tio. Jr., became a prominent player in early jazz and the tutor of such great jazz musicians as Sidney Bechet, Barney Bigard, Jimmie Noone, and Johnny Dodds.[2] In his later life, Tio Jr., sold sketches and fragments of tunes to jazz musicians. He sold some to Barney Bigard and to Duke Ellington, including "Mood Indigo."

Traveling in the opposite direction, composer Louis M. Gottschalk, born in New Orleans to a Haitian immigrant family in 1829, lived in Cuba and other Caribbean islands for extended periods in the 1850s and 1860s. In Cuba he met Nicolás Ruiz Espadero and Manuel Saumell, two musicians who would have a profound influence on his work. Saumell in particular, a master of the *danza* and the *habanera*, influenced not only Gottschalk, but also ragtime (Starr 1995, 184).

In the last decades of the nineteenth century Cuban and Mexican musicians in New Orleans composed and played Cuban *habanera*, the *danza* and the *danzón*, the latest Cuban dance rage. The strong presence of Cuban music New Orleans at that time has been credited with shaping the rhythmic styles of early jazz. Composer Jelly Roll Morton, who was raised by godparents of Cuban ancestry, learned to play Cuban *habaneras* from a Mexican guitar teacher. He claimed to always put "Spanish tinges" in his music. Drummer Baby Dodds suggested that even the style of playing the blues in New Orleans was influenced by the *habanera*. "The blues," he said, "were played very slow . . . in a Spanish rhythm" (Dodds 1959, 11).

The *habanera* rhythm was adopted by several U.S. composers such as W. C. Handy. He became familiar with Cuban music in 1900 when he traveled to the island with a band and used the *habanera* beat in his famous "St. Louis Blues." The history of early jazz in New Orleans is full of musicians with Spanish last names, many of Cuban origin. There was, for example, Manuel Perez, born in Havana in 1863. A former cigar maker, Perez played cornet with the Onward Brass Band before forming his own band, the Imperial Orchestra in 1900. The Reliance Brass band, directed by Jack "Papa" Laine often employed Cuban musicians such as cornetist Manuel Mello and clarinetist Alcide "Yellow" Nuñez, whom Pee Wee Russell named as one of his greatest influences. To sum up, the presence of Cuban musicians and Cuban musical elements in New Orleans during the incubation period of early jazz is clearly supported by the historical record.

AFTER JAZZ

On the other side of the Florida straits, shortly after jazz developed its own identity as a new genre in the early twentieth century, Cuban professional popular musicians in the island brought it into their repertoire. After the Spanish American War of 1898 the United States occupied the island, maintaining a quasi-protectorate over it until 1933. U.S. investments, professionals, and tourists flowed to the island with the sound of jazz close behind. As early as 1914 there were musical groups in existence in Cuba using the same instruments used in U.S. jazz bands, such as saxophones, cornets, and the drum set, although whether they actually played jazz is subject to speculation due to the absence of recordings. Eventually such ensembles became known as *jazzbands* in Spanish. By the 1920s hotel and show bands in Havana had certainly incorporated jazz into their repertoires. It is possible, even likely, that the kind of jazz they played resembled the "society" jazz sound favored by the likes of the Paul Whiteman Orchestra in the United States at that time (Acosta 2001a, ch. 2).

On the other hand there is evidence that some of these Cuban musicians were familiar with the sounds of the most "authentic" U.S. jazz of the time. A case in point is Alberto Socarrás who, after playing in *jazzbands* and symphony orchestras in Cuba, migrated to the United States in 1927. Socarrás toured Europe with Lew Leslie's stage music Blackbirds in 1928, and in 1929 made the first recording of a jazz flute solo, in "Have You Ever Felt That Way," with the Clarence Williams band. Thus, as early as the 1920s, a Cuban musician, a recent arrival in the United States, made a significant contribution to the history of instrumental jazz soloing (Salazar 1993). In the 1930s Socarrás played in both jazz bands and Cuban dance bands in New York. He traveled back and forth between Havana and New York, played flute for Benny Carter and wrote arrangements for Cab Calloway and Tommy Dorsey. In the late thirties he organized the Socarrás and His Magic Flute Orchestra, in which the young Dizzy Gillespie played for a while. The musical career of Socarrás, one of many Cuban jazz musicians active in Havana in the late 1920s, indicates that Cuban musicians had quickly absorbed new developments in jazz and were proactive participants in its evolution.

Simultaneous with the development of jazz, the 1920s witnessed the appearance of recordings of the Cuban musical genre known as the *son*. A fusion of Spanish and African elements, the *son* reached the United States in the early 1930s under the name of rhumba or rumba—an unfortunate nomenclature which has led to much confusion, as *rumba* is the name of a different, drum-based, Afro-Cuban folkloric genre. The first rhumba that made a big hit in the United States in 1930 was "The Peanut Vendor" ("El Manisero"), a composition by Cuba's Moisés Simons. Although Simons and his "Peanut Vendor" have always been identified as quintessentially "Cuban," he also led a *jazzband* in Havana in the 1920s, the same in which Socarrás had tested jazz waters. In the early 1930s, Simons worked for a while in Paris. There he played and recorded with a *jazzband* led by another Cuban expatriate musician, saxophonist Filiberto Rico. The latter led a band, Rico's Creole Band, which included Cuban and other Caribbean musicians, and played in a style similar to that of earlier New Orleans groups. Some of their recorded tunes included definite jazz-style improvisations. The work of Rico's Creole Band can justly be seen as one of the early precursors of the Afro-Cuban jazz explosion of the 1940s (Acosta 2001b).

The first Cuban musician from this epoch who, while remaining in Cuba, fully mastered the jazz idiom was Armando Romeu, who played saxophone and flute for American bands touring the island in the 1920s. In the 1930s he toured Latin America with his own jazz band. Beginning in

1941, Romeu's orchestra became the house band at the famous Tropicana nightclub in Havana, where he remained for the next twenty-five years. In 1967 Romeu founded a government-supported jazz and modern music band, the Orquesta Cubana de Música Moderna, in Havana. The "Moderna," as it is known for short, was the training ground for a large number of contemporary Cuban jazz musicians of note, including Chucho Valdés, Paquito D'Rivera, Arturo Sandoval, and Carlos del Puerto (Acosta 2001a, ch. 8). The story of Romeu is evidentiary material showing that the rise of these notable musicians was not an accidental fluke but rather the product of a solid, decades long tradition of jazz playing in the island.

ANTECEDENTS IN NEW YORK AND HAVANA

Cuban musicians were present when the first serious steps towards the development of Latin Jazz were taken in the 1930s in New York and Havana. During that decade, due to the impact of the rhumba's popularity, U.S. jazz musicians attempted to mix, in various degrees, Cuban melodies and sometimes rhumba rhythms with a jazz style. "The Peanut Vendor" became a favorite tune for these admixtures. Louis Armstrong recorded a version of "Peanut Vendor," as did Red Nichols and others. The same occurred in Havana: Cuban music researcher Cristóbal Díaz Ayala has pointed to a 1931 recording of the Hermanos Castro *jazzband* in which "St. Louis Blues" is mixed with strains from "Peanut Vendor" (Ayala 1998, 152). In the world of the jam sessions, other Havana musicians, including Chucho Valdés's father the pianist and composer Bebo Valdés, also began to experiment with mixtures of jazz tunes and Cuban rhythmic tumbaos, albeit in an informal manner (Valdés 9/20–21/00). Later in the decade another dance craze from Cuba, the conga, led to further cross-pollination between jazz and Cuba music. Duke Ellington, Cab Calloway, and other musicians brought tinges of the conga dance into compositions such as Ellington and Tizol's "Conga Brava." Two other significant developments paved the way for the final jelling of the new Latin jazz hybrid of hybrids in the 1940s. First, a trumpet player named Arturo "Chico" O'Farrill, who had fallen in love with jazz while studying in a military academy in the United States, began, back in Cuba, to study music theory, composition and orchestration with Félix Guerrero, a noted composer, orchestra conductor, and teacher. Through Guerrero, the young Chico O'Farrill became exposed to the experiments in arranging Afro-Cuban rhythms with European classical music carried out in the 1930s by Cuban composers Alejandro García Caturla and Amadeo Roldán. The technical knowledge O'Farrill acquired, plus his later immersion in popular Cuban tunes as a member of the international Cuban showband Lecuona Cuban Boys, would be decisive for his later contribution to Cubop and Latin jazz.

But most important of all was the relocation of Mario Bauzá from Cuba to the United States in 1930. Bauzá was born in Havana in 1911. He studied music first with his godfather Arturo Andrade, a solfege teacher, and later at a Havana conservatory. A child prodigy, Bauzá joined the Havana symphony at the age of sixteen. He also played clarinet for the *danzón* charanga band of Antonio María Romeu. In the late 1920s, while in New York on a recording date with the Romeu orchestra, Bauzá was exposed to jazz and decided on the spot to become a jazz musician. Returning to Havana, he played in local *jazzbands* for a while until, in 1930, he settled permanently in New York City. Soon he joined the Noble Sissle band, played with Fletcher Henderson and Don Redman, and eventually became the musical director of one of the great jazz dance bands of the period, the Chick Webb orchestra. Bauzá played clarinet and trumpet for Chick, and worked also with Cab Calloway in the late 1930s. The work of musicians like O'Farrill, Bauzá, and Bebo Valdés continued the tradition Cuban musicians playing jazz in and out of Cuba and laid the foundation for the appearance of a new "hybrid of hybrids" in the ensuing years.

DEFINING MOMENTS IN THE 1940S AND 1950S

The most important events in the launching of what was called Afro-Cuban jazz, Cubop, and eventually Latin Jazz took place in the decade of the 1940s and in the early 1950s. A defining moment was the foundation in 1940 of Machito and the Afro-Cubans in New York City, with Mario Bauzá as musical director and Machito as lead singer. As he played with swing bands in the 1930s, Bauzá dreamed of integrating Afro-Cuban dance rhythms with jazz-oriented sounds. With his brother-in-law "Machito" (Frank Grillo)—an experienced *son* musician from Havana—Bauzá set out with the Afro-Cubans to deliberately experiment with this new fusion. From the mid-1940s on they were supported in the task by the arrival of another Cuban musician, pianist René Hernández, who became the principal arranger for the group. Out of this experimentation a new sound emerged, jazz of a different kind, in tunes like "Tanga," "Asia Minor," and many others. This was Afro-Cuban jazz.

While Machito, Mario Bauzá, René Hernández, and other band members applied themselves to develop the mixture of jazz with dance rhythms like the mambo, another variant of Afro-Cuban jazz began to emerge via the band's female vocalist Graciela Grillo, Machito's sister, who joined the group in 1943. In the late 1940s Chico O'Farrill arranged boleros for her performances with Machito and the Afro-Cubans. With O'Farrill's direction and backed up by a superb band fluent in the jazz idiom, Graciela, by all accounts, turned the Cuban bolero into another vehicle for jazz expression. O'Farrill arranged often for the Machito orchestra, and eventually for the Benny Goodman and Count Basie orchestras. He also wrote several Latin jazz suites, including the *Afro-Cuban Jazz Suite* (1950) which featured the Machito rhythm section led by René Hernández and outstanding jazz soloists such as Charlie Parker.

The impact of Mario Bauzá's ideas, as carried into practice by Machito and the Afro-Cubans, was widely and deeply felt in jazz circles. On the West Coast, bandleader Stan Kenton recorded the tune "Machito" in honor of the Cuban musician in 1947, began his own experiments in mixing a big-band sound with Afro-Cuban rhythms, and even utilized the Machito rhythm section in several recordings in the late 1940s. Bauzá and Machito's blend of Afro-Cuban music and jazz garnered lasting popularity with both Latino and American audiences in the United States. Bauzá and Machito, who traveled often to Havana to recruit musicians and to check out the music scene there, affected musicians in Havana who had also experimented in a much more sporadic and casual ways with the notion of jazz/Cuban music fusion.

The development of the mixture of jazz with Cuban music reached a pivotal stage with the arrival in New York of Cuban drummer Chano Pozo in 1946. Pozo was a successful drummer, dancer, and composer in Havana, and had played in large *jazzbands* as well as small jazz combos in the Cuban capital. Some of his dance tunes like "Nagüe," and "Blen, blen, blen" had been recorded already by New York bands like Machito and

Xavier Cugat. When, at the recommendation of Mario Bauzá, Chano Pozo joined the Dizzy Gillespie band, jazz was changed forever. In collaboration with Gillespie, Chano wrote several tunes that became standards, such as "Manteca," "Tin Tin Deo," and "Guachi Guaro." He was an electrifying performer with Gillespie's big band, dancing, playing, and singing in creolized African languages to enthusiastic audiences in New York, Los Angeles, and major cities in Europe. Even though Pozo did not play long in the United States—he was killed by a gunman in a Harlem bar in December 1948—the fusion of jazz with Afro-Cuban music, called then Cubop, began to be played in a variety of ways in the United States, Cuba, and elsewhere. The Pozo-Gillespie alliance in effect turned jazz music in a new direction, laying the foundations for Latin jazz.

When the recording of "Manteca" was heard in Havana it filled local jazz-oriented musicians with enthusiasm. By the late forties a new crop of young artists, such as Bebo Valdés, José "Chombo" Silva, Luis Escalante, and Gustavo Mas had become fluent in the jazz idiom, kept apace with developments in the United States, and advanced their own musical agendas. In the jazz world of Cuba at the time there were two main simultaneous and overlapping currents. One was made up of "purists," who were interested in jazz as played by leading groups in the United States and for whom fusion with local music elements was of lesser interest. For example, beginning in the early 1940s, the Tropicana nightclub's orchestra, led by saxophonist Armando Romeu, played a vast repertoire from the best American bandleaders, including Duke Ellington, Count Basie, and Fletcher Henderson. A second group, among whom Bebo Valdés figured prominently, sought to bring together both traditions. In the late forties, Valdés performed at the famed Tropicana nightclub where he played piano for shows and in jam sessions with other local musicians interested in jazz and with jazz musicians visiting from the United States. What kind of a jazz musician was Bebo Valdés? Dizzy Gillespie answered that question when, in the early 1950s, after getting word-of-mouth reports, he tried to hire Valdés as a pianist for his band. But Valdés failed in his attempt to obtain an entry visa to the United States. It was the era of rabid anti-communism in the United States and the U.S. Embassy in Cuba refused him a visa on the grounds that he had associated with other musicians suspected of being communist sympathizers (Valdés 9/20–21/00)!

The recorded evidence of jazz playing by Cuban musicians is scant. There are a few "garage" recordings from the 1940s that have survived as collectors items. Thus the evidence we have offered so far has been indirect, either based on oral narratives, or on the demonstrated familiarity with jazz of Cuban immigrant musicians who settled, and worked, outside of Cuba, such as Socarrás, Bauzá, and Pozo. But a number of 1952 recordings made in Havana reveal that developments in Cuba paralleled those taking place those in New York. In that year Bebo Valdés recorded four tunes in the Afro-Cuban jazz style. Commissioned by impresario Norman Granz, they featured trumpeter Alejandro "El Negro" Vivar and saxophonist Gustavo Mas. What the recordings sounded like was aptly summarized by a review in *Downbeat* magazine (May 6, 1953) which noted, "That's life for you! After all these years of North American jazzmen trying to sound like Cubans, we finally get a jazz LP from Cuba played by Cuban musicians, and how do they sound? They sound exactly like the Norte Americanos!"

But even after that significant event, most Latin jazz recordings continued to take place in the United States and not in Cuba for a very simple reason. While artists in both countries sought to develop a musical innovation, recording companies in the United States supported the Cubop fusion because they estimated, correctly, that adding a "Latin" sound to jazz would result in a new jazz with increased sales. On the other hand, what sold in Havana was the most popular local dance music. Industry executives were not interested in recording jazz in Cuba, as its audience was very limited. The paucity of jazz recordings in Cuba is evidence of the division of markets by recording companies rather the absence of quality jazz musicians in the island (Acosta 1996, 249).

Another important contributor to the development of Latin jazz in Cuba was Frank Emilio Flynn. Blind since his birth in 1921, Flynn became known for his passion for jazz. In the late 1940s he composed his first jazz tune, entitled "Midnight Theme," and became the founder of a jazz-influenced group, the Loquibambia Swing Boys. The group included vocalist Omara Portuondo, recently of Buena Vista Social Club fame, who often sang in English (Flynn 12/18/99). One of his later compositions, "Gandinga, Mondongo y Sandunga," dating from the early 1960s, became one of the standards of Cuban jazz.

In the 1940s and 1950s American jazz musicians such as Nat King Cole, Sarah Vaughan, Philly Jo Jones, Stan Getz, and Woody Herman performed in nightclubs in Havana, participated in jam sessions with local Cuban jazz musicians, and expressed their admiration for the quality of Cuban jazz musicians (Acosta 2001a, ch. 7). Even Cuban musicians not usually identified with the local jazz scene associated and played with visiting U.S. jazz musicians. For example, Cuban music bassist Israel López "Cachao" and American bassist Milt Hinton got to know each other well and got together for small jam sessions during Hinton's frequent visits to Havana as a member of the Cab Calloway band (López 1/24–25/94). In sum, by this time jazz was a well-entrenched, time-honored part of the musical scene in Havana where proficient local musicians like Valdés, Gustavo Mas, Flynn, and others pushed jazz forward as players, composers, and bandleaders.

THE MAINTENANCE OF A TRADITION

Throughout the 1950s Cuban musicians played jazz in jam sessions in Havana and other locales in the island. Leonardo Acosta documents in his book on the history of jazz in Cuba the many groups that formed during this period, the venues which became the site of regular jam sessions and the most prominent musicians involved (Acosta 2001a, ch. 8). During this decade the Cuban *descarga* movement also developed. The *descarga* (Cuban Spanish for jam session) movement, normally associated with the names of Bebo Valdés, Cachao, Peruchín Jústiz, and Julio Gutiérrez, sought to give free rein to the improvisatory potential of Cuban dance music itself. It represented a significant instrumental exploration and development of the musics traditionally associated with Cuba: *son*, mambo, rumba, etc. Unwittingly it may have served as a further impetus to musicians interested in jazz improvisation since musicians involved in the *descargas* were often playing in jam sessions, too. Saxophonist José "Chombo" Silva is a case in point: in 1956 he recorded his sax playing for the *Cuban Jam Sessions* recordings in Havana. A short year and a half later, after moving to the United States, he recorded a superb Latin jazz album, Cal Tjader's *Mas Ritmo Caliente*. Silva's tenor solo on "Perdido" provides further indirect evidence of the proficiency of jazz musicians in Cuba at that time.

In 1958 some of the leaders of Cuba's jazz scene took an important step: jazzmen Leonardo Acosta, Frank Emilio Flynn, Jesús Caunedo, Walfredo de los Reyes, Orlando "Cachaíto" López, and Orlando "Papito" Hernández organized the Club Cubano de Jazz. An important link was saxophonist Gustavo Mas, who had moved to Florida earlier in the decade. The purpose of the club was to promote formal musical exchanges and a steady relationship between Cuban and American jazz musicians and audiences. From the United States, Gustavo Mas worked as a scout who suggested and contacted U.S. jazz musicians to travel to Cuba. Under the sponsorship of the club, musicians from the U.S. played in concerts and impromptu jam sessions with Cuban musicians in Havana. We have no recordings of these dates. But, once again, as indirect evidence of the quality of musicianship involved on the part of the Cubans, one can listen to Gustavo Mas's recordings with Woody Herman in the U.S. in 1960s. His solo sound on tenor saxophone can be heard on *The New Swingin' Herman Herd* (1960).

Meanwhile, after the initial spurt caused by Cubop in the late 1940s and early 1950s, the passion for Afro-Cuban jazz in the United States diminished somewhat in intensity. From the mid-fifties on, and for many years to come, a number of prominent Cuban percussionists helped keep the new tradition of Latin jazz alive. These drummers were of supreme importance because they provided a constant supply of rhythmic patterns, styles, and phrasing from the immense reservoir of Cuban Afro-based folklore. Among the many Cuban drummers involved in this process a few names stand out: Armando Peraza, Mongo Santamaría, Cándido Camero, Carlos "Patato" Valdés, and Francisco Aguabella. Peraza who had achieved fame as a bongo drummer in Cuba in the mid-1940s, migrated first to New York in the late 1940s before settling in San Francisco in the early 1950s. In the 1950s and 1960s he played and recorded often with George Shearing and Cal Tjader. Called "the best bongo player I ever saw" by Machito's outstanding bongosero José Mangual, Peraza was known for his impressive, flashy solos on both congas and bongos. He was the featured percussionist in two of the most important Latin jazz LPs of the period, George Shearing's 1957 *Latin Escapade* (which sold a surprising eighty thousand copies, something unheard of for a Latin jazz album at the time), and Cal Tjader's 1965 *Soul Sauce*, another Latin jazz best seller.

Mongo Santamaría, another bongosero from Cuban dance bands, was active with several groups in New York in the late 1940s and early 1950s. He played conga drums for Tito Puente for several years, before moving to the West Coast and joining the Cal Tjader Quintet in 1957. While playing for Tjader, Santamaría composed a tune that became an immediate jazz standard: "Afro-Blue." The tune was played and recorded so often by John Coltrane that many jazz fans believe to this day that it is Coltrane's composition. In the early 1960s, Mongo formed his own group. For the next three decades Mongo's band became a kind of school through which many young jazz players took their steps as professionals, among them Chick Corea, Hubert Laws, Justo Almario, Herbie Hancock (who played piano on Mongo's first recording of his tune "Watermelon Man"), and many others.

First known in Cuba as a player of the *tres* guitar in *son* groups in Cuba, Cándido Camero eventually became a successful bongo and conga player as well. He played Latin jazz in the early 1950s on both sides of the Florida Straits, with Bebo Valdés in Havana and with Billy Taylor, Art Blakey, and Dizzy Gillespie in the United States. Dubbed "the Man with a Thousand Fingers," Cándido contributed for several decades a special flavor to both Latin and straight-ahead jazz combos. In great demand as a studio musician, he played on hundreds of recordings with dozens of different groups.

Known as an innovator in conga-playing styles, Carlos "Patato" Valdés arrived in New York in 1954, and soon became the conguero for the Machito band. He toured Africa with Herbie Mann, and recorded with both Cal Tjader and as leader of his own percussion ensembles. Known for his ability to play several congas at once and for extracting melodic tones from his drums, Valdés is highly regarded within the tight circle of outstanding Afro-Cuban drummers for his gift for devising new rhythmic patterns on the congas and his expert use of the instrument.

One of the most influential percussionists to come from Cuba to the United States in the late 1950s was Francisco Aguabella. After a three-year stint with the Katherine Dunham dance troupe, Aguabella settled in the West Coast in 1957. A master of various kinds of Afro-Cuban religious drumming, including *batá*, *abakuá*, and *arará* rhythms, Aguabella played and recorded with Dizzy Gillespie, Eddie Palmieri, Mongo Santamaría, among others. Aguabella, who leads both Latin jazz and dance bands, also continues to work as a ceremonial drummer at religious events and as a teacher of Afro-Cuban religious drumming.

For several decades Peraza, Santamaría, Valdés, Cándido and Aguabella enriched the rhythmic palate of jazz, strengthened the foundation of Latin jazz, and introduced new and exciting Cuban rhythms into the jazz idiom. Their playing style and vast knowledge influenced jazz drummers and inspired an entire new generation of jazz percussionists of Afro-Cuban rhythms.

LOWS AND HIGHS AFTER 1960

Although the writing of a music history divided by decades has been aptly criticized by many, there is little doubt that the beginning of the decade of the 1960s is significant in the history of Cuban jazz in and out of the island. The advent of the Cuban Revolution signified a rupture in relations of all kinds with the United States. The fortunes of jazz were no exception. Cultural things that, in the Castro government's view, could be connected to the United States were discouraged, to say the least. The Club Cubano de Jazz ceased to exist. Many musicians left the island, and the easy flow of jazz musicians and music itself from the United States to Cuba slowed to a near halt.

Yet jazz continued to be played by groups of all kinds with varying life spans, and the world of the jazz sessions (and, with few exceptions, the general absence of recordings) continued as well. Pianist Felipe Dulzaides led a group that played Latin jazz more or less in the style associated with the George Shearing Quintet in the United States. The Dulzaides group became the training ground for a number of musicians who would later acquire international prominence as jazz musicians once they began to perform and record abroad. Such is the case for bassist Carlos del Puerto and drummer Ignacio Berroa (del Puerto 5/29/99). The young Chucho Valdés also led his first jazz trio during this period, when he wrote the tune "Mambo Influenciado" that became a "Havana standard." Trombonist Pucho Escalante led a larger group during this period that played in the swing mode of earlier times. Pianist Frank Emilio Flynn, together with drummer Guillermo Barretto and conguero Tata Güines, formed a quintet that played jazz, Latin jazz and *descarga*-style music.

If the early years after the victory of the revolutionary government were not very favorable to the further development of Latin jazz, a number of fortuitous events would allow the decades-long brewing of a jazz and Latin jazz music culture in Cuba to literally explode on the international scene. In the late 1960s Cuban officials responsible for cultural affairs created a large orchestra named the Orquesta Cubana de Música Moderna. Some of the best jazz musicians in the island were recruited into the Moderna, whose first director was the renowned Armando Romeu. This orchestra played some jazz, big band arrangements of show tunes, and whatever else could be justifiably included under the rubric of "modern music."

Smaller subsets of the Moderna began to travel to jazz festivals abroad in the early 1970s. Thus the "outside world" became aware of the existence and talent, for example, of Chucho Valdés, who appeared at the Jazz Jamboree in Poland in 1970 with a small combo. In Cuba, other members of the Moderna formed groups that focused more directly on Latin jazz, notably, Sonorama 6, led by renowned guitarist and composer Leo Brouwer, with Carlos del Puerto as the bassist. A few years later a nucleus of musicians within the Moderna recorded a couple of tunes that became instant national hits. Even though they were dance tunes, the recordings allowed these musicians to acquire an identity and a certain status, which in turn permitted them to focus their attention on the real love they had for jazz and Latin jazz. The group, led by Chucho Valdés, named itself Irakere, meaning "dense jungle" in the Cuban Yoruba Lucumí language.

Irakere mixed jazz, Western European classical music, rock, funk, and Afro-Cuban rhythms to produce a fresh and exciting new sound. The band exploded on the world stage in 1976, appeared at various festivals in the next two years, including the Newport Jazz Festival, and won a 1978 Grammy Award for Latin Music. For the next twenty years Irakere became a group that influenced jazz, Latin jazz, and Cuban popular dance music both on the island and abroad. Irakere was widely admired for its brilliant soloists, the complexity of its arrangements, and its tightness as an ensemble. It also became a school through which many Cuban Latin jazz musicians would pass during the subsequent decades. Irakere's leader Chucho Valdés, one of the most versatile musical artists in Cuba's history, made an impact not only with Irakere, but with a number of outstanding recordings in the late 1990s, both solo and with his quartet.

While Valdés still resides on the island, other members of the original Irakere group left Cuba after 1980. Two of them, Paquito D'Rivera and Arturo Sandoval, have deservedly become performing and recording names in the Latin jazz genre. D'Rivera, an outstanding saxophonist and clarinetist, has also championed bebop and South American music. After arriving in the United States in the early 1980s, he has led his own groups, and assumed the directorship of Dizzy Gillespie's United Nation Orchestra after the trumpeter's death in 1993. Trumpeter Arturo Sandoval also relocated to the United States. A multi-instrumentalist who also plays piano and percussion, he has recorded, since coming to the United States, not only Latin jazz, but also straight-ahead jazz, classical music, and popular Afro-Cuban dance music. A master of the high registers of the trumpet, Sandoval received two of the first seven Grammy Awards for Latin Jazz, which were instituted beginning in 1985.

While many jazz fans outside of Cuba tend to think of Irakere as the one Cuban jazz group of importance during this period, the fact is that Irakere was not an exception. In addition to Irakere another major group that excelled Latin jazz in Cuba in the late 1970s and early 1980s was the Afro-Cuba ensemble. And one of the great Latin jazz pianists in the history of the genre, Emiliano Salvador, was not a member of Irakere and never traveled to the United States. Salvador died in Havana in 1992 at the young age of forty one.

A new crop of post-Irakere jazz musicians, such as pianist extraordinaire Gonzalo Rubalcaba, flutist Orlando "Maraca" Valle, and percussionists Horacio "El Negro" Hernández and Dafnis Prieto, offers further confirmation that the rise of Irakere was not a one-time fluke but rather the culmination of a process that was more than a century in the making. Unfortunately, as in the past, it is mostly those Cuban musicians who play and record abroad that become known to jazz audiences and writers. But the jazz world in Cuba continues to progress, develop its own local talents, and move jazz and Latin jazz forward. In the last two decades, and despite the immense economic and technical difficulties involved, Cuban musicians have succeeded in developing an infrastructure that nurtures the continuing development of jazz musicians. For example, shortly after the early success of Irakere, Havana became the site of a major jazz festival which in its first year, 1980, featured only local, homegrown jazz and Latin jazz ensembles groups. Since then, of course, the Havana Jazz Festival in late December every year (sometimes it skips a year) has become a de rigueur destination for major jazz artists from all over the world.

The growth of Latin jazz was neither the exclusive province of Cuban musicians nor a unilinear process of development. Musicians from Puerto Rico and the United States, especially, are very much part of the story of Latin jazz. Its evolution depended as well on a constant dialogue with successive, emerging styles of jazz, such as swing, bebop, cool, and funk. Yet the history of Latin jazz, and by extension, of jazz itself, cannot be fully understood without taking into account the century-old creative contribution of Cuban jazz musicians both inside and outside the island.

DJANGO REINHARDT'S LEFT HAND

—Benjamin Givan

A half century after his death, there are signs of a renewed interest in the legendary jazz guitarist Django Reinhardt. Director Woody Allen's fictional 1999 film *Sweet and Low Down*, in which Reinhardt's off-screen presence was pivotal, introduced the guitarist's name to a wider audience, and its soundtrack, featuring the contemporary guitarist Howard Alden, spawned a Reinhardt tribute concert and accompanying memorabilia exhibit in New York during the summer of 2000. Later that year the Big Apple's first Annual Django Reinhardt Festival presented an array of modern guitarists, including Reinhardt's son Babik, who died in November 2001 (Django Reinhardt NY Festival 2001). Meanwhile, albums of Reinhardt's music were released by two very different musicians: the country singer Willie Nelson, and the eclectic jazz saxophonist James Carter (Nelson 1999; Carter 2000). And a new compact disc boxed-set of Reinhardt's own recordings became the fastest selling item in the history of the prestigious Mosaic label ("Label Watch: Mosaic Records" 2001).

Born in Belgium in 1910 to a family of peripatetic Manouche (French-speaking) gypsies, and based in France for his entire adult life, Reinhardt is the only non-American jazz musician active before World War II to be commonly mentioned in the same breath as the greatest American soloists of his day. During the 1930s he led the renowned Quintet of the Hot Club of France, whose driving, pulsating rhythm section of two guitars and a bass provided an ideal backdrop for Reinhardt's virtuoso improvisations and the freely swinging playing of his longtime colleague, violinist Stéphane Grappelli. In these years Reinhardt also played and recorded with many American musicians who passed through Paris, including saxophonists Coleman Hawkins and Benny Carter, and cornetist Rex Stewart. Stewart later wrote that "Django, in my opinion, was to the guitar about what Louis Armstrong was to the trumpet or Art Tatum to the piano. He inspired the playing and thinking of countless hundreds of guitar players all over the world" (Stewart 1991, 186).

Future generations of jazz guitarists were probably inspired even more by the American Charlie Christian (1916–42), whose principal stylistic progenitors were tenor saxophonist Lester Young, and the blues and western swing of his Oklahoma origins (Schuller 1989, 564–66). But Reinhardt's influence may even have been transmitted through Christian's playing. The guitarist Mary Osborne remembered hearing Christian replicate Reinhardt's recording of "St. Louis Blues" note-for-note at a concert date in Bismarck, North Dakota, during the late 1930s (Ferris 1975, 78). In the years after World War II, American guitarists such as Charlie Byrd, Les Paul, and Barney Kessel all sought out Reinhardt during visits to France before the latter's death in 1953 (Kienzle 1985, 116; Shaughnessy 1993, 135–36, 209; Lee 1975, 59). And the myriad other players who cite Reinhardt as a source of inspiration include hard bopper Wes Montgomery, country legend Chet Atkins, bluesman B. B. King, fusion pioneer John McLaughlin, and rock-oriented artists like Carlos Santana and Vernon Reid (Atkins and Neely 1974, 78; Obrecht 2000, 320, 327, 337; Rosen 1975, 72; Menn 1992, 160, 198, 218).

Reinhardt even inspired an entire subgenre of jazz. The "Gypsy jazz" (or *jazz manouche*) style still thrives among the gypsy communities of western Europe, and has generated enthusiasts worldwide (Silverman 2000, 288; Wilkinson 2001, 618; Jalard 1959, quoted in Jost 1997, 16), many of whom converge each summer on the French village of Samois-sur-Seine for a festival dedicated to Reinhardt's memory. Leading present-day exponents of Gypsy jazz, which generally takes the original Quintet as a model for emulation, include the French guitarists Boulou Ferré and Biréli Lagrène, Jimmy Rosenberg from Holland, and the American Frank Vignola (Lagrène 2001; Vignola 2001; see also Mackenzie 1999).

Over the years, a considerable mystique has enveloped not only Reinhardt's musical legacy, but also his singular personal history. He occupies a unique niche in the firmament of jazz by virtue of his ethnicity, but furthermore his early years were marked by a life-altering event. On the night of November 2, 1928, the eighteen-year-old musician returned to his caravan from a playing engagement (see Delaunay 1961, 43–55; Billard 1993, 53–58; and Williams 1991, 23–25). As he prepared to retire to bed, a candle's open flame accidentally ignited a large pile of celluloid flowers that Bella, his first wife, planned to sell the next day. His wife escaped from the blaze with minor injuries, but Reinhardt sustained severe burns to much of the left side of his body. At a local hospital a surgeon recommended that his left leg be amputated to prevent gangrene. Reinhardt refused, and instead underwent surgery (under chloroform anaesthetic) to open and drain his wounds, which involved the application of silver nitrate to dry the flesh and cause scars to form. During a recovery period of almost two years he regained the use of his leg, but the third and fourth fingers of his left hand were permanently damaged. That Reinhardt nonetheless managed to relearn his instrument with an entirely new playing technique has been a source of awe and mystery ever since.

Little else remains known about Reinhardt's accident, or, for that matter, his early life in general. We do know that he began his career playing the music known as *musette*, a popular form of live entertainment in France during the years after World War I. Musette, which was usually performed by three- or four-piece ensembles led by an accordionist, bears little musical resemblance to jazz. Indeed, the scholar Jody Blake notes that while, on the one hand, musette orchestras might superficially seem to be a sort of "French equivalent of the jazz band," on the other, the bals-musettes (working class dance halls) where the music was often performed were viewed by contemporary observers as the site of an authentically Gallic culture, relatively free of the American influences that permeated much French visual art and classical music at the time (Blake 1999, 102–05). In these musette ensembles Reinhardt played not the guitar, but the banjo-guitar, a now-obscure hybrid instrument constructed like a banjo, but with six strings tuned like a conventional guitar. However on all recordings made after the accident he appears on guitar. Reinhardt's biographer, Patrick Williams, raises the possibility that Reinhardt made the switch during his convalescence because the guitar required a lighter touch upon the fingerboard, and so was less physically demanding (Williams 1991, 39). And the writer François Billard points out that, in contrast to the banjo's piercing sonority, the guitar's mellower sound may have been better suited to the hospital ward where Reinhardt spent his recovery, since it would have been less disruptive to his fellow patients (Billard 1993, 58). During this same period Reinhardt was increasingly exposed to recordings of American jazz, probably including those of Eddie Lang (1902–33), the first jazz guitarist of note.[1] Thus Reinhardt adopted both a new instrument and a new musical idiom more or less simultaneously.

In the absence of concrete information, many writers have tended to romanticize Reinhardt's biography, and have often exaggerated his disability either because of misconceptions, or for rhetorical effect. Tales of the enigmatic gypsy who miraculously triumphed over dire personal circumstances make for compelling reading, but various conflicting accounts have circulated. This inconsistency is the impetus for the present article, which explores two straightforward questions: what was the nature of Reinhardt's injury, and what were its ramifications for his music? In the following pages I review some disparate existing accounts, and assess the physiological implications of injuries like Reinhardt's from a clinical perspective. I then consider primary evidence of Reinhardt's disability in the form of photographs and sound recordings. Musical transcriptions are useful for comparing recordings that he made both before and after the accident, and for contrasting his playing with that of an able-bodied performer, his forerunner Eddie Lang. Taken together, these sources help to demystify an issue which is central to both Reinhardt's life and his music.

At the very least, photographs show that the third and fourth fingers of Reinhardt's left hand were, as Ian Cruickshank writes, "deformed," or in Mike Peters' words, "partially mangled" (Cruickshank 1989, 6; Peters, notes in Reinhardt 1999). But many writers disagree as to whether the affected fingers retained any function. Mike Zwerin, like several other authors, writes that the fingers were paralyzed (Zwerin 2000, 539; Smith 1987, 30; Horricks 1983, 17; Nabe 1993, 23). Yet Zwerin adds that the guitarist was still able to use these fingers to a degree. To the contrary, Michael James, in his *New Grove Dictionary* article, states unequivocally that Reinhardt's accident "deprived him of the use of two fingers" (James 2002, 396). Likewise, Williams claims that the guitarist's handicap "allowed him only to play notes with three fingers of his hand: the middle finger, the index finger, and the thumb" (Williams 1991, 23). As we will see, a variety of evidence suggests that Reinhardt actually retained a significant, albeit substantially limited, level of function in his damaged fingers. We will be best able to assess this evidence if we first review briefly the recent medical literature on hand burns.

The anatomy of the human hand is extraordinarily complex. Its skeletal structure consists of nineteen bones and seventeen joints. Each finger contains three bones, called phalanges (the thumb has only two). The joint between two phalanges is called an interphalangeal joint. At the base of each finger the longest phalange meets another bone, a metacarpal. This joint is called the metacarpophalangeal joint. The metacarpals are in turn attached to the carpals, a group of small bones within the wrist. Motion is controlled by two sets of muscles, attached to the bones by tendons. Extrinsic muscles, located in the forearm, are responsible for powerful motion, while intrinsic muscles, located within the hand itself, control delicate, finely coordinated movements (Tubiana and Chamagne 1988, 84–86). A total of thirty-nine muscles control motion of the hand and wrist, and there is a considerable degree of functional interdependence: moving one part of the hand often affects the position of another. Movement of the fingers is described as either flexion, when joints are bent toward the palm, or extension, when joints are bent away from the palm (Tubiana 1988, 124).

When the hand is burned by flames, as was Reinhardt's, the damage is most often to the back (dorsum) of the hand. (This is "probably because the back of the hand is exposed when it is used to protect the face and because the hand closes instinctively in flash burns" [Koepke, et al. 1963, 147].) Burns are classified according to their severity as either "partial thickness," when they are fairly superficial and produce blistering and minor scarring, or "full thickness," when the skin's entire thickness is charred, leaving an open wound that heals with scar tissue that lacks the skin's former elasticity (Nichols 1955, 97). Additionally, "deep burns of the dorsum of the hand are apt to destroy the extensor tendons, especially those over the middle joints of the fingers" (ibid., 109), thus inhibiting extension of the affected digits.

Severe burns to the dorsum of the hand frequently lead to hyperextension of the metacarpophalangeal joints, and compensatory flexion of the interphalangeal joints (Boswick 1974, 171). In layman's terms, the fingers are drawn backward at their base joint while their smaller joints curl inward. The photograph in Figure 1 shows that the permanent effects of

Reinhardt's injury almost exactly correspond to these conditions: the third and fourth fingers of his left hand are bent backwards at their base at an abnormal angle, while the upper joints are partially flexed.

In recent decades, all fields of medicine have witnessed considerable advances, the treatment of hand injuries being no exception. Doctors are now often able to prevent deformities by using splints to support and protect the burned hand during recovery. But in 1928 Reinhardt

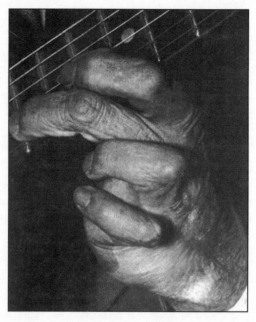

Figure 1. Courtesy Mike Peters Collection.

benefited only from care designed to stave off potentially life-threatening infections, and he was otherwise compelled to come to terms with his injuries without further treatment.

Though Reinhardt's left hand clearly was disfigured, we may still question whether he retained any function in the affected fingers. I have already suggested that the view that these digits were "useless" or "paralyzed" is misleading. In fact, the medical literature is notable for the conspicuous absence of the word "paralysis." Providing muscle tissue and tendons heal sufficiently, a burned hand may retain a significant level of motoric function within the constrictions of its deformed state.

Several commentators have rightly acknowledged that Reinhardt retained limited use of his damaged fingers. A 1966 *Down Beat* magazine article quotes the following description of the guitarist's technique from an English booklet by Billy Neil and E. Gates, published in 1944:

[Reinhardt] uses the first and second left-hand fingers most of the time in single-note work; in chord work he can make use of the third and fourth fingers to a limited extent on the first two strings. He plays his famous octave passages on any two strings, with a "damped" string in between . . ., avoiding that frenzied rushing up and down the fingerboard which would otherwise be necessary. His famous chromatic runs, if played in the first position, are *fingered*; if played up the fingerboard, they are *glissed* with one finger. He plays unusual chord shapes because of his handicap. (Hoefer 1966, 22; original emphasis)[2]

This may be an eyewitness description, though since Reinhardt spent the war years in continental Europe the authors of an English publication would probably not, in 1944, have observed him in person for at least five years. It is supported by a definite first-hand account from Reinhardt's longtime colleague, Stéphane Grappelli, in an interview shortly after the guitarist's death:

[Reinhardt] acquired amazing dexterity with those first two fingers, but that didn't mean he never employed the others. He learned to grip the guitar with his little finger on the E string and the next finger on the B. That accounts for some of those chord progressions which Django was probably the first to perform on the guitar . . . at least in the jazz idiom. (quoted in Delaunay 1961, 17)

Some recent writers, such as Mike Peters, have repeated these claims—that Reinhardt was able to use his disabled fingers on the guitar's two highest strings, but that these fingers were only used to play chords, while single-string melodies were played with only the two fully functional digits (Peters 1982, 12). Peters also notes that Reinhardt's hands appear to have been larger than average. The critic Whitney Balliett, like Grappelli, speculates that Reinhardt's physical condition may have been partially responsible for his innovative harmonic techniques: "The huge hand made the crippled fingers work nonetheless: thus the mysterious chords and melodic lines that no one had heard before" (Balliett 2000, 99).[3]

But these accounts amount to little more than brief asides. In contrast, the most in-depth consideration of Reinhardt's instrumental technique to date appears in Alexander Schmitz's and Peter Maier's biography (Schmitz and Maier 1985, 57–60). While the authors do not cite specific evidence for their findings, they nonetheless provide a rigorous, concise treatment of the issue.

Schmitz and Maier assert categorically that for chord playing, "the third finger of Django's left hand was almost always completely functional, so long as it was not required to stretch far from the middle finger" (57–58). They affirm that Reinhardt's use of his damaged fingers was primarily confined to the instrument's two highest-pitched strings (the B and high-E), thus prohibiting him from playing chords which demand considerable wrist supination in order to place the third or fourth fingers on the instrument's middle or lower strings.[4] This precludes many fingerings which are merely run-of-the-mill for non-disabled guitarists. The authors also suggest that the guitarist was occasionally able to take advantage of his disability, such as by barring across up to three strings with his third finger, which fell naturally at an angle more conducive to this technique than it would on a healthy hand (57). With these details in mind, we may now consider the historical evidence of Reinhardt's technique in practice.

A very short film clip of Reinhardt playing has recently been discovered (Reinhardt 1938). The guitarist, soloing on the theme "Tornerai" ("J'Attendrai"), is on camera for about thirty seconds, and uses almost exclusively his index and middle fingers on the fretboard. Thus the film corroborates the descriptions of Reinhardt's single-note solo technique cited above, but sheds only scant light on the functionality of the disabled fingers (he appears to use them for just two or three chords). In the remainder of this article I will first address the latter issue by examining Reinhardt's approach to chord-playing, and will then discuss some noteworthy aspects of his single-note technique.

A small number of still photographs capture Reinhardt's playing in close-up, and along with the film they provide the most reliable visual evidence of his instrumental technique. Figure 2, for instance, clearly shows Reinhardt using both his third and fourth fingers on the guitar's uppermost strings to play a chord.

But while photographs provide valuable evidence, they present only static records of a dynamic physical activity. For more clues, we must turn to Reinhardt's recordings. In order to gauge his injury's impact on his guitar technique, it seems appropriate to begin by comparing his playing from before the November 1928 accident with that of his later career. He made fifteen known recordings between May and October of 1928. On each he assumes a solely accompanimental role as banjo-guitarist within a

Figure 2. Photograph by M. Descamps. Copyright © Scoop (Paris-Match Archive). Reproduced by permission.

three-part musette ensemble dominated by an accordionist, and also featuring at various times a whistler, slide-whistle, xylophone, or other percussion. The recordings are less than ideal historical sources because the sound quality is poor, and even the original pitch is uncertain. (The original instrumental tunings are not known for sure, and, as is not infrequently the case with recordings of this vintage, inconsistent turntable speeds at any stage of the recording and reproduction process may have distorted the sounding pitch.) Furthermore, because Reinhardt is heard only as an accompanist, his playing is sometimes difficult to discern beneath the foregrounded melodic instruments. For these reasons, the transcription process involves a certain amount of guesswork.

Example 1 transcribes the opening measures of one of these early recordings, "Miss Columbia" (Reinhardt 1928a), and gives a hypothetical tablature for Reinhardt's banjo-guitar accompaniment.[5] Unsurprisingly, being at the time equipped with a fully functional left hand, Reinhardt makes use of all four fingers. His accompaniment is mostly of the "oom-pah" variety: a bass line played on the instrument's middle and lower strings on beats one and three of each four-four measure alternates with chords played on the higher strings on beats two and four. The descending bass progression E-D#-C#-B heard in mm. 5–6 and mm. 7–8 is most likely played using the left pinkie and middle finger on the pitches C# and B respectively (m. 6). These two notes are played on the instrument's A-string at the fourth and second fret while the first finger depresses the G-string at the first fret. Thus the wrist is heavily supinated, enabling the fourth finger to reach across the fingerboard. Such a fingering, while quotidian in the hands of any modestly accomplished guitarist, would have been entirely impossible for Reinhardt after 1928. But a decade later Reinhardt was still playing the same type of accompaniments, and in a jazz style that was more harmonically and texturally varied. Example 2 is a partial transcription of a 1938 recording of "It Had To Be You," in which Reinhardt alone accompanied Stéphane Grappelli's violin (Reinhardt 1938). A proposed tablature and left-hand fingering for the guitar part are also given.[6] It suggests that instead of using his weaker fingers to play a bass line within an oompah figuration, as in the previous example, Reinhardt would often play a bass line with his first and second fingers, and produce chords by barring across the higher strings with any of his first three fingers. The chord in m. 3, for instance, has the third finger barred across the upper three strings. Alternatively, Reinhardt could use his thumb for the bass line, by curling it over the guitar neck so as to reach the instrument's lowest two strings (labeled "T" in m. 2). While able-bodied guitarists can also find it convenient to use the left thumb in this way (see the prescribed use of the left thumb in Jorgensen 1996), Reinhardt probably had to rely on it more often because he had fewer alternatives.

The three- and four-note chords that Reinhardt played on "It Had To Be You" illustrate that in addition to using harmonies that required only

Example 1. "*Miss Columbia*" *(Marceau).* 1928.

Example 2. "It Had to Be You" (Jones-Kahn). 1938.

his healthy index and middle fingers, he frequently employed the disabled third finger too. None of the chords in Example 2 calls for the use of the fourth finger on the left hand (though since the indicated fingerings are merely speculative, it is conceivable that he may have used it).

More of Reinhardt's chord-playing techniques are displayed in the solo performance transcribed in Example 3, an excerpt from his 1937 recording of Lao Silèsu's "A Little Love, A Little Kiss" (Reinhardt 1937a). The passage shown is an a cappella rendition of the song's verse (again, a proposed tablature and left-hand fingering are given).[7] None of the thirty-seven chords shown in this example requires the guitarist's fourth finger (some of the chords are the same, so there are only about twenty-five or so different chords). Fifteen do, however, necessitate the use of the third finger. In each instance it is used only to depress the instrument's high E-string, with the possible exception of the final chord in m. 5. This particular chord (G-C#-E#-A) may be played with the third finger on the B-string, as indicated, although it is also playable by using the second finger to depress simultaneously both the G- and B-strings.

But if the music in Example 3 was indeed played as indicated, without using the fourth finger on the left hand, in a few instances the third finger would have had to stretch a considerable distance from the second finger. The first chord in m. 1 (G#-D-E#-C#) and the first chord in m. 2 (E-A#-C#-A), as well as the final chord in m. 4 (G#-D-F#-C#), would all require the first finger at a given fret, the second finger one fret higher, and the third finger two more frets higher than the second finger. This appears to contradict Schmitz and Maier's view that Reinhardt was unable to stretch his disabled third finger far from the second (though the guitarist's large hands may have found this less of stretch). Thus the highest notes of these chords may have instead been played with the fourth finger on the high E-string. Without visual evidence, recordings cannot always reveal conclusively how Reinhardt fingered a given chord.

We can, however, make measured generalizations about the relationship between Reinhardt's physical state and his music by comparing his technique with that of an unimpaired performer. Reinhardt's performance of "A Little Love, A Little Kiss" was very likely inspired by Eddie Lang's earlier recording of the same tune (Lang 1927). Lang's 1927 recording is an entirely solo performance (Reinhardt is accompanied by the full Quintet during the

Example 3. "A Little Love, A Little Kiss" (Silèsu). 1937.

rest of his solo, which is not transcribed here). Like Reinhardt, Lang played the song in the key of D major, and he began with a similarly free, rubato rendition of the song's verse, which is transcribed in Example 4.[8]

From a technical standpoint, Lang's version serves as a stark reminder that Reinhardt's disability was, despite his adaptability, indeed considerable. A majority of the chords containing four or more notes that Lang played would, it appears, have been impossible for Reinhardt. In purely musical terms, the result is that Lang much more frequently played chords containing intervals of less than a major third between adjacent notes. Since a guitar's strings are tuned in perfect fourths, with the exception of the major third between the G- and B-strings, in order to create intervals smaller than the interval between any two adjacent open strings the performer's wrist must be heavily supinated, enabling a given string to be stopped at a higher fret than that of the adjacent (higher) string. For instance, in m. 7 of Example 4, Lang creates a major second, G-A, by stopping the B-string at the eighth fret with his pinkie and the high E-string at the fifth fret with his index finger. This requires wrist supination enabling the fourth finger to reach a lower string than the first finger. Lang employs various other chord fingerings with similar physical demands (they are indicated in Example 4 wherever a left-hand finger-number appears beneath a lower finger-number, such as in m. 1, where the fourth finger depresses the G-string while the second finger stops the B-string). While these sorts of fingerings were possible for Reinhardt using his healthy index and middle fingers, on the whole he tended heavily to favor chords in which any two adjacent strings are stopped at the same fret (for instance by barring with a single finger), or in which a higher string is stopped at a higher fret than its neighbor. This is especially apparent when we consider the interval between the highest pair of pitches in Reinhardt's chosen chords. These are most often played on the instrument's uppermost strings, tuned at the interval of a perfect fourth. Therefore Reinhardt's chords usually contain an interval of a perfect fourth or greater between their highest two pitches. Lang, of course, often used such formations (they are, after all, also easier for a normally endowed individual to play). But he regularly used closer harmonies than Reinhardt's.

The foregoing evidence confirms that although Reinhardt's injury profoundly affected his instrumental technique, he retained a substantial

Example 4. "A Little Love, A Little Kiss" (Silèsu). Performed by Eddie Lang. 1927.

degree of function in the disfigured third finger of his left hand. And, while his disability substantially restricted the range of chords available to him, he was partially able to compensate for it, for instance by using his thumb to play bass notes on the guitar's lower strings. However, his use of the thumb and disabled fingers seems to have been associated solely with chord playing. All evidence suggests that when soloing with single-string melodies he relied on only his two fully functional fingers.

Because Reinhardt's earliest recordings, from before the accident, feature him in an exclusively accompanimental role, they present very few examples of single-string playing for comparison with his later work. But on several brief occasions the young performer departed from his customary chordal accompaniment by using arpeggiated harmonies or an obbligato-like counter-melody. Example 5 transcribes one such instance from a 1928 recording of "Moi Aussi" (Reinhardt 1928b). Here, while an accordionist and whistler play the melody, Reinhardt plays a pattern (mm. 1–2) based on rising and failling arpeggiations that somewhat resemble the more recent American bluegrass banjo style, in which the performer plucks the strings with the thumb, index, and middle fingers of his right hand. At m. 8 Reinhardt shifts to a different pattern based on rising and falling arpeggiations of a dominant-seventh harmony (B7 in the key of E major) that span a range of two octaves. The proposed fingering indicated beneath the guitar staff in Example 5 suggests that he may have played this passage with all four left-hand fingers traversing all of the instrument's strings but the lowest. This would permit his hand to remain between the fingerboard's sixth and tenth frets, obviating the need for inefficient shifting up and down the guitar neck. In the wake of his injury such fingerings were often no longer feasible.

Some examples of Reinhardt's mature solo work are seen in Example 6, which shows excerpts from his 1937 performance of "Sweet Georgia Brown" (Reinhardt 1937b). In Example 6a he plays an arpeggiation of a diminished-seventh chord that ascends almost two octaves from F# through D# (this is one of Reinhardt's favored melodic formulas). When fingered using only the index and middle fingers, this figure is most comfortably executed by progressively shifting the left hand from the instrument's fourth fret up to the eleventh (and finally the twelfth) fret. With at least three available fingers, a more orthodox fingering would allow the

Example 5. "Moi Aussi" (Marceau-Dehette). 1928.

Example 6. "Sweet Georgia Brown" (Bernie-Pinkard-Casey). 1937.

performer to execute the same figure while remaining between the ninth and thirteenth frets.

Example 6c shows the solo's closing measures, in which Reinhardt displays his trademark technique of playing in octaves. These are probably fingered by stretching three frets between the first and second (or, perhaps, first and third) fingers so as to depress two non-adjacent strings with one intervening string simultaneously damped by light pressure from the first finger, as described above by Neil and Gates. And in Example 6b Reinhardt plays an ascending triplet sequence that uses the guitar's open D-string as a repeated pedal tone beneath a series of arpeggiated gestures. These can be rendered using only the first two fingers of the left hand in alternation across adjacent strings, which requires considerable coordination to accomplish at the given tempo of quarter-note = 204.

The astonishing facility with which Reinhardt was able to execute these sorts of rapid, technically daunting effects brings us, in closing, to a key aspect of his historic significance in the evolution of guitar technique. Despite his handicap, Reinhardt can yet be regarded as a forerunner of the cult of guitar virtuosity that has emerged in recent decades. Neither his predecessors, such as Eddie Lang, nor his swing-era contemporaries, like Charlie Christian, equaled Reinhardt's technical achievements in terms of sheer physical speed. But during the post-World War II era, and particularly with the rise of the electric guitar, guitarists of all stripes—perhaps more so than most other instrumentalists—have often placed a premium on velocity. This attitude may arguably have led to the occasional elevation of superficial technique over artistic substance (Ratliff 2000). Such a broad trend cannot be credited to any single individual, but Reinhardt set an important precedent nonetheless.

On the evidence of recordings, Charlie Christian's playing showed few overt signs of Reinhardt's influence, notwithstanding the curious anecdote noted earlier. In fact, though his records were available in the United States during the 1930s, Reinhardt's reputation was still fairly modest in America when Christian began performing. In the *Down Beat* magazine poll of January 1939, Reinhardt ranked fifteenth in the guitar category, well behind artists who are virtually unknown today (17). In January 1940 Christian, having reached a wider audience after joining the

Benny Goodman Orchestra, placed first in *Down Beat*'s guitar poll, with Reinhardt ranked twentieth (13). But several other comparably influential guitarists later adopted specific instrumental techniques that Reinhardt originated. His use of octave doublings later reappeared as a signature device in the playing of Wes Montgomery, widely regarded as the greatest jazz guitarist of the 1960s. Montgomery, like Reinhardt, would often end a single-note solo with a passage in octaves, creating a more emphatic sense of closure (van der Bliek 1991, 151–52).[9] The same effect is also occasionally used by blues guitarist B. B. King. Jerry Richardson has identified several other elements of King's style that may be traced to Reinhardt, whom King acknowledges as an early influence. Foremost are King's use of certain types of melodic ornamentation, such as upper-neighbor-note embellishments and expressive pitch bends, created by "choking" the guitar strings (increasing a string's tension by bending it with the left hand) (Richardson 1999, 294–95, 288–89). King has in turn been a major influence on many leading rock guitarists (Menn 1992, 46, 76, 129, 173).

The most influential aspects of Reinhardt's guitar technique—the octaves, ornamental inflections, and phenomenal digital velocity—have little direct relationship to his physical handicap. Indeed, it is a striking paradox that one of his most historically significant technical innovations—pure speed of execution—was in an area where his injury would appear to be most disadvantageous. Persistent misconceptions about Reinhardt's disability have fostered an enduring conundrum: his disability seems in theory to have been of enormous significance, yet in practice to have been spectacularly irrelevant. This article has sought to reconcile this contradiction. Though I have argued that his injury may have been less severe than many sources suggest, we should not, however, underestimate what was nonetheless a colossal challenge. That he surmounted this challenge attests not so much to the inconsequence of his affliction as to his extraordinary feat in transcending it.

BRAZILIAN JAZZ AND FRICTION OF MUSICALITIES

—*Acácio Tadeu de Camargo Piedade*

Translation by Helen Langdon

This article is a brief ethnography of Brazilian instrumental popular music (*música instrumental*), which is known in the internationally as Brazilian jazz (see also Piedade 1999a). I intend to focus on Brazilian jazz as a musical genre of Brazilian popular music and not as a national adaptation of jazz, and to search for its main characteristics and socio-cultural nexus in contrast with North American jazz. The specific goal is to show how there is constant reference in Brazilian jazz to North American jazz, mainly in the realm of improvisations, and that these references mark the tense encounter between Brazilian and North American musicalities, a founding characteristic of this music. I begin by explaining the meaning of the term *música instrumental*, and then I trace a brief historical overview of Brazilian jazz and draft a definition of the musical field through its lines. I then explain the use of the term *bebop*, which appears frequently in the verb form *bebopear* (to bebop), and in the following section I demonstrate the correlations between Brazilian jazz and bebop. Finally, in order to account for the characteristics of Brazilian jazz, I develop the idea of friction of musicalities.

I do not intend to write a history of Brazilian jazz, but rather to begin an exploration of the theme in an attempt to gather preliminary data to help construct Brazilian jazz as an object of anthropological study. This paper is based on ethnographic data obtained in interviews and jam sessions with musicians active in the São Paulo scene, one of the most significant in Brazil (Piedade 1999b). I refer to these musicians and their audience as natives, in the sense of people who belong to a musical community. The results of this paper are also the fruit of my own musical background and professional experience as a musician in this scene.

41

Instead of Brazilian jazz, the designation of this musical genre in Brazil is *música instrumental brasileira* (Brazilian instrumental music). Naturally, in Brazil the word *instrumental* also means the music composed for and played exclusively with instruments—that is, music that does not have any lyrics or text—which includes genres from Western European "art music." However, the term *música instrumental* is the label used by the natives for the specific corpus of musical productions of Brazilian jazz. This way, the category *MPB, música popular brasileira,* taken as the heterogeneous collection of popular urban musical productions in Brazil that has been showing stability at least from the 1960s on, is taken here as a supergenre comprised of categories such as *música instrumental,* national rock/blues, *bossa nova, pagode, sertaneja* music, *samba, forró, axé* music, *lambada,* etc. Since there are many types of instrumental music, the natives are aware of the inadequacy of the term *música instrumental,* and for them the correct designation would thus be *música popular instrumental brasileira* (Brazilian instrumental popular music). The fact is, it is called *música instrumental.*

Meanwhile, in magazines and stores outside of Brazil *Brazilian jazz* is used, and especially in the United States Brazilian jazz is frequently regarded as a sub-field of Latin jazz, a generic label that also designates Afro-Caribbean genres such as salsa. However, this wide use of the term *Latin jazz,* which places Brazil in the Latin world, is not shared in Brazil, where natives use the word Latin to refer solely to Afro-Cuban rhythms. This rejection of Brazil's Latin qualities reveals a contrastive construction of cultural identities, hiding what in reality is a common ground, as for example in the idea of *mestizo* (Quintero-Rivera 2000).[1] A similar phenomenon is expressed by the natives' refusal to call *música instrumental* Brazilian jazz. According to many of them, as a category jazz is too heavy and does not encompass all the musical diversity of música *instrumental.* However, for purposes of international promotion, the label *Brazilian jazz* is accepted, especially since *música instrumental* is also an incorrect denomination, as stated above.

The ambiguous nature of the term *música instrumental* is symptomatic of the actual uncertainty surrounding the dimension of its musical field and its historical roots. In fact, most natives recognize the fluidity of the genre and ask themselves what unites musicians as dissimilar as Egberto

Gismonti, Hermeto Pascoal, Toninho Horta, and so many others. Despite this uncertainty, there is a shared tacit knowledge and a lived experience that enable the natives to recognize what is *música instrumental*, so much so that they are constantly seeking legitimation of their identity in the face of MPB and jazz, two musical traditions that are very close to *música instrumental*.

According to native interpretations, Brazilian jazz originated in the beginning of the twentieth century, with the emergence of an instrumental genre of Portuguese influence known as *choro* (weeping), which to this day is played and greatly appreciated (Cazes 1998), and widely considered by natives as the ancestor of Brazilian jazz. The history of *choro*, or *chorinho*, involves interesting facts for this discussion, and therefore I shall relate a brief history until the advent of *bossa nova* in the 1950s, when Brazilian jazz most clearly emerges, differentiating itself from *chorinho*.

In Brazil, by the second half of the nineteenth century, there was a rich repertoire of European instrumental dance music, such as *polka*, *mazurka*, and *schottisch*, rhythms that were blended and transformed in the national genres of the time, such as *maxixe* and *lundu*. At this point, the word *choro* simply meant a typical musical formation known as *trio de pau e corda* (wood and string trio), which performed *maxixe* in an improvisational manner (Reily 2000, 6); later then, *choro* came to mean a way of playing, and finally, around the 1930s, it designated a musical genre. Even though it emerged among the popular classes, *choro* established a strong connection with art music through figures such as Ernesto Nazareth and Chiquinha Gonzaga, who composed fully scored *choros*. The bourgeoisie started to appreciate this *choro* dressed as art music, and began to see it as an expression of Brazilianess, for it was eager at this time for symbols of national identity to counteract France's cultural prominence. *Chorinho* established itself through musicians such as Pixinguinha and Garoto, who paved the road for other instrumental music to conquer the public's tastes. It should be noted that the origins of *chorinho* and *samba* are deeply interwoven, and the consolidation of *chorinho* as an individual genre is perhaps related to the great shift in style that occurred within *samba* in the 1930s, when the old *samba-maxixe*, dating from the mid-1800s, gave way to the more "whitened" *samba* of the *sambistas* of Estácio (Sandroni 2001).

In the 1920s, more precisely in 1922, during the *Semana de Arte Moderna* (Week of Modern Art) in São Paulo—a fundamental moment for modernism in Brazilian art (Wisnik 1977)—the band Pixinguinha e os oito Batutas was returning from a sojourn in Paris, during which it seems to have fallen in love with jazz. While jazz was exploding commercially in the United States, in Brazil Batutas was heavily criticized for having adopted a jazzy style, for having been contaminated by jazz (Menezes Bastos 2000, 20; Vianna 1995, 117). I take this to be the first important moment of friction of musicalities in Brazilian jazz. Already present at this time is an Adornian and pessimistic view of popular music, one that seems to endure throughout the history of MPB and is based on the idea of musical autonomy (Middleton 1990, 41–45). The persistent view of some critics, who relied on what Hamm calls the modernist narrative of authenticity (1995), also stems from this. According to this narrative, folk music and music from different peoples are more valuable depending on the degree of non-contamination: the presumption here is that a culture is only authentic when it does not mix with others, leading to the notion that a commercial product and authenticity are irreconcilable. By the end of the decade, important intellectuals such as Gilberto Freyre were criticizing jazz and the influence of North American culture on Brazil (Vianna 1995, 182), in the same tone in which José Ramos Tinhorão would later criticize *bossa nova*.

In sum, the natives consider *chorinho* to be the great ancestor of Brazilian jazz, even though the latter only properly emerged as the heart of musical experiences of the *bossa nova* period. The natives have much respect for *chorinho* performers, especially great masters such as Pixinguinha, yet they explain that contemporary *chorinho* has become too much of a conservative genre in general terms. The natives accept this fact because they attribute to *chorinho* the role of a root music, which must be preserved from exotic influences. However, this native thinking hides a certain rivalry that results from the *chorinho* musicians' self-conscious strategy to stay away from the jazz influence, which touches on several symbolic points to which the natives are sensitive. According to native discourse, even though *chorinho*'s symbolic advantage of being root music and not having undergone the influence of jazz causes a certain tension between *chorinho* and Brazilian jazz, the natives absorb a lot from *choros* melodic patterns. This is very interesting when seen as a rebirth of the old concept of *choro* as a way of playing, prevalent in the early 20th century. Personally, I think that what confers the seemingly conservative face of *chorinho* is actually a structural characteristic of this genre, which evokes nostalgia, simplicity, virtuosity, and cosmopolitanism. I think this thematic stability makes *chorinho* subject to eclipse phases, which in fact occurred from the 1940s, when it scarcely developed, until the 1970s, when *choro* festivals started boosting the re-emergence of the genre. Currently *chorinho* is undergoing an impressive revival, mainly in the cities of Rio de Janeiro and Brasília, with the emergence of the groups Trio Madeira Brasil, Arranca-toco, trio Brasília Brasil, artists such as Maurício Carrilho and Yamandú Costa, as well as the specialized record label Kuarup Discos. The music of art music composer Radamés Gnatalli plays a central role in this rekindling of *choro*. Contemporary *choro* explores new repertoires, however, attempting to maintain the traditional sound and typical distance from jazz. It has been a separate musical genre from Brazilian jazz since at least the 1950s, yet despite this differentiation *choro* musicality is an important element in the compositions and improvisations of Brazilian jazz. This musicality is primarily enacted through melodic characteristics, which emerge in the typical shaping of the melody and use of *appoggiatura* and *arpeggios*, often in *scherzando* spirit.

In the 1930s the repressive dictatorship of Getúlio Vargas began, lasting until 1945 and marked by nationalist discourse. In this so-called radio era, many groups—referred to as *regionais*—showed up to play live for radio broadcasts. During this period the Rio de Janeiro carnival was glorified, helping to transform *samba* (which until then had been rejected and execrated by the elites) into Brazil's national music, through the interaction and dialogue between Afro-Brazilian musicians and intellectuals and artists of the city of Rio de Janeiro. This is what Vianna terms "the mystery of *samba*" (1995). Meanwhile, the presence of American culture in Brazil was intensified during this period, mainly through movies and dance music. Brazilian *samba* was represented in the United States primarily by the figure of Carmen Miranda and *Bando da Lua*, interestingly exhibiting a fairly Mexicanized image. Miranda created a particular view of Brazilianess, strongly criticized in Brazil because of the anti-American climate disseminated by the nationalist thought of the 1940s (Vianna 1995, 129–31).

While, since the end of the 1920s, many dance bands in major Brazilian cities had played fox-trot and other North American music in dance salons (Kiefer 1979, 60–61), in the 1930s they started to play Brazilian rhythms, such as *chorinho*, for dancing. This tradition led to the *gafieira* bands of the 1940s that played instrumental music based on arrangements of popular songs and instrumental compositions that were different from both fox-trot and *chorinho*. Despite exploring Brazilian rhythms, many of these bands began calling themselves jazz bands, but only because the term gave the band a modern touch, not because it was musically influenced by jazz (Cazes 1998, 61). Despite its huge success, this instrumental dance music left the scene in the 1960s and only returned, mainly in São Paulo in the mid-1980s, with the revival of the *gafieira* (Piedade 1999b).

Another important fact of the 1940s was the avant-garde art music group surrounding German composer Hans-Joachim Koellreutter, called *Música Viva*, which represented a great renovation of the language of the previous nationalist paradigm, headed by Villa-Lobos. Popular music and atonalism profoundly influenced *Música Viva* composers such as Claudio Santoro and Guerra-Peixe, and the *gafieira* maestros K-chimbinho and Severino Araújo were among their students, as well as future exponents of *bossa nova*, such as Moacyr Santos and António Carlos Jobim. Yet this was an avant-garde movement. At the time much nationalistic criticism was directed against its advances, and Brazilian art music was marked in the following decade by the outcome of a new nationalism (Neves 1981, 77–106).

During the post-World War II years, nationalism was on the rise in many countries, accompanied by an impressive consolidation of North American jazz in the international arena, and at this time many "nationalized" jazz styles emerged. In the midst of this scene, *bossa nova* was born and artists such as João Gilberto and António Carlos Jobim appeared, constituting a landmark in Brazilian and world popular music (see Castro 1990). At the end of the 1950s and early 1960s, names such as Laurindo de Almeida, Charlie Byrd, and Stan Getz made *bossa nova* known to the North American audience. While the world was discovering *bossa nova*, an entire generation of instrumentalists profoundly influenced by jazz got involved with this music, creating mostly instrumental *bossa nova* trios, such as the Milton Banana trio, Tamba trio, Jongo trio, and bigger groups, such as J. T. Meireles and the Copa 5. All these groups frequently played at bars and jazz clubs, such as Bottles and Farneys bar in Rio de Janeiro. West Coast jazz was heavily appreciated and played, and in fact its influence on *bossa nova* is undeniable, even though the cool element of *bossa nova* may have an older connection with the 19th century *modinhas* in Brazil (Menezes Bastos 1999a). While João Gilberto's famous guitar beat came from the rhythmic patterns of *samba* (Garcia 1999), *bossa nova* harmonies were derived not only from jazz, but were also congruent with Brazilian urban music of the 1930s and 1940s, especially the dance band arrangements (Pinheiro 1992). Despite this, in the 1960s *bossa nova* was strongly criticized, accused of being elitist and resulting from the Americanization of MPB (especially by Tinhorão 1974, 1998). This was counteracted by critics who affirmed the modernity of *bossa* (Campos 1974), and by *tropicalismo* (Veloso 1997). The crystallization of Brazilian jazz as a musical genre occurred precisely in this environment—in the instrumental universe around *bossa nova*—and thereafter it developed apart from *chorinho*, which would cultivate its conservative nature, and apart from instrumental dance music.

Throughout the 1960s, *bossa nova* was still appreciated within Brazil and was legitimized by its international success, but it began to fade away until its revival in the 1980s (Castro 1990). In addition to *bossa nova*, several simultaneous waves occurred in MPB in the 1960s: the movement known as *jovem guarda*, which assumed a well-behaved romantic rebellion with its bolero-like rock & roll songs (Menezes Bastos 1999b); protest music, which affirmed a necessary political engagement of art (Tinhorão 1974); and finally, the *tropicália* movement, which synthesized all these waves (Dunn 2001; Sanches 2000; Calado 1997; Veloso 1997). *Tropicalismo* is an attempt to articulate modernity and tradition, hence touching deeply on what Da Matta termed the Brazilian dilemma: the founding dichotomization of Brazilian ethics between the rural-traditional-holistic and the urban-modern-individualistic worlds (1979). In the midst of these various waves, the emerging Brazilian jazz was growing, sustained mainly by *bossa nova* and its reflections in the United States, where the celebrated meeting of João Gilberto and Stan Getz symbolized the encounter between the Brazilianess of *bossa nova* and the Americanness of jazz, launching a dialogue of musicalities that would become central to Brazilian jazz. The compatibility of Getz's solos with the groove of *bossa nova* created a sound that would be explored also by cool jazz artists.

In addition, Airto Moreira, Flora Purim, Oscar Castro Neves, and other Brazilian musicians who lived in the United States started bringing to jazz Brazilian rhythms such as *baião*, and percussion instruments such as the *pandeiro* and *berimbau*. The occasional inclusion of these exotic elements in American jazz reflexively stimulated natives and changed their way of playing, while legitimizing the continuity of Brazilian jazz. In other words, elements of Brazilian music, because of the way in which they were incorporated into North American music, return to their original source legitimized by international recognition, and thus end up reinserting themselves into and reinventing tradition. A recent example of this reflexivity is the North American drummer's typical way of playing *samba* and *bossa*, heavily drawing on cymbals, which influenced the style of many Brazilian drummers, who in turn create new ways of playing. This reflexivity seems to me an essential constituent of the cultural systems of reappropriation and rearticulation of globalized musicalities, since the world's musical genres are composed mutually and dialogically. MPB itself results from a notable interaction with Caribbean, Paraguayan, and Argentinean music (Menezes Bastos 1999b), with bolero playing a central role (Araújo 1999).

In the 1970s, despite the constraint in Brazilian culture caused by the military dictatorship that began in 1964, independent record labels came out in Rio de Janeiro and São Paulo, such as Lira Paulistana, dedicated to promoting Brazilian jazz. In other regions of the country the genre also developed significantly: in Minas Gerais, where the *Clube da Esquina* movement and groups like Som Imaginário and Azymuth emerged; and in Pernambuco, where the *Armorial* movement arose, blending the traditions of popular Northeastern culture with avant-garde art.

In the 1980s, Brazilian jazz began to appear in international jazz festivals such as the one in Montreaux. At the same time that the success of national rock was dawning (Dapieve 1995), Brazilian jazz seemed to have achieved maturity with the music of Hermeto Pascoal and Egberto Gismonti, forming a musical unity that remains to this day relatively homogeneous in thematic, structural, and stylistic terms, and consisting therefore of a genre of recent tradition. In addition, one must not forget the important role of brass bands, mainly in small Brazilian towns, which until at least the 1960s frequently played in park bandstands. For example, many musicians from the Mantiqueira band, an important current exponent of Brazilian jazz, began their musical experiences in connection with these bands, as is the case of saxophonist and clarinetist Nailor Proveta. With the maturity of Brazilian jazz in the 1980s, the following decade represented a period of impressive growth, recounted later. I shall now examine the lines and tendencies of Brazilian jazz.

I identify three terms representing the main tendencies of Brazilian jazz: *brazuca*, *fusion*, and *ecm*. According to the natives' view, these are three of the so-called main *linhas* (lines) of Brazilian jazz. Native discourse refers to these lines not as closed monolithic labels, but as open and flexible thematic musical fields, where the three lines intermingle and dialogue with each other, though one of them—depending on the artist—remains salient. For this reason, the natives do not say that a given artist is *brazuca*, but that he is more *brazuca*, which does not exclude his *fusion* and *ecm* qualities.

The more *brazuca* line—a term obviously derived from Brazil—consists of national rhythms such as *samba*, *baião*, *frevo*, and *maracatu*, and articulates the jazz language in a dialogue with expressive elements of these rhythms. The most prominent exponent of *brazuca* is Hermeto Pascoal, and its oldest referential is the legendary Quarteto Novo. Northeastern musicality (that is, musical material that originated in the Brazilian Northeast region and widely disseminated in all Brazilian music) plays a central role in this line: the extensive use of the mixolydian mode, with optional augmented fourth, or the dorian mode, with various melodic riffs, and the beat of *baião*. Another influence in the *brazuca* line is the melodic style of *chorinho*, with its typical ornamentation and its playful ethos. In a discussion among natives, one can say a given song has a "very *brazuca*" theme, or that a saxophonist has a "really *brazuca*" style of composition; that is, s/he does not simply "bebop" but has a very "roots" sound.

In the *fusion* line, the mixture of *samba* and funk predominates, based on the musical movement Black Rio and on the danceability of *carioca* funk and soul music from Rio de Janeiro. This aesthetic celebrates a predominance of corporeality, a roguish swing of *samba*, and a funky dance drive. The defunct band Cama de Gato crystallized this line, which encompasses musicians such as Leo Gandelman, Marco Suzano, and others. One of the most explored facets of the *fusion* line is the rhythmic structural similarity between *partido alto samba* and funk. One of the best known groups of this line is Aquarela Carioca, which uses the cello and *pandeiro* and creates a new, yet deeply *carioca*, sound (Connel 2001).

The *ecm* line is more jazzy and meditative, influenced by European avant-garde and world music. The word *ecm* refers to the style of the music recorded by German record label ECM, which, beginning in the 1980s, included artists such as Egberto Gismonti and Naná Vasconcelos. In this *ecm* sound there is a certain disregard for danceability, yet at the same time tremendous freedom and much room for improvisations and exploratory solos. This demands much musical background from the musician, including knowledge of art music. The inclusion of South American indigenous musicality and instruments, such as the rain stick, is typical of this line, and helps create an atmosphere of suspended time, evoking rituality and mythical temporality.

As stated above, the natives believe that in Brazilian jazz there is no repertoire whose tendency is solely and purely *brazuca*, *fusion*, or *ecm*. These three tendencies are part of a pragmatic knowledge and may be articulated by the same artist or group, or may even appear in different moments of the same composition, or in a single improvisation. For example, the Cama de Gato sound, classified as a more *fusion* line, also expresses *brazuca* tendencies, but the *fusion* tendencies are dominant. These lines may be seen as styles of the Brazilian jazz genre. My understanding of a musical style is inspired by Bakhtin's (1986) ideas about styles of language and functional styles, which consider generic styles for certain spheres of human activity and communication. As typical forms of communicative spheres, styles are inseparably linked to particular compositional units. That is, they are connected to certain types of constructions, as parts of a totality, yet they also act over them as if polishing their surfaces. *Brazuca*, *fusion*, and *ecm*, inseparable from the repertoire of Brazilian jazz, are mental constructions that are articulated and communicatively recognized by the natives, and they cross the Brazilian jazz musical genre without touching on the deeper aspects of its structure.

There is a particular kind of symbolic relationship uniting these three lines: more *brazuca* points inwardly, to what is internal, to the regional identity of its rhythms; more *fusion* evokes a corporeality common to *samba* and funk, symbolizing a viability of musicalities that highlight blackness and hence tradition; while the more *ecm* line, directing itself outwardly—towards globality and intersubjectivity—points towards globalization. Such directions show how the lines of Brazilian jazz mirror Da Matta's aforementioned "Brazilian dilemma."

I should reiterate that currently there is much more instrumental music being cultivated in Brazil in addition to Brazilian jazz, such as *chorinho* and the dance music of *gafieira*, both classified by the natives as within a possible line termed *resgate* (rescue). By looking into the multiplicity of current tendencies of MPB (Mello 2000), today it is possible to find recordings of a variety of regional instrumental musics, such as the music of *viola caipira* player Helena Meireles, electric trios from Bahia, and experimental groups such as Uakti.

In native discourse, *bebop* is a musical language connected to the North American jazz bebop tradition developed from the 1940s on, but mainly its melodic dimensions. The *bebop* serves as a basic springboard for Brazilian jazz musicians to create a type of methodology, indicated by the large-scale use of the famous compilation of jazz songs called the "real book," and Charlie Parker's solo transcriptions, the "omni book" (Gutstein 1978), referred to as a "bible" by many saxophonists. What is worth noting here is that the jazz language is extremely structured and normatized, and therefore strictly conventional, as Berliner (1994) demonstrates. Berliner reveals the development of a unique improvisational jazz voice, considering it to be an aesthetic and a tradition—what I call a musicality. Brazilian jazz natives are aware of this normative aspect of jazz, and they use the verb *bebopear* (to bebop) as meaning "to articulate phrases according to this style," which means it is necessary to know, respect, and follow its rules. Here I shall limit myself to exposing a few meanings of *bebopear*, gathered from the clues of native discourse:

- *suingar* (to swing), which is to imprint the jazz feel (Brazilian musicians interpret this as the predominance of 12/8 meter). Each beat should express two notes most of the time, the second corresponding to the last ternary subdivision of the beat. This note should be lightly accentuated in order to get *suíngue* (swing). While the bass should strictly hold the pulse by always playing on the beat, the drums should "think in front," that is, play ahead of the beat, and the phrases *suingadas* (swinging) of the soloist should hold it, that is, to force back by playing behind the beat. This way, the group shall be really *suingando* (swinging). This native meaning of swing can be compared to U.S. jazz natives' notions of swing, groove, and feel, approximating an interesting definition by Van Praag (cited by Keil): "swing is a physical tension that comes from the rhythms being attracted by the metre" (Feld and Keil 1994, 59);

- the wide use of patterns or standardized harmonic sequences of the II-V-I type, also with substitute chords;
- the use of typical melodic cliches, or riffs, which are ready-made musical phrases to be engaged in specific harmonic patterns;
- the manner of linking the notes available for improvisation to the type of chord in the harmonic basis and to the chord alterations;
- the way of attacking these notes by employing chromatic and diatonic approximations;
- the creative interaction between the rhythm section and the soloist, as shown by Monson (1996).

All these points are meanings that the natives employ in their use of the concept of *bebop*. Transgressions of the system, such as the use of poly-tonality and the so-called outside scales, are accepted in this *bebop* aes-thetic of Brazilian jazz.

The object of this article is not the Brazilian interpretation of jazz, but a specific genre, Brazilian jazz, which is born within the instrumental world of *bossa nova* and involves from the outset an encounter of the Brazilian and North American jazz musicalities, which I term friction of musicalities. Several studies on music show that genres are cultural constructions classi-fied by natives and that the borders between musical genres are flexible and mutable, and therefore questionable under several points of view. Genres in popular music are subject to intense fluidity: new genres with new labels emerge constantly, often through the intersection of multiple existing genres, or from the reevaluation of their symbolic borders. Likewise, there may exist musical genres that are performed but which have no label, as occurs with literary genres (Ducrot and Todorov 1972, 147). To approach musical genres as discourses is one way of trying to unfold the cultural meanings that underlie their construction (Walser 1993). The notion of genre employed here is inspired by the ideas of Bakhtin about speech genres (1986): a musical genre is like a set of musical and symbolic elements that presents stability in terms of thematics, styles, and compositional structures.

Genres are therefore like spheres of popular music that incorporate relatively similar musical productions during a certain period of time and are constantly subject to changes. All over the world, musicians are constantly creating new fusions and connections, and for this reason the study of genres in popular music is a difficult and constant task. Supergenres are the categories that somehow encompass several musical genres, and Brazilian jazz, as we saw above, is a musical genre that belongs more to the supergenre MPB than to the supergenre jazz.

I view musicality as more than a musical language: it is a set of musical and symbolic elements, deeply interconnected, that constitutes a system which rules the musical world of a given community. It is also the competence of musical hearing and practicing enacted through this musical-symbolic system, a capacity that derives largely from a learning process. Even though it results from a particular manner of ordering the audible world achieved through cultural transmission, it is not monolithic and exclusive: as a repository of cultural meanings, constituting a kind of "cultural memory" (Floyd Jr. 1995), a musicality can be approached by means of observation and participation. Thereby, an individual can reach a certain competence in different musicalities, similarly to what Hood (1960) termed "bimusicality." An example of this is Brazilian jazz natives' efforts to attain competence in jazz; so are the efforts of some North American jazz natives in relation to Brazilian music.

Bebopear is the expression of the Brazilian reading of the jazz musicality, yet it is simultaneously both valuable and fearsome for most Brazilian jazz natives: it demonstrates technical know-how and mastery of the jazz language, which symbolically is a passport to global communicability, but at the same time it teleologically points to the need for dissolving *bebop* itself and expressing what distinguishes it from Brazilian jazz, that which is nearer to a root of Brazilian musicality and therefore more authentic. There is an important contradiction here, which refers to the already mentioned modernist narrative of authenticity. However, along with the drive to avoid contamination from the *bebop* paradigm and to seek an expression that is more rooted in Brazil, there is an absolute cannibalization of the jazz musicality, explicit in the natives' discourse about their favorite jazz masters and the wide use of jazz methods for instrumental improvement, such as the aforementioned books and workbooks.

The moment of improvisation clearly exemplifies these considerations: when a native soloist has a free space for expression, there are moments when he gives himself frankly to *bebop*, seeking the weight of the jazz tradition that gives him legitimacy and confers on him the symbolic status of global improviser; but at the same time he tries to express something more Brazilian, making use of traits of other Brazilian music genres, such as *chorinho*. A very frequent resource at this time is the use of Northeastern musicality, considered to be a "root" musical universe and a safe ground for authentic expression. The idea of valuing "roots" is still very strong in Brazilian music, and its origins are probably found in nineteenth-century German romantic thought, with the congruence between the concepts of popular, nation, and rural (Middleton 1990, 4). This relationship to the Northeast as source of authenticity is historical, and recalls the foundations of Brazilian modernist thought of the 1920s and 1930s (Menezes Bastos 2000, 23–24). Therefore, in Brazil "roots" are found in the countryside, in rural areas, in rustic simplicity, as opposed to the complexities of the urban world. Other possible resources to escape *bebop* involve hybrid languages of the urban world—such as romantic lyricism from contemporary Brazilian songs—as well as the "atonal moments" of outside scales, and the expression of other Brazilian musicalities connected to regional musical developments in the country, such as music from Bahia, from the Amazon, and from Rio Grande do Sul (Lucas 2000). I argue that these fields express their own musicalities, which are here re-enacted in a new context.

I am attempting to show that the musicality of Brazilian jazz is comprised of an amalgam of regional musicalities—Northeastern, *chorinho*, *samba*, Afro-Bahian, free (urban atonalism, outside scales)—that is placed in a relationship with North American jazz musicality that is both tense and synthesizing, near-coming and distance-taking, and that this relationship is charged with native discourses regarding cultural imperialism, national identity, globalization, and regionalism. In order to understand this dialectic relationship that constitutes Brazilian jazz, I came up with the concept of friction of musicalities, which was inspired by Brazilian anthropologist Roberto Cardoso de Oliveira's theory of interethnic friction (1964, 1972). Cardoso de Oliveira developed this theory beginning in the 1960s, in order to capture the unequal relationship between the indigenous and Brazilian societies, which he saw as marked by contradiction. The conflict, inherent to the reality of interethnic friction, is explained by the diverse interests of the societies in contact and their irreversible entanglement and interdependence. Cardoso de Oliveira stays away from the ideas of transmission, acculturation, or assimilation, linked to the previous culturalist paradigm, and directs the focus away from cultural change and towards the continued interaction between the two societies that forms an intersocietal system. This system exhibits, in its core, inequality. It is not my intention to present here the discussions about this concept, carried out in Brazilian ethnology, but to show how it can inspire a new look at this tension between Brazilian and North American musicality in the heart of Brazilian jazz.

As I have already stated, I understand musicality to be an integrated set of musical and symbolic elements that manifests itself in a human community. In the case of jazz, this community is currently international and culturally pluralistic, and according to the native discourse, this community shares what could be called a *bebop* paradigm, that is, a jazz musicality that enables a global musical communicability. Yet Brazilian jazz, as I attempted to demonstrate, while devouring this *bebop* paradigm, incessantly seeks to distance itself from North American musicality, by enacting a Brazilian musicality. This tension is congenital and essential to Brazilian jazz as a musical genre, as long as it remains stable in terms of thematics (the friction of musicalities is constituent here, exposing itself more clearly in the improvisations), styles (the regional lines and idioms, such as Northeastern musicality), and compositional structures (in the musical code proper, such as in the rhythmic patterns and use of modality). The clash between the Northeastern mixolydian and the blues scale is part of this stability; it is a fundamental distinction of Brazilian jazz. Here, the musicalities converse but do not mix; their musical-symbolic borders are not crossed but instead are objects of a manipulation that end up reaffirming the differences. The mechanical metaphor of friction implies that the objects in contact touch and rub each other's outer layers, perhaps exchanging particles, but the substances of the hardened nuclei tend to be preserved. That is why we should not speak of complementarity, as many discourses naively do, since the nature of this friction is not constructive but deconstructive, full of tension and flexibility, and often of irony, such as in the examples of friction of musicalities involving irony and parody in jazz (Monson 1996, 106–25).

Despite the fact that native discourse occasionally affirms that such tension is undesirable—that is, a decharacterizing element that tends to disappear in an ideal future fusion—I think it is actually a very salient constituent part of the genre, a strong identity mark that gives it its national and global character. This friction is related to the common-sense narratives of North American cultural hegemony in Brazil and hence to the association of jazz as something invasive and unwanted in Brazilian culture. The symptomatic rejection of jazz is connected to anti-American sentiments that partially developed in Brazil, mainly beginning with the nationalism of the 1930s and the leftist discourse of the 1960s, when the cultivation of jazz was associated with the Brazilian economic elite, where jazz was supposed to be considered refined or *chic*. To listen to and know jazz was a sign of status, culture, cosmopolitanism, and participation in North American culture—a cultural passport to belong to a global elite—and a sign of alienation and disregard in relation to Brazilian culture. In this manner, while the feelings that manifest the repudiation of jazz are directly connected to the sociological aspects above, the cannibalism of Brazilian jazz points to a dissolution of the nationalist and patriotic discourse and leads to the idea of multicultural participation in the formation of the genre.

Any analysis of Brazilian jazz must examine the musical elements at play, such as motives, scales, chords, chord patterns, riffs, improvisations, forms, dynamics, as well as the embodied meanings in them (Meyer 1967). I find it very important to transcribe improvisations, to play in jam sessions, and to analyze native discourse. The fact is, in Brazilian jazz there are specific rhythmic-melodic inflections and beat de-synchronizations that may evoke a certain looseness, coherent with the open and relaxed nature attributed to Brazilian music in general, and nevertheless there is much normatization in such elements. All this is full of cultural significance and ideological implications. For example, the several kinds of drums *levadas* (leadings), the exact point at which a beat should occur, the often asymmetrical cymbal strokes—seemingly flexible aspects—are actually shared skills and involve much precision. As Keil (1994) proposes, they are participatory discrepancies. The discourse of natives—recalling that it includes not only musicians but also listeners and experts—is full of metaphors central to an understanding of the aesthetics of Brazilian jazz, and its study, along with the analysis of emerging musical processes, can demonstrate how Brazilian jazz communicates criticism, emotions, and moral and political sensibility. The shared skills are therefore also of a socio-musical order and can lead to the knowledge of the essential gestures of the genre, that is, the rhetorical topics (Agawu 1991) central to Brazilian jazz.

To conclude, I do not think there is such a thing as authenticity per se, or universally authentic cultures or traditions. I assume traditions are inventions (Hobsbawm and Ranger 1982) and cultures are best seen not as patterns of behavior, but as sets of symbolic control devices that exist for a community to govern its behavior (Geertz 1973, 218). In order to choose what is to be considered authentic, the artificial of the past must be seen as natural in the future. Authenticity is therefore a kind of veiling of previous conventions, or as Peterson (1992) puts it, a social construction that partially deforms the past. With this view of authenticity, it becomes harder to see globalization as a destructive process in which there is a flow of transnational influences that fully commands the sensibilities of the so-called "peripheral" cultures, making them increasingly non-distinct from the center. In other words, the ideas of assimilation or homogenization seem no longer appropriate, since there is neither an actual authenticity to be preserved nor a supposed authenticity of hegemonic cultures. The "peripheral" cultures (Hannerz 1991) can recolonize this flow through local responses, thus dissolving the view of a center-periphery polarization and of a unilateral direction of cultural exchange. In my opinion, there always was and always is cultural change and exchange, and a veiling of what is to be elected as the "authentic" or the "roots" of culture. In this sense, I think globalization is not something that has erupted in recent history, but an intensification of a process that originates at least in the heart of the Western modern world (Giddens 1991).

In the past ten years, the number of Brazilian jazz musicians and bands has increased in an impressive manner, even though space in the media and the amount of record labels, producers, specialized studios, and places to play have perhaps not accompanied this pace. The new generations no longer voraciously pursue *bebop* as the previous ones did. For this reason, Brazilian jazz is increasingly less jazz and more *música instrumental*. The mythic references today are much more Hermeto Pascoal, Egberto Gismonti, Pixinguinha, Radamés Gnatalli; that is, the pillars of this musicality are found mostly in Brazilian artists.[2] Regional instrumental music is growing and as a consequence so is decentralization in relation to the Rio de Janeiro/São Paulo axis, and yet an increasing number of young people are playing *cavaquinho*, *viola caipira*, *zabumba*, and the accordion, instruments that until recently had been left out. A much less prejudiced and more advantageous relationship with the world of art music has also been established, and groups of chamber music, such as clarinet quintets and guitar quartets, have emerged, dedicated to playing *música instrumental*. Indeed, the scenario is undergoing notable internal expansion.[3] It seems that starting in the 1990s, while the growth of the world music consumption in the United States and Europe was reflecting an openness to different musical cultures, Brazilian musicians were looking inwardly towards their own traditions, discovering and appreciating their "roots," or rather, recreating them under a new perspective. What is now maintained from the spirit of jazz is much less the *bebop* phrasing and the worship of great jazz masters and much more the freedom of creation and improvisation. In this deeper sense, Brazilian jazz continues to be jazz, a transnational musical movement. Throughout the twentieth century, North American jazz expanded around the world and elicited diverse responses. Today jazz belongs to the world and needs to be studied as a transnational reality: it is global culture.

JAZZ IN INDIA

Perspectives on Historical Development and
Musical Acculturation

—Warren R. Pinckney, Jr.

Excerpted from an article published in *Asian Music* 21.1 (Fall/Winter 1989/1990): 35–77. Reprinted with permission of the author and the Society for Asian Music.

The aim of this essay is to analyze the unfolding of American jazz in India. I conducted field work for this study in Bombay in February and March 1988, during Jazz Yatra, India's biennial international jazz festival. The idea of conducting jazz research in India first occurred to me during a European lecture tour I made in 1986. While searching for albums by European jazz musicians in a record store in Cologne, I discovered the album *Jazz and Hot Dance in India—1926–1944*, which contained dance band arrangements recorded in India during the swing era, and which featured musicians from various countries including the United States, Canada, and India. I decided to contact Jazz India, a nonprofit organization for the promotion of jazz in India, to arrange attendance at the Jazz Yatra festival as an observer, and to set up interviews with jazz musicians and aficionados. I tape-recorded interviews, videotaped the festival, and collected recordings, articles, and artifacts.

The relationship between jazz and Indian music has received some degree of scholarly attention, particularly in the recent past (see Cole 1976; Berendt 1987; Farrell 1988). These studies have provided useful insights into the influence of North Indian classical music on modern jazz in the United States. Because North Indian classical music has played a singular role in shaping modern jazz, it seemed appropriate to begin my study of Asian jazz in India, even though the Indian jazz community is relatively small and obscure compared to that of Japan or the Philippines. (This issue is addressed briefly at the end of this paper.) To my knowledge, there has been no scholarly research on jazz in India itself. This paper will attempt to fill this void and at the same time to complement Western views on the interrelationship of jazz and the urban meta-culture of India by providing a new perspective on this interrelationship. The main question I wish to address in this study is why and how jazz has been assimilated in India. It is my hypothesis that for some Indians, particularly the Westernized upper-middle classes in Indian cities, jazz represents modernization and progress. The cross-cultural nature of this essay can be of significance for the sociological study of jazz in a broader sense. This paper will 1) provide an historical overview of jazz in India through a discussion of the careers of individual musicians, 2) explore various approaches to Indian jazz, and 3) examine the attitudes of Indians regarding jazz in their country.

HISTORICAL LANDMARKS

European colonial influence on the Indian subcontinent provided the channels through which Afro-American music was introduced into India. According to jazz researcher Rainer E. Lötz,

Wm. H. Bernard was the greatest interlocutor, or middleman, that black-face minstrelsy has ever known. In 1849 he arrived in Australia and subsequently went to India, being the first to introduce minstrelsy there. Ever since, India has been visited by Afro-American and blacked-up artists. . . .[1]

Jazz first arrived in India in the 1920s, when visiting bands from overseas and local Indian bands began to perform. During the big-band era numerous European, Canadian, and American ensembles toured on the dance-band circuits, performing at most of the major hotels in Asia—in Colombo, Bombay, Calcutta, Singapore, Bangkok, Kuala Lumpur, and Shanghai (liner notes, *Jazz and Hot Dance In India*). Among the best-known foreign bands that performed in India around this time were Jimmy Leguime's Grand Hotel Orchestra and Abriani's Six. Accounts of dance band performances in India during this period suggest that the music served primarily as entertainment for Europeans living in India at the time, and that such performances had no meaningful effect on the indigenous population (Lötz 1984).

According to one of my respondents, however, numerous Indians from Bombay and other cities also attended jazz performances during this

period. Several Indians promoted jazz in the 1930s and 1940s, according
to another respondent. He said that Indian maharajahs discovered Afro-
American jazz musicians while traveling in Europe, particularly Paris, and
upon their return arranged for hotels to hire the musicians for parties
and other social functions (Jhaveri 3/5/88). Around this time several Afro-
Americans, including Leon Abbey and Crickett Smith, both of whom
worked at the Taj Mahal Hotel in Bombay, led bands in India.

Goan musicians led dance bands in India as early as the 1930s. One of
the most popular was trumpeter Chick Chocolate who, judging from photographs of the period, bore a striking resemblance to Louis Armstrong as
well as emulating Armstrong's demeanor and style of playing the trumpet.[2] Newspaper reviews and articles indicate that Chocolate was indeed
a celebrity in India, performing at prestigious hotels including the Taj
Mahal in Bombay. Several other Goan musicians, including bassist Tony
Gonsalves and saxophonists Paul Gonsalves (not the same Paul Gonsalves
who joined Duke Ellington's band in 1951) and Rudy Cotton, recorded
with Indian swing bands in the 1930s and 1940s. Niranjan Jhaveri, secretary general of Jazz India, told me that Cotton had brought twenty two
pairs of shoes back to India following performances in Sumatra, the implication being that jazz was a lucrative business in those days.[3] It is not clear,
however, whether Cotton performed primarily for Dutch colonists or
Indonesians, or for both.

Musicians from various areas of South Asia recorded in India at this
time, including clarinetist Reuben Solomon and guitarist Cedric West, both
from Burma, and George Banks, from Nepal, and some musicians even
emigrated to India. The only western jazz musician known to have settled in
India was black American pianist Teddy Weatherford. Born in West Virginia
in 1903, Weatherford moved in 1915 to New Orleans, where he made his
professional debut, and in the early 1920s to Chicago where he established
a reputation as an outstanding pianist. Later in that decade he traveled to
California and soon thereafter toured Asia, performing in Japan, China, the
East Indies, and India. Weatherford settled in the East Indies in the 1930s
and was active as a recording artist with big and small ensembles in Calcutta
from 1942 to 1944. His direct, authentic style of playing blues and jazz,
characterized by a forceful left hand, and his high visibility as a recording
artist helped establish him as a central figure in the Indian jazz community.

The musicians and fans with whom I spoke all knew of Weatherford's achievements in India.

The era of live big-band jazz in India began drawing to a close soon after Weatherford's death in Calcutta in 1945. It became increasingly difficult to earn a living playing jazz in India at this time; hence many jazz musicians went into film music. In the early 1950s, the prohibition movement in India following Indian independence, and ensuing reaction against Western ideas, led to the decline of live jazz; the loss of popularity of big-band music in general also contributed to this decline.

Anglo-Indian bands began to dominate the local jazz scene in India in the late 1940s and early 1950s.[4] The Bombay Swing Club, founded in the 1940s, featured several outstanding musicians such as saxophonists Norman Mupsbee (Mosby?) and Hal Green, and was largely patronized by Anglo-Indians. By the 1950s, jazz had come to be associated with the Indian upper class, for whom Western classical music concerts and ballroom dancing in private clubs—such as the Cricket Club of India, the Radio Club, the Willingdon Club in Bombay, and various hotels—were regarded as desirable social activities. The dance music was generally performed by string orchestras that played Western popular music, Latin American music, and jazz-tinged arrangements. It was also considered a status symbol to hire an Anglo-Indian jazz band for social functions such as weddings and parties. By the mid-1950s, however, many Anglo-Indians had emigrated to England after India finally achieved independence from Great Britain; this contributed to the closing of the Bombay Jazz Club and left a temporary void in the Indian jazz scene. Some Anglo-Indian jazz musicians continued their careers in England, a subject addressed in the novel *Queenie* by Michael Korda.

During the 1950s and 1960s, and with the beginning of modernization, the U.S. State Department sponsored tours by American jazz musicians to many parts of the world including India; there were concerts in cities such as Bombay, Madras, and Bangalore. With about one concert a year, this was one of the main sources of live jazz in India during the 1950s. Among the American musicians who performed in India during this time were Louis Armstrong, Jack Teagarden, and Red Nichols.

The 1950s marked the beginning of the career of Goan saxophonist Braz Gonsalves, one of the first Indians to play modern jazz. Gonsalves was born in the territory of Goa in Western India, one of the more European-oriented communities in the country, where his father directed a music program in a church, composed music, and played the piano. Gonsalves discovered jazz as a teenager through friends who owned American jazz recordings, and his father helped him focus his interest by giving him a jazz arrangement recorded by the Artie Shaw band. Attracted to the challenge of jazz improvisation, he first learned to play jazz by copying recorded solos note for note, and eventually he created his own solos (Gonsalves 3/5/88). Every church in Goa, according to Gonsalves, had its own music school where parishioners could learn to play instruments and study music theory. He himself played the clarinet and saxophone in church and at private social functions, and he credits Shaw, Charlie Parker, John Coltrane, and Sam Most, whom he met in Bombay and studied with informally in the 1960s, with influencing his style of playing the saxophone.

Gonsalves regards the 1950s and 1960s, during which time he exclusively played jazz in Calcutta, Delhi, and Bombay, as "the best days" of his professional career. He told me that Calcutta in particular was an active jazz city in the late 1950s, and in addition to his regular job playing jazz at Magnolia's Restaurant, Gonsalves participated in many all-night jam sessions with Indian as well as foreign musicians—from Australia and Great Britain, for example. After moving to Delhi, where he played jazz at a restaurant for six months, Gonsalves traveled to Bombay and formed a group which featured drummer Leslie Godino, pianist Xavier Fernandes, and bassist Anibal Castro.

In the early 1960s Duke Ellington's band came to Bombay, an event that Gonsalves believes contributed significantly to the assimilation of jazz in India. In addition to scheduled concerts, every night following the band's performance sidemen such as Cat Anderson, Rolf Ericson, and Paul Gonsalves would play at the Venice Restaurant in Churchgate (a shopping mall and train terminal) to capacity crowds. Braz Gonsalves performed regularly with them. The jazz sessions continued at the Venice Restaurant for nearly five years after Ellington's departure, and attracted numerous college students. According to Gonsalves, the fans tended to prefer dixieland and swing, and requested standard tunes such as "Take the 'A' Train," "Satin Doll," and "Misty."

In the 1970s Gonsalves began to perform outside India. In 1977, the Hong Kong Jazz Club invited him to play there, and to participate in a concert with a local band led by Tony Carpio in the Portuguese colony of Macao. Gonsalves estimated that two thousand Portuguese Chinese filled the auditorium. The Portuguese emcee, impressed by Gonsalves' playing, invited him to perform at a jazz festival in Portugal in 1978 alongside the Thad Jones-Mel Lewis Big Band and saxophonist Dexter Gordon. Gonsalves also performed in Warsaw, Belgrade, and Debrecen, and has toured Germany. He is regarded as India's best-known musician on the international jazz scene, but he has also continued to perform in his native country, albeit with greater emphasis on commercial music. He has made several appearances at Jazz Yatra, and is presently performing with his popular music band in the resort community of Juhu. Another prominent musician on the modern Indian jazz scene is pianist-composer Louis Banks, son of Nepalese trumpeter Pushkar Bahadur, who had settled in Calcutta in the early 1940s after receiving an invitation to play there with a European band, and changed his name to George Banks in keeping with the Western music he was playing (Bose 1988, 44–49). Dambar Bahadur, George's son, became Louis Banks.

After receiving piano lessons from his father and playing in his band, Louis Banks entered college and continued to study piano. He was influenced by several pianists including George Shearing, Oscar Peterson, Bill Evans, and Herbie Hancock. After several years of teaching school, Louis traveled with his father's band back to Nepal, where he decided to become a full-time musician. But in 1971 he returned to India, where he formed his own band, which performed at the prestigious Hindustan Hotel in Calcutta.

Banks' growing reputation resulted in an invitation to play at the Blue Fox, one of the most prestigious night spots in Calcutta, and to accompany touring jazz musicians from overseas. It also led to opportunities to play at the Oberoi Hotels in Calcutta and Delhi. Although Banks maintained an active performance schedule, financial compensation in those days was inadequate for musicians specializing in jazz; thus in the 1970s he began composing film music and music for television commercials and stage musicals. Louis Banks is considered to be one of the most accomplished jazz musicians and studio composers in India. When not working as a film composer, Banks performs with various local jazz musicians, including one of India's best-known jazz vocalists, Pam Grain. With Braz

Gonsalves, he has served as co-leader of the Jazz Yatra Sextet, which performed at the festival in 1980.

In addition to the Indian jazz musicians mentioned above, there are other local musicians who have contributed to the Indian jazz scene including pianist Baby Menezes, clarinetist Johnny Baptist, saxophonist Joe Santana and pianist Stuart De Silva from Sri Lanka.

Many Indian jazz musicians regard Jazz Yatra as a focal point for live jazz in India and an expression of the Indian perspective on the global jazz scene. The festival is only one of many contributions to jazz by its founder, Niranjan Jhaveri (Jhaveri 3/5/88). Born in Bombay in 1929, Jhaveri became involved in jazz in the early 1940s when he heard Latin American dance recordings by the Xavier Cugat orchestra and boogie-woogie arrangements performed by American swing bands. He studied the history of jazz by reading books such as *From Congo to Swing* by Robert Goffin and *Le Jazz Hot* by Hugues Panassié. Around this time Jhaveri began studying the trombone, inspired by recordings of American trombonists Kid Ory and George Brunies.

In the early 1950s, Jhaveri founded and edited the first Indian jazz periodical, *Blue Rhythm*, which published such articles as "The History of Jazz in South China" by Tony Lopes (May/June, 1953), and he established a jazz society by the same name. In addition to domestic subscriptions, *Blue Rhythm* had subscribers in Pakistan, Burma, and Ceylon. In conjunction with the Blue Rhythm jazz society, Jhaveri invited jazz musicians such as pianist/violist/drummer Victor Feldman to perform in India during the early 1950s, but by the mid-1950s Jhaveri had turned his attention to a career in business, thus precipitating the end of *Blue Rhythm*. His business career occupied him until the early 1970s.

Meanwhile in the United States during the late 1950s several jazz musicians had begun drawing inspiration from Indian classical music, particularly the spiritual qualities of Indian music as exemplified by John Coltrane in the song "My Favorite Things," and the tonal resources of ragas and talas as in the music of Don Ellis and others. These new experiments inspired many American jazz musicians to begin exploring Middle Eastern and Indian music, and some of them, such as saxophonist Sonny Rollins and trumpeter Maynard Ferguson, visited India in the late 1960s to explore Indian music and culture.

As the cross-pollination of jazz and Indian music continued, the year 1975 seemed a propitious time for Jhaveri and other individuals to found Jazz India, the organization that sponsored the first Jazz Yatra in 1978. Jazz Yatra is regarded as the most "international jazz festival in the world," having hosted hundreds of musicians from countries such as Brazil, West Germany, England, Sweden, Australia, Japan, the United States, Yugoslavia, Bulgaria, and the Soviet Union, among others. Jazz Yatra is also one of the most eclectic jazz festivals anywhere. Over the years, the festival has featured styles of music as diverse as Hindustani classical music, Carnatic classical music, Afro-American gospel music, samba, New Age music, South American folk music, Indo-jazz, and virtually every style of conventional jazz.

The Jazz Yatra 1988 program guide contains a statement by the Universal Soundship Foundation that illuminates the concepts behind the festival's eclectic approach:

In the course of history, especially during our century and particularly after the last world war, people are becoming aware of each other in a hitherto unknown light. . . .

This statement suggests that the Second World War was a turning point for humanity because the war actually enabled people to see beyond purely national goals to a "global consciousness," one which concerns itself with "the prosperity of the whole of mankind." The Universal Soundship Foundation believes that music can express a new "global consciousness" because "(music) is loved and practiced everywhere," and therefore can foster "understanding, togetherness and unity" among all people, objectives which political and ideological alignments have yet to fully realize. The music that represents this "new consciousness" is a type of music that people everywhere can call their own, music which "reveals this earth (as) the place of love and peace it is meant to be." The Jazz Yatra program committee, obviously influenced by the views of the Universal Soundship Foundation, has regularly invited groups from around the world that perform a variety of different styles and genres. In this way, the committee hopes to symbolically represent and unite all musical idioms. Jazz Yatra 1988 continued the eclectic tradition of past festivals. . . .

The festival, which marked the tenth anniversary of Jazz Yatra, introduced a new era in the history of the event, for this year Jazz Yatra was also
held in Bangalore, Goa, and Delhi, thus exposing more Indians to jazz than
in previous years. Live performance appears to have been one of the primary means by which Indians became exposed to jazz, but the mass media
have also served as an outlet. Though historically the supply has been limited, American jazz recordings have been available in India for many years.
Indians who have traveled abroad have often purchased records to listen
to with their friends upon returning to India. Rhythm House, the largest
record store in Bombay, has a jazz section that includes albums by American
artists such as Billie Holiday, Dave Brubeck, and Weather Report.

Recorded jazz has also reached many Indians via radio, particularly
during the Second World War. One of the most listened-to stations was
the Armed Forces Radio Services of the Southeast Asia Command in
Ceylon, headquarters of the Mountbatten Royal Command. According
to Niranjan Jhaveri, the station broadcast American jazz for two hours a
week to "GIs and Tommies" throughout Southeast Asia. The broadcasts
consisted of traditional and modern segments, each announced by disc
jockeys with expertise in one of the respective periods. In 1953, British
announcer Deryck Jeffries presented a one-hour jazz program over the
Bombay station All India Radio, presenting an historical overview of jazz
(*Blue Rhythm* May/June 1953, 18). Several other such programs followed.

According to jazz musician Anibal Castro, during the 1960s and 1970s
jazz was broadcast by Voice of America; the consensus among those who
addressed this matter, however, was that Indian radio stations broadcast
very little jazz. Some recent jazz performances have been televised in
India, and in addition to news coverage of Jazz Yatra, a television network
has broadcast videotaped highlights of the festivals.

Indian film music and films in general have been influenced by jazz.
Film critic Shantanu Bose told me that in general film music in India is
a mixture of Western and Indian influences. According to Bose, studio
pianist Kersey Lord introduced jazz to Bombay film music composers
and conductors such as Rahul Dev Burman and Laxmikant Pyarelal who
in turn employed jazz elements in their scores. In the 1950s and 1960s,
according to Bose, approximately thirty percent of Indian film music had
"little bits of jazz"—for example, a trumpet, guitar or drum solo. The films

themselves often included closeups of a "blaring trumpet" or "the flailing sticks of a jazzy drum solo." Bose also said that in some films the heroes played the saxophone or the trumpet. The various references to jazz in Indian films seem to have been a result of the expanding role of Western musical influences in India. Peter Manuel (1988, 164) has indicated:

The postwar period also saw an increased use of Western musical elements, despite efforts by the government to reverse this trend. The most visible borrowed elements were: 1) instruments like the violin, clarinet, conga and saxophone; 2) rhythms like the foxtrot and polka, and 3) chord harmony. . . .

The film industry must have indirectly introduced many Indians to the jazz idiom.

The 1970s marked the beginning of jazz education programs in Bombay. According to Tony Fernandes of the American Center in Bombay, the United States Information Service in Washington began sending books and other source materials on jazz to the Center in the early 1970s. He said that around this same time, relatively little live jazz was being played in India until the advent of Jazz Yatra in 1978. Even though the festival was a success, the local jazz scene was relatively inactive.

As a result, James Dandridge, the Director of the American Center, began exploring ways in which the Center could encourage local jazz musicians and at the same time make better use of its materials on jazz. Dandridge, in cooperation with jazz expert Yusuf Ghandi, the Bombay Madrigal Singers Organization (BMSO), and student jazz fans at Saint Xavier's College, decided to establish a jazz club at the Center every Sunday morning from 1982 to 1986 where local musicians could gather to perform. Another phase began in 1982: a jazz workshop consisting of lectures on the history of jazz by Yusuf Ghandi and performance classes taught by Louis Banks, culminating in a concert by the participants. The workshop ended in 1983, but was considered a success in terms of its achievements in jazz education, the enthusiastic response of the participants, and the quality of the music produced (Fernandes 2/25/88).

The American Center and the BMSO also sponsored a three-day jazz workshop in December 1983, featuring American saxophonist Charlie Mariano, and in 1987 the Center featured an Indo-jazz group co-founded by American guitarist Robert Giannetti (known as D. Wood) and Indian bamboo flutist Nityanand Haldipur. In addition to guitar and flute, the group included a *tabla* and a *tambura*. Wood, a graduate of the Berklee College of Music in Boston, began searching for new sources to enrich his improvisational jazz techniques, and spent a year in the West African country of Togo studying African drumming. Since that time, he has been living in Bombay, where he studies with noted Indian classical singer K. G. Ginde.

The particular approach of the Wood/Haldipur band to Indo-Jazz fusion stems from the distinctive sound of the bamboo flute and Wood's experimental conception of playing the electric guitar, which he says is an attempt to express Indian vocal and instrumental techniques in jazz-oriented improvisations. Wood's approach to playing the guitar consists in part of coordinating finger and slide techniques to create *meend*, an Indian musical effect similar to melisma. . . .

INDIAN JAZZ AND INNOVATION

It is useful at this point to consider the fundamental interrelationships between jazz and North Indian classical music in order to put the musical achievements of contemporary Indian jazz musicians in perspective. Advancements in blending jazz with North Indian classical music have taken place for the most part in the United States and Europe. The approaches are numerous and quite varied, but can be reduced to two basic categories: 1) modern jazz enriched with concepts borrowed from North Indian classical music, and 2) Indo-jazz fusion. In the former, the musicians play modern jazz but incorporate "Eastern scales" in their solos, or use "Eastern-sounding" instruments such as the oboe or the soprano saxophone. Indo-jazz, on the other hand, is characterized specifically by the use of Indian melodies and an ensemble comprising both Western and Indian instruments, such as the sitar, tabla, and other instruments (Gonsalves 3/5/88).

In his book *Nada Brahma—The World Is Sound*, Joachim Berendt (1983, 200–12) explores various interrelations among jazz, North Indian classical music, and Indian culture. Berendt suggests that jazz musicians may have been drawn to Indian music because jazz and North Indian classical music are similar in certain basic respects such as modality (a key aspect of North Indian classical music), embellishments, tone colors, micro-tones, improvisation, awareness of playing with one's own personal sound, and an underlying vocally conceived form of expression even in instrumental music.

American saxophonist John Coltrane's 1960 recording "My Favorite Things" is generally recognized as one of the most effective cross-fertilizations of modern jazz and concepts borrowed from North Indian classical music. Other American jazz musicians such as pianist Dave Brubeck have also blended modern jazz with elements of Indian classical music. The Dave Brubeck Quartet became one of the first modern jazz groups to tour extensively outside of the United States. The quartet performed in Bombay in 1958, and was a great success. The album entitled *Dave Brubeck Quartet*, a pastiche gleaned from the indigenous musics of Calcutta, Afghanistan, and Turkey, resulted from the band's tour.

Brubeck's performance in Bombay and the success of Coltrane's various recordings inspired by North Indian classical music may have contributed to sitarist Ravi Shankar becoming interested in jazz. In 1961, Shankar made a record with American jazz saxophonist/flutist Bud Shank, thus becoming the first major Indian musician to record with a jazz musician in the United States. There followed numerous Indian musicians who have become involved with blending elements of Indian classical music and modern jazz in the 1970s and 1980s, such as *sarod* player Ali Akbar Khan, who has recorded with American jazz saxophonist John Handy, and violinists Lakshminarayana Subramaniam and his brother Lakshminarayana Shankar, both of whom have led their own Indian jazz/rock fusion bands and made numerous recordings.

The Indo-jazz fusion scene in Europe began in the 1960s when composer John Mayer from Calcutta met Jamaican-born jazz saxophonist Joe Harriott in London, where they subsequently recorded an album entitled *Indian-Jazz Suite*. In 1967, Joachim Berendt produced an album entitled *Jazz Meets India*, which featured an interplay of a Swiss jazz trio led by pianist Irene Schweizer and an Indian trio led by sitarist Devan Motihar. And, in 1976, British jazz/rock guitarist John McLaughlin founded the band Shakti, which featured Lakshminarayana Shankar. The band made several recordings which are generally regarded as among the most important Indo-jazz fusion albums of the 1970s.

Native Indian jazz musicians have achieved particular distinction in developing Indo-Jazz. Most innovative concepts can be attributed to musicians such as Shankar Jaikishan, Braz Gonsalves, Louis Banks, Dinshah Sanjana, and enthusiast Niranjan Jhaveri. The 1968 album *Raga-Jazz Style* is probably one of the earliest Indian recordings of Indo-jazz. The music, composed by Shankar Jaikishan, was recorded by a group of Indian studio musicians. The eleven songs on the album are scored for alto saxophone, trumpet, piano, bass, drums, guitar, sitar, tabla and tambura. . . . Some of the songs begin with the sitar or saxophone creating arpeggios from the notes of a raga accompanied by the droning tambura. The melodies of the songs on this album are all based on ragas, and the harmonies sound like vertical structures derived from the notes of a raga. Most of the songs are in 4/4 time, although some employ 3/4, 5/4, or 7/4 time. The swing rhythm is employed, but not during sections that feature the Indian ensemble, and most of the improvisations are played on the alto saxophone or the sitar. Occasionally there is a guitar or drum solo.

The practice of improvising jazz on the basis of ragas was brought to a peak level of development by Braz Gonsalves, who is credited with being one of the first saxophonists to master the art of raga-based improvisation in the modern jazz style (Jhaveri 3/15/88). In this regard, he is considered to be without equal anywhere in the world. Gonsalves grew up listening to Hindustani religious music, in particular the sound of the *shenai*, which he says he has attempted to copy on the saxophone. His interest in Indian music led him to study it with a *vena* master. Braz Gonsalves composes intuitively, saying that "melodies and harmonies just come to me. . . ."

During the early 1980s, Braz Gonsalves became involved in the realization of Niranjan Jhaveri's concept of Indo-jazz. Jhaveri believed that the same high level of technical sophistication characteristic of modern instrumental jazz had not been achieved in the vocal jazz medium. To address this disparity, he suggested to various local jazz instrumentalists and singers that they consider experimenting with the more advanced Indian vocal techniques in a jazz setting. In essence, Jhaveri wanted Indian vocalizing to be employed in jazz arrangements in which the singing and the jazz elements would maintain their own purity of style and form. To a large degree, his intention of preserving the characteristics of Indian music grew out of a sense of respect for the masters of Indian music. A reason for Jhaveri's desire to explore new directions in Indo-jazz was that many visiting musicians from the West had told him that they were surprised that Indian jazz musicians, who were "sitting right on top of a wealth of traditional music," seemed uninterested in mixing that music with jazz.

In 1980 Jhaveri began searching for the musicians to form the kind of band he envisioned. He auditioned two singers—one trained in the Hindustani music of North India, the other in Carnatic music of South India. In consultation with Louis Banks and Braz Gonsalves, Jhaveri decided that the Carnatic singing style of vocalist Rama Mani had more in common with the jazz idiom than the Hindustani music of the other singer. According to Banks, Carnatic rather than Hindustani music is the driving force behind the concept of the Jazz Yatra Sextet because of its strong rhythmic elements (Banks 3/3/88).[5] The particular approach taken by the Jazz Yatra Sextet was partly a result of the influence of the group Shakti. Banks said that Shakti's style was based on a ratio of 90 percent South Indian music and 10 percent jazz. Shakti without John McLaughlin, according to Banks, is "totally South Indian Carnatic music" (see Farrell 1988). Banks wanted to attempt a different approach from that of Shakti—one that, in essence, corresponded to Jhaveri's concept, with periodic "meeting points" of the two main influences within a song.

One of the sextet's arrangements, called "Payan," exemplifies this type of musical fusion. It begins with an *alap* featuring Rama Mani improvising vocally on the notes of a raga. Later Banks enters, accompanying her on the piano in a modern jazz style. (According to Banks, the musicians agreed in advance that Rama Mani would "not listen to the piano," to ensure that she would maintain a pure Carnatic singing style. Banks also said that he accompanies Rama the way he would a jazz singer singing a ballad.) Gradually the piece progresses to a "rhythmic section," after which the soprano saxophonist and the vocalist state the raga-based theme in unison while the other instruments accompany with a rock-and-roll-sounding riff that leads to the improvisation section—a modal jazz-style saxophone solo based on a raga followed by a modern jazz piano solo which, in contrast, "goes chromatic." The ensemble then enters with the original theme accompanied by the same riff. A tabla solo follows, and the ending is a fade-out. "The singing," according to Banks, "was pure Carnatic. No one could point a finger and say that she had desecrated the raga. . . ."

The achievements of the Jazz Yatra Sextet set the stage for another progressive Indian band, Divya (Radiant). Unlike the Jazz Yatra Sextet, which was formed primarily to realize a particular musical conception, Divya is the culmination of several musical stages explored over many years by its leader, keyboard player Dinshah Sanjana, who grew up listening to North Indian classical music. Sanjana first studied Western music theory in the early 1960s at the Bombay extension of Trinity College, and in the early 1970s he developed an interest in popular bands, especially groups such as the Beatles and the Rolling Stones. These groups and others inspired him to study the piano, the guitar, and the use of electronic keyboards in a rock context. Around the same time, Sanjana began studying the tabla to accompany his wife, Sandhya, who sings North Indian classical music. . . .

In order to further explore jazz performance, Sanjana formed his own band, which began working at Trincas, a restaurant/nightclub in Calcutta known for musical entertainment. According to Sanjana, the band was free to play jazz material during the first and third sets, though during the second set, at the peak level of audience attendance, they were required to play more familiar songs. As Sanjana's interest in playing jazz continued to grow, he began composing original material that reflected the similarities between jazz and North Indian classical music.

Following numerous performances in Calcutta, Sanjana returned to Delhi, where he met Steve Longo, an American jazz drummer who jammed with Sanjana's band. This was a turning point for Sanjana who, because of the "thrill of spontaneous playing" he experienced during the jam session, decided to devote himself full time to "creative music." Sanjana and Longo met again in Bombay, where in 1979 they formed Holy Smoke, which Sanjana calls "my first progressive band." During the next six years Sanjana led several editions of this band, which included some of the top jazz musicians in Bombay, such as drummer Ranjit Barot and bassist Xerxes Gobhai.

Sanjana established an international reputation in 1984 when he participated in the Singapore Jazz Festival and traveled to Holland, where he recorded an album with local musicians, and to Sweden for a performance at the Fashungs Jazz Club. That same year he accompanied Don Cherry at Jazz Yatra. The following year he formed the band Ultimatum, which would go on to explore Indo-jazz in depth. A pivotal event occurred in 1987 when Sanjana formed the Indo-fusion band Divya specifically for the purpose of participating in an international jazz competition in Belgium. The group won a prize at the festival—the first Indian band to do so—and subsequently was invited to perform at the Jazz Jamboree in Warsaw. Here Sanjana met Alice Coltrane, who expressed admiration for his band's sound. Divya has also performed at Montmartre, a jazz club in Copenhagen.

The distinctive sound of Divya is based largely on a synthesis of Hindustani and Carnatic singing and percussion styles and modern Western idioms such as jazz and rock. Technically, Sanjana does not regard the band's music as jazz; rather he refers to it as "contemporary Indian music. . . ." One of the main differences between Divya and the Jazz Yatra Sextet is that the former emerges more from hard rock than from jazz. Also, Divya's album does not contain any vocal arrangements, although the band's performance at the festival featured several vocals. Carlos Monteiro, jazz critic for the *Indian Express*, wrote on February 20, 1988:

Perhaps Divya may hold the key to Indo-jazz. Last year they broke fresh ground on the European circuit with their unique melange of Hindustani-Carnatic jazz sounds. This band epitomizes the music of modern India (4).

JAZZ AND INDIAN SOCIETY

While the importance of jazz to Indians in general is a subject beyond the scope of this paper, my conversations with various individuals have shed some light on this question. Indian jazz critic Carlos Monteiro has referred to jazz as "the most potent musical language of the twentieth century," and Niranjan Jhaveri's characterization of the significance of jazz in Indian society singles out several particular aspects of jazz that he believes are most meaningful:

India and its culture feel a special kinship to America's great art music. We are thrilled by the spirit of freedom expressed in jazz. We have reason to envy the honesty, in a most basic sense, prevailing in jazz. Often this quality seems to elude our music in reality, although its existence is essential as per our ancient teachings and traditions. We admire and can learn from the wider range and variety of tones, sounds and textures of jazz than exists in Indian music today. We are also becoming aware, through jazz, that musical experiences which uplift the soul need not be induced by solo performances alone but equally by the collective efforts of a group. . . . (Jhaveri 1985, xvii, 18)

The notion of fusing jazz and traditional Indian classical music has its share of detractors. Some of the respondents I interviewed said that "East is East, West is West," and therefore jazz and Indian music should not be mixed, or both styles will be ruined. Several informants said that Indo-jazz has no future because improvising on the same notes of a raga is too limiting. A theoretical basis for the affinity of Indian classical music and jazz is that both art forms have grown out of contact between diverse ethnic groups. A synthesis of the Aryan culture of North India and the Mogul culture of Central Asia produced North Indian classical music, and a synthesis of West African and European cultures produced jazz. Another respondent pointed out that "reverse preservation" was an underlying aspect of the affinity of jazz to North Indian classical music. He defined "reverse preservation" as a phenomenon in which a musical idiom is perpetuated by an ethnic group that has adopted it, rather than by the ethnic group which actually created it. According to the respondent, "in the United States it is primarily Euro-Americans who preserve Dixieland jazz—an authentic form of jazz created by Afro-Americans; in India it is primarily Muslims who preserve Dhrupad, an authentic form of North Indian classical music created by Hindus."[6] The respondent suggested that "reverse preservation" supported the judgement that jazz in general had an affinity to North Indian classical music.

A quality that may contribute to North Indian classical music and jazz being perceived in a similar way, according to one of my respondents, is that jazz and North Indian classical music are both more popular in other countries than in their native countries. Whether or not this is entirely true, North Indian classical music is certainly finding acceptance outside of India. One respondent viewed the popularity of jazz as an indicator of a country's prestige in the international community. He said that most progressive countries have made significant achievements in jazz, and that India has been slow in this regard, possibly because India's rich historical musical tradition is of such depth that it will take jazz musicians a longer period of time than with other musical traditions to properly understand and make use of it.

The level of jazz appreciation in India is difficult to gauge. One respondent indicated that while some Indians seem to express enthusiasm for jazz at festivals, the real reason many of them attend such events is that it is fashionable; the music is secondary. In contrast, another respondent said: "Four or five nights of Jazz Yatra penetrate quite deeply into our hearts. People are learning how to listen and to sort it all out. They come to listen." One respondent told me that of all the Western music enthusiasts in India, Western classical music has the most fans, then rock and roll, then jazz. This view helps to put the role of jazz in India into perspective. But in a broader sense, another respondent said that most Western music in India—including Western classical music, rock and roll, and jazz—is on the decline. He suggested that this may be due in part to government regulations on the importation of certain Western instruments. The perception that Western music is on the decline also may be a result of the enormous popularity that Indian film music is currently enjoying among the general Indian public. But there is no consensus on the status of Western music in India. Some respondents believe that it seems to be holding its own, and, in some cases—especially that of rock and roll—that it is actually increasing in popularity. One respondent said that interest in jazz among Indians has not grown significantly over the years, perhaps because of a common perception that unlike the United States where the music originally "trickled up" from the poor to the middle and upper classes, in India jazz is perceived as an elitist phenomenon. . . .

The presence of jazz in India has not escaped controversy. Though there appears never to have been a mass expression of opposition to jazz in India, there are some who believe that it can cause Indian youth to stray from traditional values—as one respondent put it, "from sitar music to guitar music." In response to this concern Niranjan Jhaveri said: "If our musical culture is so weak that some guitar player can come along and sweep us off our feet, and if we are such fools to allow ourselves to be swept off of our feet, then probably we don't deserve better."

The Indian government initially seemed skeptical of India's increasing involvement with jazz and as a result withheld support to some organizations and musicians during the 1970s and 1980s, according to one respondent. However, at present many government agencies and business organizations in India and overseas endorse Jazz Yatra, and the Indian government sponsors tours by local jazz musicians. This attitude may be due in part to the fact that jazz is not viewed as having any political or social significance in India. According to one respondent, "It's just music, you either like it or you don't."

Several respondents said that some young musicians have a desire to learn jazz, but there are no schools where they can study it; they said that such a school, providing instruction by noted jazz musicians, would do very well in India. A major dilemma is that Indian jazz musicians do not ordinarily record albums. One respondent said that people will not buy albums by Indian jazz musicians; this is especially true of college students, who tend to think of jazz in terms of American musicians such as Grover Washington, Jr., and Al Jarreau.

SUMMARY AND CONCLUSIONS

In this study I have attempted to analyze the unfolding of jazz in India; specifically, my aim was to explain why and how jazz was assimilated there. My research was based on the hypothesis that the Indian jazz scene is an expression of modernization and progressiveness, values held by the Westernized urban upper-middle classes in Indian cities. It is the perception that jazz is "the music of the times" that enables it to function in this way, as opposed to, for example, Western classical music, which is generally associated with a different era. The degree to which jazz has been assimilated in India, relative to the size of the general population of that country, is small; it has caught on with a certain sector of the public rather than with the average person. Indian jazz fans experience aspects of Western values through jazz in the intercultural contact that this music fosters between Indians and Westerners and between Indians and Western musical concepts. In this sense jazz serves as a means by which a segment within Indian society can identify with certain aspects of Western culture.

The role of jazz as a channel for cultural identification and contact has been manifested in several other ways. From the earliest years of the presence of jazz in India, jazz musicians from Western countries and local Indian jazz musicians have performed in India, and members of Western and local Indian bands have frequently worked together. Such performances have increased the presence of Western musical influences in Indian society and have broadened the musical taste of some Indians. This basic intercultural performance relationship between Western and Indian jazz musicians continues to be a vital part of the contemporary Indian jazz scene. Teddy Weatherford's presence in India during the swing era gave impetus to the Indian jazz scene much in the same way that Duke Ellington's presence did during the modern era. The numerous jazz tours sponsored by the U.S. State Department and branches of other Western governments have played a key role in fostering the live jazz scene in India.

The development of jazz in India can be viewed in terms of a diverse series of events organized around a common thread—the diverse events being the various musicians and their activities, and the common thread, the constant influence of Indian jazz musicians from the Goan community throughout the evolution of jazz in India. The most successful periods in the history of jazz in India correspond to the most successful periods of jazz history in the United States: the swing era of the 1930s and 1940s and the jazz-rock fusion era of today. Each period in the history of jazz in India has produced outstanding musicians, from Chick Chocolate to Braz Gonsalves and from Louis Banks to Dinshah Sanjana.

Jazz Yatra represents the culmination of at least sixty years of jazz in India and provides one of the main settings in which the achievements of Indian jazz musicians can be presented in a public forum. The festivals highlight the achievements of the Indian jazz community as well as expose the limitations of jazz in that same community. Moreover, Jazz Yatra, which is unique among international jazz festivals in its highly eclectic programming, suggests the possibility that jazz *per se* has not reached the level of self-sufficiency in India. The fact that jazz has not been broadcast widely on Indian radio or television may explain why it has not reached a high level of acceptance there. The absence of formal musical instruction in jazz is responsible for the fact that most Indian jazz musicians are self taught, in complete contrast to the rigorous training with a guru that is characteristic of traditional methods of instruction in Indian classical music. . . .

Like many countries outside of the United States involved with jazz, India has brought its own traditional musical heritage to bear on jazz in ways that only Indian musicians can truly implement. Indian jazz musicians have drawn from both Northern and Southern Indian music; within these two basic approaches, the musical style known as Indo-jazz focuses on vocal techniques, especially the Carnatic singing style. The incorporation of Indian vocal techniques into Indo-jazz was an attempt to introduce the same level of technical sophistication in vocal jazz arrangements that has characterized instrumental jazz arrangements. The use by Indian jazz musicians of Indian vocal techniques and raga-based soloing in a modern jazz context makes it possible to better understand the scope of the interplay between jazz and Indian music—from modern jazz tinged with Indian musical concepts, which involves a relatively minimal interplay of the two forms of music, to Indo-jazz, which involves a more extensive interaction between Indian music and jazz. Several respondents in this study emphasized the conceptual and formal similarities between jazz and North Indian classical music—viewpoints that enhance our understanding of the "elective affinities" shared by these two forms of music. The forward-looking approaches to jazz employed by Indian jazz musicians to date suggest that these musicians attach the same importance to advancing jazz as their colleagues in other parts of the world.

INTERPRETING THE CREATIVE PROCESS OF JAZZ IN ZIMBABWE

—*Linda F. Williams*

THEORIES ON CREATIVITY

Many fallacies surround the subject of creativity, especially as practiced in jazz improvisation in cultures outside of the United States. One misconception is the notion that improvisation is indeterminate. Another misunderstanding involves the assumption that jazz improvisation is a process distinct from composition. Yet, others presuppose that somehow or other the creator is actually being "pulled" into the music by the transcendent product that he or she has not yet produced (Dutton and Krausz 1991; Nettl 1974). All such assumptions imply an unconscious process in which the musician is propelled beyond his or her conscious mastery of what s/he is producing. My research in Zimbabwe (1991–93) investigates ways in which individual jazz artists interpret processes of their development while attaining goals of becoming innovators in their own rights. The essay further defines significant distinctions between jazz in Zimbabwe and American jazz.

Zimbabwean songwriter and guitarist Michael Lannas discussed several stages of the creative process: "Creativity tends to occur whenever a musician is attempting to solve a musical problem." The process involves sustained preliminary stages, followed by a transformation period. Lannas explained the initial stage of creativity as a "subconscious motivating force," followed by an understanding or "conscious insight of what you're doing," which leads finally to a manifestation of the creative process:

As a jazz artist who is sometimes concerned with the creative process and my inner voice, I define the *subconscious* as a latent sense of my awareness. While improvising, I often attempt to bring on a unity of the subconsciousness with consciousness. . . . One must experience it in order to understand. (interviewed 10/14/92)

Consistent with Lannas' analysis, the late Zimbabwean jazz saxophonist Simangaliso Tutani maintained that creativity ranges on a continuum from minimal to total awareness. While this process may seem abstract to non-musicians, many Zimbabwean jazz artists clearly perceive the distinction between conscious and subconscious levels of creativity.

Other Zimbabwean musicians I interviewed maintained that their most significant creative ideas emerge when they work out specific difficult issues in the music itself. For example, a musician might move into uncharted directions during a song, or band members might serendipitously end a song on different beats. During spur-of-the-moment *gestures*, for example, musicians put aside their commonplace mindset to react to the challenge of an unexpected situation. An investigation focusing upon the appropriate *timing* of an event is necessary to provide clues in understanding nuances of creativity. Thus the crucial factor is precisely the same as in American jazz, since musicians are already expected to improvise as part of what makes *jazz* distinctively *jazz*.

My research in Harare presents evidence usually missed by many theoretical studies on jazz creativity: that creative processes, like jazz musicians who employ them, do not exist in isolation, but within their sociocultural environment. Improvisation is, of course, an essential aspect of Zimbabwean music and culture. Ethnomusicologist John Kaemmer (1980) states, "In many societies, including our own, the performer is distinguished from the composer, but societies with a strong tradition of improvisation frequently do not make that distinction" (64). Ethnological analysis of both professional musicians and music students suggests that the sociocultural environment provides the conditions for promoting improvisational creativity. While teaching in Harare, I noted that my ten- to fourteen-year-old students, whom I taught to read notes first, had difficulty when attempting to improvise. Those students with whom I began aural imitation exercises in improvisation, however, adapted to written notation without much difficulty. The musicians who began formal training in school were more apprehensive about improvisation than those who had consistently listened to recordings to emulate their favorite artists carefully. I attribute this distinction to the differences in initial music acquisition. The following discussion emphasizes the voices of Zimbabwean musicians and their interpretations of social and pedagogic methods in the acquisition of their musical skills.

MUSIC ACQUISITION AND MEANING IN ZIMBABWEAN MUSIC

Many of the comments I received from Zimbabwean professional jazz musicians and music educators revealed an underlying thesis: "playing by ear" is indispensable to the creative process in Zimbabwean music. Many musicians believe this phenomenon to such an extent that they repudiate other methods of musical pedagogy. Jazz guitarist Jonah Marumahoko objected to prevailing methods of music acquisition and expressed the need to explore personally constructed pedagogic methods: "Once you've figured out how to transfer the sound from your ears to your fingers, and not rely heavily on those instructional books for notes, the music becomes embedded within your own system" (5/9/92). Jazz organist Bruce Sasikwa maintained that he effectively relied on his "ear" to manipulate the organ keys, claiming that reading notes essentially impaired his ability to improvise. For Sasikwa, as with many Zimbabwean jazz musicians, personally constructed pedagogical methods of learning rely on the art of whistling or singing, and even dancing, as fundamental devices in preparing musicians to understand intervals, patterns, and motion (the rhythmic pulse) in music. Such personal development is vital in order to "find your own voice in music." Throughout Zimbabwe, young musicians begin their musical education by singing, dancing, or playing drums, tambourines, or *hosho* (rattles). Their creativity emerges when children begin to imagine sounds and construct instruments suited to their own musical tastes. During adolescence, they are encouraged to experiment with objects such as cans, gourds, and planks of wood, pebbles, and fish twine to construct instruments and identify with individual sounds.[1]

Zimbabwean guitarist Louis Mhlanga explained the significance of such early musical experiences:

Early, I tried playing the guitar but my hands and fingers were too small. So I started out by playing drums and much later, transferred those rhythms on drums to my guitar when I became older. I made my drums from empty food cans that I covered with hard cardboard using cellophane tape to reinforce it to determine the different pitches. During my very early stages, I learned how to search for a distinctive sound. (1/26/92)

Development of a unique personal sound implies culturally significant meanings in the lives of many Zimbabwean musicians. A passionate search for individuality emanates from the early creative stages of music acquisition in Zimbabwe. Thus, the jazz musician's emphasis on personally constructed pedagogic approaches reinforces how the creative process functions within the Zimbabwean music system. As explanation of reasons behind such emphasis on individuality, I focus on the observation of Friday Mbirimi:

In most families, there are so many children that the search for a separate identity becomes a common cause among musicians. With four boys, four girls, and my parents, even our household was considered relatively small in comparison to others in the township. (10/9/92)

While many Zimbabwean musicians attribute individuality to the creation of personal sounds, a reverse phenomenon may direct their musical paths during intermediate stages of their musical development: the emulation of musical models. Guitarist Andrew Chakanyuka describes a classic example of how emulating an artist provided the foundation for his development prior to establishing his personal identity on guitar.

At first, my mother would not allow me to *touch* the guitar. Therefore to convince her to let me play guitar, I came home one Sunday and said, "Hey, Mom, I saw a woman in church singing and playing the guitar." And, she said, "Yeah, but she was playing for God." And I said, "Well, I can play for God also." On the following Sunday, my mother asked the lady to help me learn the guitar. So, the lady instructed me to duplicate her voice on guitar as she sang. Immediately, I picked up the guitar and imagined the guitar strings as her voice while I played the melody. As a result the guitar became an extension of my own voice. (6/2/92)

The importance of a personal identity—even if obtained via imitation— may perhaps explain why the widespread availability of jazz recordings in Zimbabwe made such an impact on urban culture.

Unlike their counterparts in the United States, Zimbabwean musicians are taught to recognize and duplicate intricate rhythmic patterns as an introduction to music, a phenomenon that is lacking in many Western musical cultures. The goal of a beginning musician in Zimbabwe is to imitate pitch and rhythm. Rarely does this imitative exercise take place on a series of quarter, half, or whole notes. Instead, intricately diverse rhythmic and tonal repetitions are embedded in the music structure to allow for more musical improvisation during early musical development. It is not until much later, during the intermediate level of musical training, that the analysis of noted rhythms and their fractional relationships becomes a musical issue. The entire approach is based on an auditory-transmission process.

While Zimbabwean musicians attribute their basic training to listening and to emulation, there are perhaps limitations to these approaches, as guitarist Andrew Chakanyuka later explained at length. Having knowledge of chord changes and harmonies allows musicians to communicate more fully:

I never knew what notes I played until much later in my career as I began to recognize the limited capacity of aural methods. Many years back, a guitarist from South Africa came to a club where I performed, and asked to play my guitar. So, I gave him my guitar. My God what he played! And, from what he was playing, I asked him, "What's the name of that chord you were playing?" But for apparent reasons, the guy didn't want to show me the chord, and he kept performing and saying, "This one?" I said, "No, no." "This one?" I said, "No, no." "That one?" I said, "No, no, no." And he said, "How can I show you the chord if you do not know the name of it?" Fortunately, the keyboard player knew that I was serious, and he said, "Hey man, stop teasing the boy and show him the chord, okay?" And the guitarist played the chord and said, "This is D-minor seventh." From there I kept the guitar out of the case and went home holding the guitar with my fingers wrapped around that D-minor seventh chord. (6/2/92)

Limitations of auditory-transmission processes in jazz, as demonstrated above ("How can I show you the chord if you do not know the name of it?"), may potentially cause problems in music communication; thus, during advanced stages of music acquisition, Zimbabwean musicians are encouraged to seek mentors and arrange for tutorials or professional instruction. Although jazz musicians are encouraged to adapt personal sounds in their beginning stages and "play by ear" during their intermediate levels, reading music becomes a requirement during the advanced period.

THE "TRIPLET-RHYTHMIC EFFECT": CHARACTERISTICS OF INDIGENOUS JAZZ

Although certain aspects of the creative process vary with context, there exist elements common to each individual's experience in jazz improvisation. A distinct improvisatory feature of many Zimbabwean musicians is the concept of rhythm informing the melody. Guitarist Andrew Chakanyuka maintained that, while melody and harmony are central markers of the music as in American jazz, Zimbabwean artists couldn't possibly create without understanding the rhythmic principles in music.

Zimbabwean pianist Christopher Chabuka explained how rhythm, texture, and creativity work in conjunction.

During my solos, and before I reach the climax, I find myself concentrating on the tension between rhythm and texture. At this point, I sometimes reach my creative peak. Of course, every night is different, but whenever I stop concentrating on detailed aspects of my performance, and merge several ideas, I find myself becoming more creative. (10/19/92)

Central to the views voiced in the foregoing discussion, trumpeter Paul Lunga discussed how the concept of rhythm allows improvisation to become more spontaneous. Lunga contends that without rhythm, improvisation may become quite inflexible:

Imagine if you had to improvise by playing only straight melodic lines. You would end up sounding like a Gregorian Chant or something similar; you know what I mean? But for me, it is the rhythm that allows me to create effectively. Mostly, I imagine a set rhythm in my head, and then I start with an idea based on a certain chord progression, or I may use a series of fourths and fifths to create an effective rhythm. Who knows? What I think one night is different the next night. (11/4/92)

As Lunga mentioned, improvisation differs with context. Thus, improvisation is *never* the same at any two moments of its temporal development, and yet it is continuously appropriating past practices, becoming cumulatively different at each level of creativity.

Guitarist Samuel Banana Gwanzura argues that improvisation becomes *less* creative when musicians have to follow strict harmonic guidelines: "All of us musicians are different, and I for one need to be free of following chord changes. When I improvise, I depend on certain rhythms in the piece. The chord changes gets in the way sometimes" (5/7/92). As with jazz performances in the United States, however, necessary guidelines in improvisation govern rhythmic patterns, melodic phrases, and harmonic or substitute progressions. For example, when a group performs a song, it becomes the objective of each musician, if desired, to create a corresponding solo to the harmonic progressions of that given in the song. Thus, when a musician within a group asks, "What are the changes?" he or she is referring to a preexisting set of changes, or chord progressions, which give musicians the artistic freedom to build new musical ideas upon established guidelines for distinct chords or chordal progressions.[2] Jazz in Zimbabwe has, therefore, a major premise in common with improvisation in other parts of the world: the concept of combining rhythm with melody to underpin an unvarying harmony.

Distinctly significant to jazz in Zimbabwe is an undercurrent triplet-rhythm. Unlike jazz in the United States and in many other countries, in which duple rhythmic emphasis upon the two and four concept is embedded in the overall sound, the triplet foundation informs Zimbabwean sound sensibilities. Without the pervasive triplet motif, jazz in Zimbabwe could not be distinguishable. As bassist Bryan Paul explained:

There's a lot that happens in our music, and it can become very confusing. Particularly in the sense of understanding the embedded-triplet-rhythm. Without that, jazz in Zimbabwe won't sound Zimbabwean. In South African jazz everything is basically on the beat and it's all fours; in American jazz, a heavy emphasis is on two and four; but in our music, the emphasis is placed between a *triplet rhythmic* undercurrent. (5/1/92)

Figure 1 demonstrates this unique feature:[3]

In Zimbabwe, the musical culture places great emphasis on the unifying triplet-rhythmic motif. Descending pentatonic scale structures and alternative suspending patterns of compound-triplets are secondary to the entire process of improvisation. Zimbabwean jazz musicians believe that the triplet-rhythmic motif in their music is the most noticeable

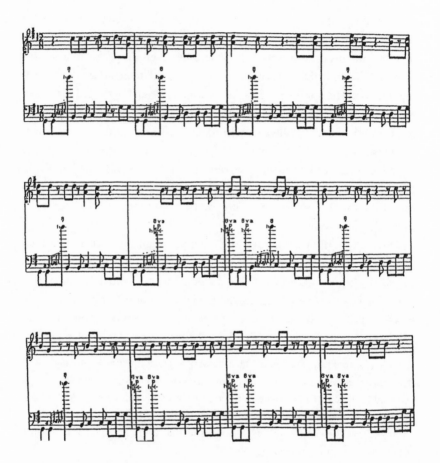

Figure 1. Triplet-Rhythmic Motif.

element that distinguishes jazz in Zimbabwe from jazz in other parts of the world.

Throughout each 12/8 metric-measure in a standard Zimbabwean instrumental vamp I analyzed, an overlaid triplet pattern is distinguished while a second triplet pattern adds resonance to the cymbal pattern in the drum line. Triplets occur and recur in the instrumental lines between the first and second guitar parts. Lesser emphasis is placed on triplet rhythms as additional instruments are added to the overall sound in subsequent measures. The continued dotted-quarter note pattern in the bass drum unit figures prominently throughout the piece, while interplay between wind instruments and guitar parts underscores an implicit triplet effect. Guitarist Jacob Mhungu explained how the overlaying of rhythms emerges as musicians intentionally seek uneven patterns as a point of departure within triplet-rhythmic frameworks:

We are deliberately trying to find an odd rhythm. And we get these rhythms by crossing them over with discrete triplet notes that are played on different instruments. Generally, the drums start with a beat on a certain triplet pattern and the guitar comes with something else. As an outcome of these patterns, little triplet figures dominate the form throughout the whole song. (9/4/92)

Similarly, saxophonist Cleveland Marshall maintained:

It's a distinct, parallel rhythm going on. If you listen to it very closely, intrinsically you'll hear the 4/4 meter and you'll also hear 3/4 meter. And that's going on simultaneously, bringing about what I call the triplet pulse. That's how we reach the climax; it is through those two rhythms synthesizing. Yes. We try and place these rhythmic figures together to create a certain amount of tension in the music. (6/10/92)

While each musician takes an independent role in the overall organization of a musical creation, an overlay of triplets emerges invariably in each measure throughout most songs. Two independent sections emerge as instrumental lines complement each other. This structure does not produce *call-and-response* patterns with independent parts one following another, but rather polyrhythmic interplays between two individual parts. Percussionist Jethro Shasha postulates that "Triplet rhythms in Zimbabwean jazz are used distinctively to enhance the music, as well as to create other rhythms that can be expressed in 12/8, 6/8, and perhaps in the 7/8 rhythms" (4/22/92). In 12/8 time signatures, the duality of three sets of triplets over four distinct and consistent dotted-quarter notes (per measure) leads to an illusion of two or more meters. The duality of three sets of triplets may emerge from two electric guitars, while the bass guitar creates an underlying triplet pattern, with or without the aid of a drummer. Added tension can be sustained as melodic figures fluctuate from distinct triplet groups into indistinct groups as demonstrated in Figure 2.

Increased tension from the drums, *hosho* (rattles), or other percussion instruments interlocks the triplets within the overall musical form, producing cross rhythms or multisonic patterns.

Michael Lannas discussed cross rhythms as a major component to distinguish the triplet-rhythmic effect:

There are distinct cross rhythms in the music that come together ultimately as triplets. In other words, we try *not* to duplicate similar patterns because the music becomes redundant. A drummer may decide to begin a song using 6/8 as a guide and another musician counterbalances the sound by crossing 6/8 with another rhythmic pattern. Complementing both of these sounds, a third musician may lock in between the two preceding sounds, and what happens? Each additional person in the group becomes obligated to listen closely and find an independent meter to sustain all of the patterns. So eventually, these cross rhythms circumscribe an overall compound triplet effect that leads us to the rhythmic pulse. (10/14/92)

Similarly, bassist Bryan Paul discusses cross rhythms as a technique employed by Zimbabwean musicians to connect or fuse contemporary jazz styles with their earlier music traditions.

Odd rhythms in our music occur at various points in a song. For example, a guitarist accents a distinct rhythmic pattern while another musician demonstrates a completely different rhythmic figure that sometimes, depending on the individual, may be used right through the entire song. Then someone else will come in with his or her own pattern on the shakers [*hoshos*] for instance; you know like, fusing the modern ideas in jazz with traditional styles of music. So by crossing these rhythms over each other, we create undercurrent triplets. (6/10/92)

Figure 2. Distinct and Indistinct Triplet Groups.

Many Zimbabwean musicians believe that cross rhythms and triplet rhythms are implicit within the sound, and "mere talk" or studying transcribed music "on paper" destroys the essence of understanding their music. According to Christopher Chabuka, an underlying compound triplet is embedded in the overall production:

> It's not the triplet rhythm that's important while playing music. It's only important when you put it on paper, but it's not that simple. Like in American jazz, people think that in order to *swing*, you have to place a dot behind the quarter note and play an eighth note, followed again by a dotted quarter note consecutively and repeatedly. That's not it! What American jazz musicians do is take two eighth notes and place an extraordinary emphasis on the second note of each eight note grouping to create an added tension in connecting each phrase. It's precisely this same element that we find in our music. (10/19/92)

"Mere talk" is also framed in Samuel Banana Gwanzura's explanation as he explains:

> You know what happened with our music is, we were not allowed to attend college in the first place. For someone to know what's a triplet-rhythm is really hard for us here. Most of the people never went for any lessons or things. It's only now that we are given entrance into colleges here. For people to understand a thing like a triplet would be impossible. (5/7/92)

However, a few Zimbabwean musicians believe that in order to properly codify the triplet-*rhythmic* effect in Zimbabwean jazz, there has to be a systematic attempt to formulate a method that most indigenous musicians could readily understand. Zimbabwean bandleader and trumpeter Paul Lunga discussed the disadvantages of *not* having a codified system:

> It would be very difficult for me to explain to you the dimensions of my musical scores unless I sing it and attempt to involve all the instrumental sounds simultaneously. Would I be in a position to verbalize properly or connect each sound in a comprehensible fashion? If I could, then I'd be a genius. That's why many Zimbabwean musicians fail in their attempts to express the intricacies of our music. If we could codify our system, the music would be more explainable. (11/4/92)

MELODIC PRINCIPLES IN
ZIMBABWEAN JAZZ STYLES

Another distinguishing musical characteristic Zimbabwean jazz musicians often expressed is the descending solo line. Similar to the performance of jazz in the United States, emphasis is placed on descending elements of the minor pentatonic/blues scale with the added flat 5th degree (or sharp 4th—tritone) of the descending scale. The scale is constructed as follows: 8ve-b7-5-b5-4-b3-1.

Descending melodic contour is also a noticeable characteristic of the early music of many parts of West, Central, East, and Southern Africa (Nketia 1974; Rycroft 1977; Williams 1997). The idiosyncratic use of this same contour in Zimbabwean urban music and jazz is yet another example of reciprocal influence between African America and Africa.

Similar to the descending pentatonic pattern found in American jazz, a dominant descending pattern *governs* and defines the principle upon which most Zimbabwean jazz musicians engage while soloing. Discussing his approach while performing, jazz pianist Nelson Mapango explains:

After I play an introduction and the standard melody on piano, I usually begin improvising by starting on a higher interval and moving up *a fourth, fifth, flat five*, or a *dominant seventh* to begin a series of descending patterns. Now listen to this. [Mapango plays.] Now listen also to how I am able to use these same descending links to construct my entire solo. (8/3/92)

In a very similar manner, guitarist Jacob Mhungu demonstrated his approach to formal principles of soloing in his original composition, "Gift," a dedication to his parents.

To me, every improvised solo becomes a gift. From where it comes, I do not know; perhaps a gift from God? But whenever I am inspired, I create my solo by using half-step-descending tones to combine phrases—sometimes repetitive and sometimes not. Here's how I do it. [Mhungu plays the entire song.] Do you hear how those descending tones fit smoothly into each melodic pattern? (9/4/92)

Mhungu's explanation involves descending melodic concepts. With solo guitar lines, the triplet-rhythm emerges from the drum line.

SUSPENDED PATTERNS AS IMPLICIT WITHIN JAZZ STYLES OF ZIMBABWE

While many Zimbabwean jazz musicians attest to the fact that using descending tones underscores both the formal and generative principles of jazz in Zimbabwe, Louis Mhlanga discusses the relationship of "suspended time" to descending patterns of melody:

You'll find a lot of the African bands here with three or four guitarists on stage. And, everyone is playing a different *descending* pattern. Although the main accents are *strictly triplet* within a certain time frame, generally, musicians do not play the same melodic pattern. Some musicians actually suspend time by prolonging the rhythm. And somehow they seem to correlate harmonically. (1/26/92)

Different lines emerge within the instrumental interplay of voices to create an illusion of bi-tonal sounds. Since instrumental lines are consecutively overlaid, suspended patterns serve as a guide to generate rhythmic vibrancy. Guitarist Jonah Marumahoko explains similar suspended patterns in jazz styles of Zimbabwe:

As long as the drummer is playing a straight bass drum which is like four on the pedal, while the high hat cymbal is emphasizing three, everyone will lock in to the beat, and find their own pattern. It's like alternating suspensions and triplet rhythms throughout the entire music score. (7/26/92)[4]

"Alternating suspensions," Marumahoko explains, are triplet patterns overlapping between instrumental parts resulting in compound-triple effects. Understanding these alternating suspensions involves an effort by most Zimbabwean musicians to think of music in terms of patterns, rather than to recognize meters in relation to rhythm.

CONCLUSION

Jazz in Harare emerged largely from musicians accepting certain African-American musical elements into their local music as expressive forms. Combining their own traditions with American jazz cultural models, Zimbabwean jazz musicians created a distinctive style of music, transferring American idioms into an African expression. Fusing traditional triplet-rhythmic patterns with American jazz harmonies resulted in "triplet-rhythmic" concepts in Zimbabwean jazz. While jazz improvisation in Zimbabwe is characterized by many elements found in American jazz, differences are marked by a distinct rhythmic approach. Unlike American jazz, in which melody and harmony are prevalent identifiers of the music, triplet-rhythmic motifs distinguish Zimbabwean jazz styles from jazz genres in other parts of the world. This embedded concept of rhythm allows the transference of the creative process in Zimbabwean jazz styles to emerge. Triplet-rhythmic motifs lend themselves to layering and displacement of polyrhythmic concepts within Zimbabwean jazz styles. While many music cultures accentuate beats one and three as important to establish continuity, American jazz depends upon the emphasis of beats two and four. Unlike the performance of jazz in other parts of the world, Zimbabwean musicians rely upon triplet rhythm patterns on each beat as guiding forces. As Zimbabwean drummer, Jethro Shasha argues,

Unique to South African jazz musicians is all four beats. South African musicians actually swing on all beats, and can blow any musician off the stage from Timbuktu to America. Singularly important for Zimbabwean musicians is their dependence upon the drummer's insistent expression of the triplet concepts underscoring all songs. We Zimbabwean musicians, we fall in the middle and between all beats from 4/4 time to 12/4 time with triplet rhythms of the drums supporting the entire ensemble. Yes, jazz is unique in Zimbabwean traditions, because while we attempt to maintain our own identity in music, the music of Black jazz musicians in America seems to be our guiding force.

While many commercial popular styles moved to the forefront of Zimbabwean musical consciousness immediately before and after independence in 1980, the audience for jazz remained limited to a small class of Zimbabweans, expatriates, and visiting foreigners who frequented the jazz bars, nightclubs, and hotels in downtown Harare. Since the late 1980s, however, jazz has begun to grow in popularity, attracting enthusiastic audiences from all classes and age groups. Many jazz musicians study abroad and bring back ideas that they couple with what is already in Zimbabwe to foster new explosions of creative energy.

Two African musicians, the late Fela Anikulapo-Kuti and Jethro Shasha, provide testimony to the transatlantic reciprocity of African and African-American music. According to Shasha, a jazz percussionist, the reason Zimbabwean musicians are heavily influenced by African-American musical styles is the aesthetic framework found in the creative expression of jazz:

For one thing, like African Americans, we Zimbabweans can attest to the fact that a good musician cannot possibly create unless he feels strongly about the melodic and rhythmic features in music. African-American music in the United States has an aesthetic framework in which Zimbabweans can relate. The creative freedom in jazz is very important for our musical development because while learning to play jazz, we find ourselves not only as entertainers, but we become artists. (2/4/92)

Fela Anikulapo-Kuti remarked, "I had been using jazz to play African music, when really I should be using African music to play jazz. So it was America that brought me back to myself" (quoted in Collins 1987, 189).

MUSICAL TRANSCULTURATION

From African American Avant-Garde Jazz to
European Creative Improvisation, 1962–1981

—Christopher G. Bakriges

This article investigates how African American avant-garde musical sensibilities have been received and transformed by European musicians, producers, and culture vendors. The thesis that guides this article is that an important black music variant, variously known as Free Jazz, Energy Music, Great Black Music, or the "new thing," has had to leave America in order to perpetuate itself. Over time, this music has changed its original name, while simultaneously expanding its meaning outside of the United States. Under consideration is how American musicians transmitted this new music beginning in the early sixties and how it was received in Europe, by using primarily Dutch musicians and producers in the Netherlands as case studies. I argue that this musical emigration redefines the meaning of *diaspora* in African American expressive culture.[1]

This diasporic condition may be labeled transcultural, with its practitioners participating across national lines. The musical and extramusical processes set in motion by the culture contact that occurred among American, Canadian, African, and European artists in Europe is called "musical transculturation" (cf. Kartomi 1981 and Kartomi and Blum 1994). George Yudice defines *transculturation* as a dynamic whereby different cultural matrices impact reciprocally, though not from equal positions, on each other, not to produce a single syncretic culture, but rather a heterogeneous ensemble (Gross, McMurray, and Swedenburg 1994). African American musicians were involved with creating a music that was considered a mutation of jazz practice. The available performance venues for this music were often bohemian haunts, coffeehouses, churches, artist lofts, part of an imperative to counter the waning jazz club scene in the United States throughout the sixties. In the infancy of the avant-garde movement, they felt not unlike James Baldwin relating his feelings on living in America and Europe in the preface to *Notes of a Native Son*:

... the most crucial time in my own development came when I was forced to recognize that I was a kind of bastard of the West; when I followed the line of my past I did not find myself in Europe but in Africa. And this meant that in some subtle way, in a really profound way, I brought to Shakespeare, Bach, Rembrandt, to the stones of Paris, to the cathedral at Chartres and to the Empire State Building, a special attitude. These were not really my creations, they did not contain my his-tory; I might search in them in vain forever for any reflection of myself. I was an interloper; this was not my heritage. At the same time I had no other heritage that I could possibly hope to use—I had certainly been unfitted for the jungle or the tribe. I would have to appropriate these white centuries, I would have to make them mine—I would have to accept my special attitude, my special place in this scheme—otherwise I would have no place in any scheme. (Baldwin 1963, 6–7)

Artists like Archie Shepp, Bill Dixon, Cecil Taylor, Makanda Ken McIntyre, Milford Graves, George Russell, Marion Brown, Andrew Cyrille, Ishmail Wadada Leo Smith, Bobby Bradford, John Carter, Anthony Braxton, Yusef Lateef, Sam Rivers, Reginald Workman, Clifford Thornton, William Shadrack Cole, George Lewis, Anthony Davis, John Handy, Charles Gayle, and Raphe Malik lead or have led academic lives in the States while conducting their recording and performing careers almost exclusively in Europe.[2] These and scores of other artists, many of whom have expertise in other areas of the arts besides musical performance, have moved between two or more national spaces since at least the mid-sixties. By the early seven-ties this music, known by a variety of names, became essentially a diasporic music, transplanted to Europe where there awaited an eager production and artistic infrastructure. Between 1969 and 1981 over ninety record labels were established in Europe to document the new music (see chart below). What was known either as black music or the culturally androgynous "new thing" in the United States became essentially a separate genre in Europe known as "creative improvisational music," an idiom whose discography this author, in earlier consultation with scholar John Szwed, now estimates at over twelve thousand albums (pers. com. 1995).

Essentially abandoned by American jazz critics, other journalists, and producers, practitioners of the "new thing" were unable to maintain longevity in their various attempts at artistic and economic self-determination. Charles Mingus's Jazz Workshop, John Coltrane's innovative quartet with Eric Dolphy, and Sonny Rollins' pianoless trio were among those groups whose experiments were exposed across the Atlantic by the early sixties. Dutch and German adherents of the jazz workshop concept would organize themselves shortly thereafter (see Van Eyle 1981, 127; Paulot 1993, 201, 257; Jazz Workshop 1962; and Jazz Workshop Ensemble 1966). An example of a musician who was influenced by these developments is Amsterdam-born Herman de Wit. Once the director of the Big Band Orchestra of the youth movement of the Dutch communist party, de Wit began running workshops for the Youth and Music Association in Zeeland, Utrecht, the Hague, and Amsterdam in the early sixties. De Wit's philosophy was "to accept the idea that the jazz workshop is an indivisible part of our music" (Tra 1978c, 13). To coordinate activities throughout the country, all the workshops worked on the same pieces so that, on occasion, a big band could be put together. Repertoire was made up of different numbers such as blues, cha-chas, Kurt Weill's "Mack the Knife," Ornette Coleman's "Free Jazz" and "home products" like "March of the Anti-Fascists" by saxophonist Eva Bouman, or Jan Rood's arrangement of Dutch folksongs (for example, "Ik wou dat ik een vogeltje was" ["I wish I were a little bird"]).

Musical transculturation emerged from a spatial transposition from one cultural context to another. The New York-based Archie Shepp-Bill Dixon Quartet introduced the new music in Helsinki, Finland, in 1962, where they met the Danish-Congolese saxophonist/composer John Tchicai, whom they encouraged to come to the United States (Noglik 1981, 404–06). In New York, Tchicai and Shepp organized the New York Contemporary Five, which also included Don Cherry (who took over for Bill Dixon, although Dixon remained the group's principal composer), Ronnie Boykins or Don Moore, and Sunny Murray or J. C. Moses. Tchicai took the group on an extended tour of Germany and Scandinavia in 1963 (pers. com. 1999). In Sweden they recorded their music for the film *Future One.* Back in New York, Tchicai co-led the New York Art Quartet with Roswell Rudd, Lewis Worrell, and Milford Graves. All were active in the Jazz Composers' Guild Orchestra and made appearances at Newport 1965 and at the Museum of Modern Art in New York in July of that year. Albert Ayler and

Cecil Taylor recorded a live album at Copenhagen's Jazzhus Monmatre in fall 1962. George Russell, whose sextet toured Europe in September and October 1964 with George Wein's History of Jazz package show, remained in Europe playing clubs and appearing on television in Scandinavia and Germany as well as touring Swedish schools. Russell taught his lydian concept of tonal organization in Stockholm and was interviewed with Karlheinz Stockhausen at a concert that featured the music of both (Feather 1966, 254). By 1965, Ornette Coleman, Marion Brown, and the many Americans practicing the new music poured into Europe. A survey of the recording activities among several generations of leading lights and lesser-known African American avant-gardists (among them, Cecil Taylor, Marion Brown, Bill Dixon, Anthony Braxton, George Lewis, Alan Silva, Frank Lowe, and Frank Wright) indicates this shift in recording activity across the Atlantic.

The proliferation of European recording companies between 1969 and 1981 is shown in the following list:

> *Italy:* Black Saint, Soul Note, Fore, Horo, Ingo, Jazz, Oxford, Ferrari
> *Germany:* Birth, Ring/Moers Music, Free Music Productions, New Artists Guild (precursor to FMP), Po Torch, Mood, MPS, Futura GER, Mouloudji, Sound Aspects, Saba, Calig Verlag, Praxis, Konnex, Sandra, European New Jazz Association (ENJA), ECM, Japo
> *Sweden:* Jazz Society
> *England:* Incus, Leo (2), Ogun, Bead, Matchless, Black Lion, A Records (later called Arc), Rough Trade, Emanem
> *Denmark:* Steeplechase, Dane, Brazillus
> *Switzerland:* GNM, hat Art United Composers and Artists, Hat Hut
> *Austria:* Reform Art Unit, Pipe
> *Holland:* Instant Composers Pool, BvHaast, Claxon, Attacca, Broken Records, Coreco, Hummeloord, Kloet Muziek, Ooyevaar Disk, Catfish, Waterland, Timeless, Criss-Cross, Circle, KGB/Snipe Sound, Peace, Altsax, Osmosis, Fontana, Relax, Renais Sense, Elf Provincien, Intercord Freedom, Artone, Vara, Wergo
> *Finland:* Leo (1)
> *France:* BYG Actuel, Freedom/Intercord ITC, Affinity, Toho, Pathe, Frame, America, Futura, Black & Blue, Calumet, Free Lance, Red, Palm,Blue Marge, Shandor, Calumet, Fractal, Sun, Center of the World and Goody/Gravure Universelle.

The work of several African American avant-garde artists also served as the debut releases for several European companies. *Black Glory (La Glorre Du Noir)* by pianist Mal Waldron (who, like Max Roach, Charles Mingus, Abbey Lincoln, and Herbie Nichols, was a precursor of the avant-garde), recorded live at the Munich jazz club Domicile in June 1971, was the inaugural album for Horst Weber's and Matthias Winckelmann's European New Jazz Association label (ENJA 2004 ST). Saxophonist Marion Brown's critically acclaimed album *Afternoon of a Georgia Faun*, a self-described tone poem depicting the nature and environment in Atlanta, was essentially the first production in 1970 by Manfred Eicher for his Edition of Contemporary Music label (ECM 1004 ST), which, up to then, had primarily been a basement industry in Munich operating as Jazz by Post, or JAPO. Technically, Eicher's first release was *Free at Last* (ECM 1001) by Mal Waldron, which was recorded in November 1969 in a limited edition. Bertold Hummel's German classical, folk, and African music label Calig-Verlag also recorded Marion Brown. In fact, Brown's 1968 release *Gesprachsfetzen* (CAL 30601) was the company's first attempt at jazz recording. In 1971 saxophonist Billy Harper released the first album on Italian Giovani Bonandrini's Black Saint label and its affiliate Soul Note Records, *On Tour in Europe* (BSR 0001). Swiss pharmaceutical executive Werner Uehlinger's hat Hut label was formed in order to document Joe McPhee's first recording efforts entitled *Underground Railroad* (hat A) around 1970. Uehlinger's company, formed in West Park, New York, became a transnational enterprise with the opening of offices in Switzerland in 1981.

A music that was once the sole domain of America was quickly transformed into having two alternative meanings in Europe. One was Sunny Murray's declaration of "un hommage au son universel de l'homme noir" (homage to the universal black man) in liner notes he wrote for his first album produced for the BYG-Actuel label in France in 1966. The other was what Eric Dolphy, while residing in Europe in 1964, called "Human Jazz . . . the other name for the New Thing" (Miller 1966, 182). *Human Music* became the title for Don Cherry's 1970 release on Flying Dutchman Records, which featured the electronic music of Jon Appleton. These two meanings are manifest in how the new jazz intervened in contemporary musical life in the Netherlands.

Early jazz history in the Netherlands followed roughly the same pattern as in most surrounding European countries (van Delden, v.13, 1986, liner notes). Although jazz was first introduced as a popular dance style around 1919, it was the artist Piet Mondrian who wrote an article in 1927 in the international magazine out of Holland *i-10* on the differences and similarities of Neo-Plasticism and jazz. Mondrian stressed the rhythmic aspect of both and, later in the article, their reiterative, universal qualities:

Jazz and Neo-Plasticism are highly revolutionary phenomena. They are destructive-constructive. They do not destroy the real content of form. They merely deepen form in order to elevate it to a new plane. They cut through the binding effect of "form as a separate element" to pave the way for universal unity. (Koopmans 1976, 6)

The Dutch sociologist and jazz critic Rudy Koopmans, once the editor of *Jazzwereld* and one of the founders of the Amsterdam music center Paradiso—a major performance and recording venue for many an expatriate musician (Gordon 1969)—praised Mondrian for being able to identify the commercial corruption that posed a constant threat to jazz. The Decca recording company made it their practice to record foreign visitors in the thirties like Benny Carter and Coleman Hawkins, usually backed by Dutch groups. By the sixties, an overtly imitative rendering of jazz musical style and sound in the hands of Dutch musicians became an attempt at autonomous musical conception.

Amsterdam's pianist/composer Misha Mengelberg, whose father is the pianist/composer/conductor Karel Mengelberg, was a student of composition from 1958–64 under Kees van Baaren (1906–1970) at the Royal Conservatory in The Hague. Van Baaren's influence on Dutch music became apparent after World War II with his founding of constructivism at the New Vienna School, the period before 1950 when dodecaphony was not accepted. This movement evoked strong reactions in the Netherlands and elsewhere and ultimately gave rise to a complex known as the crisis of tonality (van Baaren 1972). Towards the end of his stay at the conservatory, Mengelberg became active in the "Fluxus movement," inspired by the Dadaism founded in 1962 in Germany by the Lithuanian American musician George Maciunas. Mengelberg formed the Mood Engineering Society while also performing as a pianist with his own jazz quartet. His first recording was with drummer Han Bennink on what would be American saxophonist/composer Eric Dolphy's last studio date in June 1964. Inspired by Dolphy, Mengelberg, Bennink, and saxophonist Willem Breuker formed the Instant Composers Pool (ICP) in Holland in late 1966, eventually becoming prime movers of their own brand of what they termed "creative improvised music" (cf. van Eyle 1981, 66, 149; Hylkema 1992; Dolphy 1964a and 1964b).

Han Bennink recalls Mengelberg's proposition that "in speech people constantly think of things on the spur of the moment. Structured thinking in music goes a little further, that is, instant composing" (pers. com. with Han Bennink 1997). The formation of the ICP, one of the first of many Dutch "new artists guilds" patterned after short-lived but influential American artist organizations like the Max Roach/Charles Mingus Jazz Artists Guild (1960) and the Bill Dixon/Cecil Taylor Jazz Composers Guild (1964), came in the wake of Mengelberg and Bennink having been invited to perform at the 1966 Newport Jazz Festival, where they witnessed some of the most diverse samplings of jazz approaches perhaps ever assembled on one stage in American music history (Goldblatt 1977, 271). Rudy Koopmans said that it was Mengelberg, winner of the 1966 Wessel-Ilcksen prize, the Netherlands Jazz Society's annual award, "who initiated the metamorphosis of jazz into improvised music pure and simple" (Koopmans 1982, 35). Mengelberg was more explicit in identifying this metamorphosis, agreeing with John Tchicai about how to consider "Africanizing the 12-tone row" (Whitehead 1998, 49).

This musical "metamorphosis" appears to have resulted from several suppositions. Although Mengelberg maintains that music in itself has no political dimension, music forms a part of the musical "scene," which is subject to political influences. Consequently, he was active in restructuring the music business including subsidy and program selection. Mengelberg objected to the subordination of music to more general policy, and to the subordination of culture to social and economic policy. Along with Willem Breuker and others, Mengelberg introduced the unique phenomenon known as Dutch music theater that, with its use of musical improvisation, brought together people who were intent upon the creation of artistic acts containing musical, theatrical, and socially critical elements (see for example Koopmans 1975, 20; and De Voldharding 1992). It was the musicians themselves (Mengelberg, Breuker, Willem Van Manen, Maarten Van Regteren Altena, and others) who took control of the Netherlands Jazz Society and who founded the Association of Improvising Musicians (Beroepsvereniging voor Improviserende Musici) in 1971. The musicians obtained seats on the National Arts Council, a body set up to advise the Ministry of Cultural Affairs, and on the Amsterdam Arts Council. Willem Van Manen, who occupied the ICP seat on the Councils, said that "Amsterdam provided the first grants for improvised music in 1973" (Tra 1978a, 7). Although artist subsidy plans have changed over time, it was not unusual to see as much as 20 percent of arts funding going to improvised music in the Netherlands in the formative years of the Instant Composers Pool and BVHaast, an artist-driven label run by Willem Breuker after he departed from the ICP.

Another supposition occurs in relating music and language. The narrative aspects of Mengelberg's work can be traced back both to his jazz background and cultural concerns as "jazz is, after all, largely a question of 'talking music'" (Koopmans 1982, 35). In the Instant Composers Pool Orchestra's tribute to Thelonious Monk, eventually released as *Two Programs: The ICP Orchestra Performs Nichols-Monk* (ICP 026 1984, 86), one can hear serial elements, musical allusions to Mengelberg's teacher Kees van Baaren, George Russell's pantonality, as well as Monk's own rhythmic and harmonic dissonance. It is no wonder that Mengelberg relates the story of having first heard Monk on U.S. Armed Forces radio in Europe in 1953, thinking that it was the Firebird music of Igor Stravinsky (ICP 026 1984, 86, liner notes). Mengelberg cites Thelonious Monk and John Cage, whom he heard in Darmstadt in 1958, as the two musicians in whom he was then interested.

American trombonist and composer George Lewis, who lived in Europe and played with the Instant Composers Pool on the ICP's Monk and Nichols project, said:

... When I came [to Europe] ... I came here in 1985 and stayed until '87 ... I didn't understand the culture, and so I didn't understand the music. ... After awhile I started to see what the culture was like, and how it enters the music. ... The thing about ICP—Misha serves literally the same function as Muhal [Richard Abrams] in Chicago. ... When I was in ICP, he [Misha] was literally teaching them Thelonious Monk. ... Misha puts together his ironic stance toward European classical music and its class pretensions, with the heart of jazz and theater, and he puts it all on a Monk tune. It's a band where people can play and learn. . . .

I started reading a lot about African history here. After seeing how it was possible for Misha, Willem Breuker and Maarten Altena to have a Dutch identity, I looked for ways to make my own music reflect where I'm coming from. Then I saw it already did. I just hadn't known where to look; extreme contrasts, a lot of colors, multiple rhythms all around. Confronting their culture in a deep way made me confront my own. A typical expatriate experience I think. No one ever said I had to leave, it just became an imperative. (quoted in Whitehead 1998, 150–51)

Lewis's imperative was put into perspective by Misha Mengelberg at a forum focusing on the uniqueness of European jazz at the Jazz Institute in Darmstadt. Replying to a question regarding his association with Eric Dolphy and the meaning of African American music on his work, Mengelberg's take is both retrospective and provocative because of its artistic inclusiveness:

It wasn't just Eric Dolphy. You can add Duke Ellington, Thelonious Monk, Herbie Nichols, Anthony Braxton, George Lewis, just off the top of my head. But their work has ceased to exist as being meaningful. I think jazz is the music of black people in ugly America [bosen Amerika]. It's great and very exciting music. Those were fantastic times, all that jazz music at that time. (quoted in Knauer 1993, 180)

The marquis events that signal the change from "jazz in Europe" to "europaischer Jazz" emanate from the aftermath of the free movement of the sixties. It is in the wake of this period when the terms "German Jazz" or "Italian Jazz" come to the fore, as the perception of national jazz traditions are formed. These traditions are a result of the development of a jazz self-consciousness in Europe, a parallel, albeit later, development to the mainstreaming of a jazz tradition in America. Utilizing folk music traditions with musical improvisation and the jazz language (*Jazzbereich gefunden*) have served both to expand the borders of jazz, and to demarcate what many argue are distinctive national musical spaces in Europe. Free jazz is the emancipating agent that invigorates distinctive national elements in European jazz. Some European record labels, like Silkheart (Sweden), hatOLOGY (Switzerland) and CMP (Germany) have even created separate American "creative music" catalogs to further enhance these national distinctions. Composer/trumpeter/painter Bill Dixon supposes that the European reception of creative black musicians has ultimately changed and shaped European consciousness:

I mean a lot of European musicians are resenting the heavy influence and the heavy influx of black musicians at what they might feel is at the expense of their own musicians and they are now more formally and more overtly addressing themselves to the tenets of what they are referring to, as improvised music—as if, in the final analysis, all music wasn't improvised. . . . In fact, had it not been for the fact that a lot of black American music was totally unsupported and unacceptable in America . . . I would hazard a guess . . . that the idea of a European concept of improvised music would not be serving up its contemporary existence. (Dixon 1980, liner notes)

Ekkehard Jost, the premier academic spokesperson on American free jazz and the development of contemporary European jazz (1974, 1982, 1987), has not been able to ascertain the full dimension of African American innovation on his continent. As late as 1993, while acknowledging ties with the political and social upheaval in Europe in the sixties and oppositional artistic trends in the United States, like the Living Theater or the Mothers of Invention, Jost could not completely gauge the African American contribution except by observing that, "drawn to the traditional jazz up to the sixties, nearly all of the noteworthy innovations of American jazz have come without question from African Americans" (Knauer 1993, 234). He can, however, account for the distinctiveness of European jazz due to three historical conditions.

First, Jost connects European contemporary new music to the sixties free jazz movement in the development of a collective-group concept using mostly linear or continuous melodic form. This new development was spearheaded beginning in 1966 by European-international networking in newly formed festivals and meetings such as Free Music Production's Total Music Meeting in Berlin, Derek Bailey's Company Week in London, King Kong-Veranstaltungen in Antwerp, and the Controindicazioni Festival in Rome.

Secondly, European jazz further distinguishes itself because of its use of European folk music materials. These folk materials actually have precedent in the United States with Miles Davis's "Dear Old Stockholm," which uses a

Swedish folk song "Ack Varmeland du skona," or Coltrane's "Ole," which uses the Spanish song "El Vito" and privileges modalism. European jazz is derived both from distinctive European and West African folk features and the tapping of the indigenous music reservoir of the world. Jost and his colleagues at the Jazz Institute in Darmstadt believe that a kind of "imaginary folklore" has manifested itself in Europe through a jazz lens. In other words, folkloric elements in improvisation "sound" an imaginary folklore. This folkloric quality is a precursor to the development of national schools of jazz. Jost concludes that it is European pre-industrial folk, rather than a high art mentality, which reaches into the national underbelly to foster distinctiveness.

The third condition, perhaps spearheaded by Coltrane's version of "My Favorite Things," is the use of verbatim themes from the canon of European popular songs, operas, dance music, and musicals just as Tin Pan Alley, Broadway, and Hollywood are used in American jazz repertories. Although Django Reinhardt's "Marseillaise" ("Echoes of France") set this precedent, using European popular music was not in vogue until free jazz artists began using these materials, often satirically. Jost uses his own *Weimar Ballads* (Fish Music FM 005) as an example of this burgeoning tendency in jazz towards cultural representation.

In this instance, we cannot simply speak of a union of disparate elements from American and European sources. More appropriately, we can speak of the consummation of a unique musical product because, as Bruno Nettl has argued, where the "borrowing" of expressive culture ends, creative musical change begins (cf. Nettl 1985). The process of intercultural musical synthesis sets into motion an essentially creative process, in what Margaret Kartomi describes as the transformation of complexes of intersecting musical and extra-musical ideas. This flow of transnational to transcultural dialogue produced a new music and, in the process, the "new thing" eventually developed a transidiomatic musical perspective in its new locale.

When former childhood prodigy Joachim Kuhn made his escape from East Germany to Paris in 1966, at age twenty-two, his flight from an international competition in Vienna was inspired, in part, by the music of Ornette Coleman. Coleman's concepts of free, non-hierarchical music shattered the attitudes of many musicians, but none more so than those growing up with severe restrictions of artistic freedom and civil rights, living in fear of the Stasi secret police, behind the Berlin Wall. Kuhn recalls, "I heard some guys mention his name, and they said, 'This guy plays without chord changes,' I said, 'Wow, this is someone I have to hear' . . . [Ornette's early albums] changed everything for me . . . it was those records that encouraged me to play free music" (quoted at Harmolodic website 1995). Indeed, music bars could not contain Kuhn, nor could the Stasi. As a refugee in Paris, Kuhn finally met Coleman, who wrote some harmolodic scales and exercises for him to practice. He would eventually team with Coleman on a critically acclaimed duo recording released in 1997. Kuhn went on to perform with musicians as diverse as Gato Barbieri, Don Cherry, Michael Brecker, and his own creative music trio with bassist J. F. Jenny Clark and drummer/painter Daniel Humair.

By the end of the seventies several thousand recordings utilizing the expanded language constructs of the African American avant-garde (seen in pitch logic, time, sound color, texture, process, performance ritual, parody, historicism, and uses of tradition) were in evidence, with the majority of its production occurring after 1969 in Europe. This musical transculturation happened because of the transnational networking by the founders of the "new thing" in their ongoing attempt to establish an infrastructure for the music. Creative artists in the Netherlands, just as in other European centers for this new music, negotiated in their own unique way a worldview towards music history and performance practice espoused by American new music practitioners established prior to their dispersion across the Atlantic.

Shifts from one jazz era to another are often seen as knee-jerk stylistic reactions in the modernist landscape (Harvey 1990). Authors have suggested that periods of stylistic innovation in the history of jazz have simultaneously forced periodic reassessments of the tradition. However, historians do not account for the discourse that occurred during the formative years of the "new thing." Instead, these historians often look at the music as an autonomous, unilinear metonym for yet another sixties social movement and use the oxymoron "free form" in describing a music produced by "angry young men." African American avant-garde musicians developed their musical methods and materials in an effort to shrug-off the forced alignment of jazz with American popular song forms. The popular feeling in critical discourse is that jazz identity is somehow dependent on tunes from Tin Pan Alley and Broadway to such extent that shedding the skin of the American popular song form is tantamount to committing jazz hara-kiri. New music artists constructed a worldview on events begun at least as early as the bebop "revolution" (which wasn't enough of one, according to this vanguard) in the late thirties. The African American avant-garde continue the tradition of the slow, incremental dissolving of the American popular song form from the jazz repertoire in order to advance the art form.

European musicians are of the belief that "creative improvisational music" is the result of the failure of American jazz and of Western classical music. This aesthetic posture may be seen in the Netherlands, a country that launched around two dozen new music labels between 1966 and 1981. Musicians and music critics from the Netherlands and other European countries call this transition from American "free jazz" to "creative improvisational music" a "metamorphosis." Today, the Swiss-based United Composers and Musicians of Hat Art Records, whose corporate sponsor until recently was UBS, formerly the Swiss Bank, maintains an artist roster of nearly one hundred musicians, over forty percent of whom are Americans.

Another important African American avant-garde worldview adopted by many artists is that this music advances only when the idea of black music and the idea of jazz are at their furthest points of cultural aesthetic separation. Moreover, the times that black music and jazz blur are the times that inevitably represent stasis and commodification benefiting culture vendors, but not culture producers. It is only by separating African American musical production from the genre in which it is steeped, and up to this period totally dependent on, that one can understand why there are certain anomalies in jazz history that are dismissed or rebuked offhandedly. For example, Duke Ellington preferred the term "Negro music" to "jazz" and served as a model for American "new thing" players because of his organizational capabilities, methods of writing for and conducting his orchestra, and his aesthetic platform, that is, the methods and materials he used in making music. Sun Ra, once Fletcher Henderson's staff arranger, would subsequently don space attire and depart into intergalactic realms, far away from the prevailing music industry, so as to express himself. John Coltrane's albums for Impulse between 1965 and 1967 utilized the methods developed by first-generation "new thing" practitioners. This work has not been acknowledged as having the validity of his earlier, more "mainstream" material. Bill Dixon, one of the architects of this new music who had established what is to this author's knowledge the only Black Music degree program in the United States, has been almost entirely written out of jazz history. His artistic production since the early seventies has mainly been in Europe, often for the Italian Black Saint and Soul Note companies out of Milan. Aside from his courses at the New England Conservatory, George Russell's music theories and artistic production are mere footnotes in the United States, while being greatly utilized by Swedish Radio Orchestras and other European organizations as early as 1965. The European State mechanism supports new music because, as the French drummer and painter Daniel Humair states, "jazz is considered an art form in Europe," and European musicians have forged crucial links with receptive state and corporate mechanisms (quoted in Hylkema 1992; see also France 1986). An alternative sentiment is articulated by Anthony Braxton, who says the "history of the music is a history of tampering" (quoted in Rosenburg 1993, 50).

A third notion of the African American avant-garde worldview upheld the primacy of improvisation as being 1) the only creative musical process that could not easily be appropriated, or as being 2) representative of the cataclysmic music of the universe. Joachim Ernst Berendt, the German writer, educator, and record producer who founded the World Music Festival in 1965 and organized the first New Jazz Meeting in Baden-Baden in 1966, calls jazz, "an indicator of the social, political and spiritual consciousness of the twentieth century" (Berendt 1984, 12). America could no longer remain the territorialized harbinger, nor the sole innovator from this point on, with the founding of the International Jazz Federation in Venice, Italy in 1966, which became a member of the International Music Council of UNESCO by 1973.

European and American players, in some way, are part of a larger community which becomes the receptacle of the shared values and perspectives that shape the artists—a like-minded vision and connectedness where Black Music finds its kindred spirit as a world music. Different musicians with different agendas come together in the interest of constructing a new code, the guidelines of which may be continued or discarded thereafter. As Jacques Attali explains, these new codes are not simply random or gratuitous acts among players: "Composition [read: Improvisation] does not prohibit communication. It changes the rules. It makes it a collective creation, rather than an exchange of coded messages. To express oneself is to create a code, or to plug into a code in the process of being elaborated by the other" (Attali 1977, 143).

The Globe Unity Orchestra, founded in 1966 by German Alexander von Schlippenbach (a later manifestation of this group is called the Berlin Contemporary Orchestra); The Brotherhood of Breath, formed in Great Britain in 1970 by South African expatriates Louis Moholo, Chris McGregor, and Dudu Pukwana; American (Bermuda-born) Alan Silva's Celestial Communications Orchestra organized in France around the same period; U.K.'s John Stevens' Spontaneous Music Ensemble; John Tchicai, who led the workshop ensemble Cadentia Nova Danica in Denmark from 1967–71; Pierre Dørge's Dutch New Jungle Orchestra; German Gunter Hampel's Galaxie Dream Band and New Eternal Rhythm Orchestra in 1971; and Manfred Schoof's European Echoes which recorded for Free Music Productions in Berlin in 1969, the year in which he joined George Russell's Orchestra USA; these are just a few of the many bigger ensembles, not to mention smaller groups, organized in Europe which fomented a relationship among improvising musicians of all nationalities and were modeled after U.S.-based groups like Sun Ra's Arkestra, the aforementioned New York Contemporary Five and New York Art Quartet, or the Jazz Composers Orchestra Association, all of which became transnational organizations.

Europeans in general were able to internalize the worldview of the African American vanguard by acknowledging that place, that is, locality or local factors, shapes the production and consumption of music. The European Jazz Federation was founded in the mid-sixties to promote cooperation between all European countries in the field of jazz. The development of European "national schools" of jazz, an outcome of African American penetration across the Atlantic, was as much an ideological marker as a musicological one. These schools based their distinctiveness on the assumption that sound and location is connected to identity. Manfred Eicher, owner of the aforementioned German record label Editions of Contemporary Music (ECM) established in 1969, states that the music he records, his company's engineering and production values, and even its record covers, reflect a "new ecology of catching sound" and are evocative of northern

European spaces—"of a certain quality of light and air in that region" (Bergerot and Merlin 1991, 97).

It is not uncommon for players to state that the music they play is "Italian jazz," or "Swedish jazz."[3] By contrast, American "new thing" players, by defying place in order to lead a successful artistic and economic way of life, become part of a transnational phenomenon that alters our way of thinking about diasporic entities. Musicians "live in America" and "work in Europe." No longer can we construe jazz music as speaking for a people struggling with the "double consciousness" of which W. E. B. Du Bois wrote, how to be black and an American at the same time. Instead, we have witnessed a music that, if not heir to the jazz tradition, surely must be seen as its transcendence. The levels of (dis)location, rhetoric, politics, meaning and locality in which the African American avant-garde have resided have all contributed to the historical development of a musical idiom born, but largely disowned in America, while being nurtured and, consequently, inherited in the European new music scene. Perhaps it is as Bronowski says in talking of Pan-Africanism, that "when we discover the wider likeness, we enlarge the order in the universe . . . and moreover, we enlarge its unity" (Brokensha and Crowder 1974, 11).

GIANLUIGI TROVESI'S MUSIC

An Historical and Geographical Short-Circuit

—Stefano Zenni

Translation by Luigi Monge

The Italian jazz scene is one of the most lively and variegated in Europe: one can find active musicians following the most diverse stylistic trends ranging from modern mainstream to New Orleans revival, from swing to historical free jazz. Some of the most original contributions have come from musicians such as Gianluigi Trovesi, Eugenio Colombo, and Bruno Tommaso, who emerged in the mid-1970s and nurtured personal, original styles in the 1980s. Their work stands out because of their clear-cut abilities to synthesize markedly different materials, make the most of the Italian folk music heritage, and mix popular and cultured sources of inspiration, both European and American.

Together with Eugenio Colombo, Gianluigi Trovesi is perhaps in this respect the most successful composer and improviser. Born in 1944 in Nembro, a small town near Bergamo in Northern Italy, Trovesi was trained as most post-war Italian country town musicians were. He studied and practiced the clarinet in the town marching band, studied in a Bergamo music school, and then attended the conservatory at Piacenza, where he got a diploma in 1965, and finally studied composition from 1969 to 1972. In the meantime, Trovesi played in bands and pop music groups, then in local jazz groups and orchestras, and entered Giorgio Gaslini's sextet in 1977. It was here that his talent as an alto saxophonist and clarinetist became noticed. He formed his own trio with Paolo Damiani on cello and contrabass and Gianni Cazzola on drums, making an impression as an extremely energetic improviser strongly influenced by Eric Dolphy but at the same time rediscovering the folk tradition of Northern Italy, especially of the Bergamo area.

115

In any case, Trovesi did not deny himself any experience. He played in the RAI—the Italian Broadcasting Corporation—section orchestra in Milan and played solo concerts in which he used electronic instruments. His records as a leader won prizes from Italian critics. At the beginning of the 1990s, he collaborated with two long-established permanent groups, Tiziano Tononi's Nexus (1989–1991) and Paolo Fresu's quintet (1991–1995), now a sextet. In 1992, he formed his own octet, made up of his own reeds, trumpet, trombone or tuba, cello, two contrabasses, drums, and percussion, increasingly devoting himself to alto clarinet as an alternative to bass clarinet. Together with the octet, Trovesi recorded two CDs for Soul Note, which achieved great critical acclaim. In the mid-1990s, a duo with accordionist Gianni Coscia was formed. The climax of the latter's growing success was a CD recorded for ECM. Since 1998, the octet has been supplemented by a new nonet made up of jazz (reeds, guitar, drums), folk (accordion, contrabass, tambourine), and classical (two violins and a cello) trios, for which Trovesi wrote a repertoire drawing inspiration from Shakespeare.

From Trovesi's maturity emerges a concept of music that transcends the traditional notion of jazz. First of all, it takes root in Northern Italian folk traditions, in its old tunes and country dances, a repertoire with which Trovesi is acquainted due to both actual music practice and academic study. Beginning from the 1990s, European compositional techniques and references to Renaissance and Baroque music have taken on greater importance. As "the folk tradition in North Italy has been contributing for centuries to the flowering of so-called 'classical' music (the birth of modern violin and its repertoire is one example)" (Piras 1992), by adopting classical techniques being used in the sixteenth- and seventeenth-century and folk repertoires, Trovesi devoted himself to rediscovering some crucial points of Italian and European music history.

After invisibly communicating for centuries or traveling in time and space, some cultures sharing compositional and improvisational techniques have changed without losing their distinctive features. Some European traditional dances present the same characteristics as the jazz idiom. For instance, it was just in the sixteenth century when musical forms such as *passacaglia* or *chaconne* first appeared. They consisted of a harmonized bass chorus of lute or harpsichord overlapped by a few extemporaneous variations from a soloist (voice, violin, or the harpsichord itself) as in a sort of jazz improvisation ahead of its time. As already proven by Curt Sachs (1933), it is beyond all doubt that *sarabande, chaconne,* and *passacaglia* are originally from Central America and contain African elements, a fact confirmed by literary, musical, and dance sources. Indeed, in the strong thrust to be given to the movements of the pelvis and in the independent movements of trunk and legs it is possible to trace an African origin (Piras 1997 and forthcoming). In addition, the way to perform it by running over the strings is very similar to the way of playing the lutes, such as the *halam* (or *xalam*), in Senegal and Senegambia (Piras 1994, 39). Moreover, it has recently been discovered that it is in this kind of repertoire and not in the monodical songs performed by the Florentine Group of Bardi that the modern notion of harmony takes shape (Preitano 1994), which probably owes its origin to the Mediterranean culture medium more than to Giulio Caccini. It must also be borne in mind that *folia, passacaglia,* and *chaconne* introduced to Europe the form and practice of the "chord changes" or "chorus"—which was unknown to the European cultured tradition until then—a form recalling the repetitive circularity of African dance music genres. Yet, as for the exact origin of these dances, it is not at all clear whether they came to Portugal and Spain directly from Africa alongside the thriving cultural exchanges and trade in the Mediterranean Sea or—more likely—whether the meeting took place in the New World when the cultures of the Hispanic conquerors and the African slaves came into contact and subsequently returned to Europe. Whatever the case, *folia, passacaglia, chaconne,* and *sarabande* undoubtedly mark one of the most spectacular encounters between African and European music cultures.

   That being stated, it comes as no surprise that a few jazz players turned their attention especially to *folia* in order to find new directions in composition and improvisation. The term *folia,* which refers to a dance and its accompanying music, appeared in Portugal at the end of the fifteenth century. Its etymology is controversial. According to the tradition, the term refers to the fact that in the heat of the dance it seemed as if dancers went out of their minds; more recently, it has been related to fourteenth- and fifteenth-century *folie* and *sotie* (a sort of burlesque farce), thus tracing it back to medieval parties such as the "donkey's party" and the like. In any case, the dance spread from Portugal to Spain into France and Italy together with the Spanish guitar, which provided its instrumental accompaniment alongside the lute. *Folia* was essentially based on chord changes, that is, a real chorus where variations were being improvised and soon started to be put down in writing. Its golden age in writing started after 1630 and reached its height in 1700 at the time of the variations composed by Arcangelo Corelli for the last part of his *Sonata for Violin and Basso continuo op. 5 no. 2*, which became so famous as to be broadly copied (for instance, by Vivaldi and Geminiani among others).

Among jazz players, it was George Russell who, in 1989, carried out the most difficult task of composing (and later recording) *La Follia: The Roccella Variations* (see Zenni 1996). Instead, Gianluigi Trovesi systematically uses harmonic riffs deriving from the European popular and cultured tradition. For instance, his *C'era una strega, c'era una fata* ("Once upon a time there was a witch, there was a fair," which brings fairy tales to mind), composed in 1980 and recorded in the same year with his trio for the first time (on *Cinque piccole storie*), is conceived as a series of variations based on chord changes typical of *folia*. In his 1995 duo version with accordionist Gianni Coscia, the accordion starts playing the chords in *tempo rubato*, then, when the clarinet comes in, the 3/4 meter typical of *folia* is established. In order to make his execution sound jazzier, Trovesi makes a slight change at the end of the chorus, adding a vamp of Dm and G7 chords. Starting from the clarinet improvisation, the tempo turns into a typical 4/4 swing feel, and Trovesi's solo veers to jazz phrasing with strong bluesy accents in the vamp section. In the final part, after the accordion solo, the connection with the popular world becomes clear: the two performers need only change rhythm, and it is here that the *folia* is transformed into a driving mazurka typical of an Italian dance hall atmosphere. Obviously, there is no "scientific" connection between *folia* and Italian popular dance hall music, but this transformation reflects a deep-rooted cultural connection and illuminates a standard historical process of exchange and derivation through which old popular dances have become a useful subject for composers of classical music, at the same time surviving and transforming themselves through the performance of popular dances. It takes a composer and improviser such as Gianluigi Trovesi—whose culture is at the same time steeped in mountainous as well as urban areas, in dance as well as concert halls, in marching bands as well as jazz big bands—to bridge the chasms between elite and popular cultures, between

African-American music and European popular dances. Sharing the same ideas (without skimping on humor and irony), Trovesi and Coscia managed to find a contact point for jazz, country tradition, as well as Central and Southern Italy dance halls, where mazurkas, waltzes, tangos, ballads, and a certain kind of jazz end up being on the same plane.[1] If compared to works performed by bigger groups, the simultaneous fusion or "short circuit" dimension is absent here. It is rather the succession of ideas and atmospheres, and of stylistic references, that prevails, even though approaches and transformations occur in a very refined way and often with surprising results.[2]

"Hercab" is as interesting a case. Conceived as the closing piece of the octet's first concerts (it is included at the end of the masterpiece *From G to G*), it starts as an overwhelming and melancholy brass band march in minor that Pino Minafra's vocal gags on megaphone, like a clown's grimace, make even sadder. But as it develops, it gradually reveals its submerged Dixieland vein. "Hercab"'s circus-like character, pervaded with 1920s novelty, disappears in the duo version: the accordion lets a country-style, feast-like, frontyard aspect come to the surface.

"Hercab" represents only one of Trovesi's use of march rhythms. "Now I Can" (again on *From G to G*) perfectly exemplifies the overlapping of march rhythm and fragmented phrasing, which in the second theme is rearranged according to a 7/4-meter post-bop line, but with folk overtones. Later on, the march rhythm takes on a much funkier progression. In the nonet's repertoire, *Animali in marcia* presents the word "march" in the very title, but has a more homogeneous progression and mixes the usual comic vocalizations (here a series of tongue-twisters and nursery rhymes, many from Southern Italy) with two themes, both in minor, which are not subjected to any particular treatment or change except for a variation for stringed instruments at the end, the whole thing being dealt with in the habitual refined and joyous humor.

The link among the three worlds—African-American, classical European, and folk—becomes more evident in the version of *C'era una strega, c'era una fata*, performed by the nonet and recorded in 1999. As a matter of fact, the composition for the string trio follows the seventeenth-century Italian model, while the presence of a jazz rhythm section accentuates African-American swing. The arrangement starts with a cadence for violin solo, written by violinist Stefano Montanari according to Arcangelo Corelli's style, and leading to the string trio's development of the theme. The theme's original coda is picked up by the accordion which, thanks to its "folk" intercession, favors a quick transition to the 3/4 swing development of Trovesi's clarinet; and here is the vamp blues. Trovesi's clarinet solo and Jean-Louis Matinier's accordion solo follow. Then, still on the swinging waltz time, the string trio, Trovesi, and Matinier chase each other. The stringed instruments make some tension-filled—though classically styled—sixteen-bar variations, written by Bruno Tommaso especially for this arrangement. In a jazzier vein, Trovesi and Matinier follow up playing eight bars each. After two such rounds, the chase exchanges become shorter. Still in a classical style, Montanari's solo violin exchanges eight, then four, and then two measures with Trovesi and Matinier, and concludes with a solo lowering in the final cadence, which closes the piece just as it had started.

In *C'era una strega, c'era una fata*'s duo as well as nonet versions, the different musical worlds are side by side rather than overlapping. In the nonet version, their relationship is more blurred due to both the mediating role of the accordion—which sounds folkish but whose phrasing is jazzy—and the constant presence of the jazz rhythm section, which links up and mixes the different languages. The chase of the string trio and the two soloists represents the closest possible point between the cultured version of a folk dance having distant African American origins and jazz improvisation.

Trovesi finds inspiration in the medieval folklore of the Bergamo area as well. On his first album as a leader, *Baghèt*, recorded in 1978, he electronically worked out a famous medieval *saltarello* that originally came from Northern Italy. On the CD recorded in 1999 with his new nonet, *Round a Midsummer's Dream*, Trovesi's "imaginary folklore" (Piras 1992) finds a historically much more defined source, a dance from Bergamo, the *bergamask*, which, as its name implies, originated from the author's native area. The choice of the *bergamask* comes from a verse in Act V, Scene I, of William Shakespeare's *A Midsummer Night's Dream*: "Will it please you to see the epilogue, or to hear a bergamask dance between two of our company?" The *bergamask* was an acrobatic, improvised dance accompanied by a tune with a very simple chord changes (I-IV-V-I). Not only is its melody documented in dance collections, but it was also used by composers such as Girolamo Frescobaldi (in *Fiori Musicali*) for complex elaborations; it became popular in Germany and was also employed by Bach in the *Quodlibet* closing the *Goldberg Variations*.

For his record Trovesi elaborates the *bergamask* as a twentieth-century artist who has several languages at his disposal. So, in the *Adagietto bergomasco*, the theme and harmonies of the Renaissance dance are subjected to a series of transformations involving the string trio, the folk trio, and the jazz trio. At the beginning, the traditional tune is performed by the clarinet in its folk naturalness, but the modified stringed instruments' response lets classical memories come to the surface immediately. It is the accordion that brings it back to the folk context. When the bass starts swinging, the connection of the *bergamask's* harmonies with the calypso's traditional ones emerges, and Trovesi starts to improvise on the Caribbean rhythm. A little later, the soloist and the stringed instruments start a tight dialogue on the folk theme, now on the calypso rhythm, perfectly linking up different worlds and cultures as in a circle. At this point music radically changes from calypso to soul music, and the stringed instruments ironically interplay with a typical soul music riff in the background of the clarinet solo. Paolo Manzolini's electric guitar solo lowers into a cadence going back to the folk theme and the classical variation used at the beginning.

Trovesi's view ranges beyond the traditions of his native land. For instance, he grasps the modal qualities of the ostinato basses that enable him to sketch jazz modal improvisations as well as pure folk melodies. It is through this modal component that Mediterranean melodic elements are linked to 1960s jazz improvisational techniques, a method which was adopted by many Italian jazz players such as Paolo Damiani and Eugenio Colombo. The use of asymmetrical and additional rhythms serves to overcome historical and geographical references and to include the Balkan and Near East worlds as in a short circuit, suddenly revealing the deep-rooted connections among different and distant music genres. Such revelations of a shared nature among seemingly different traditions does not occur through a naïve approach of elements or the mere overlapping of style, but is rather the fruit of a complex compositional process that digs deep into the original material. In order to understand its nature and scope, Gianluigi Trovesi's *Dance for a King*, included on the CD *Les Hommes*

Armés (1996), is analyzed below. The "king" in the title is Eric Dolphy, to whom the composition is dedicated. The piece is made up of four component parts:

- D tonic bass including improvisations by wind instruments (section A)
- Rhythms and Balkan melodies including meter changes (sections C and C')
- Writing and orchestration of wind instruments, which draw inspiration from the Venetian Renaissance tradition (again sections C and C')
- Melodies taken from the theme and solo on Eric Dolphy's "Miss Ann" (sections B, D, F)

The bass in section A creates a swinging and elastic atmosphere for improvisations by Trovesi on alto clarinet, and Pino Minafra on flugelhorn, and Rodolfo Migliardi on trombone. In these passages Trovesi depicts an ambiguous atmosphere in which melodies alluding to the East digress into free jazz passages. These references to the East take concrete form in section C, where Trovesi plays unquestionably Balkan rhythmic and melodic tunes, though still rich in overtones going back to the Italian popular tradition.

Obviously, Trovesi's Balkan folklore is far from being philologic: his melodies present some general features, such as odd rhythms, descending profile, and some slight embellishments, which may be found, for example, in the dance *Le petit cerisier*, which is drawn from the collection *Bulgarie—Musique du pays Chope: Anthologie de la musique bulgare vol. 1*. Trovesi also adopts the multi-thematic form typical of folk dances in many parts of the world. In *Dance for a King*, section C consists of a number of alternating and repeated short themes (a, b, c, d) just as in *Ratchenitsa*, one more Bulgarian dance in the CD mentioned above. Moreover, it is also possible to find the call-and-response technique present in *Le petit cerisier*, which Trovesi employs in the C sections alternating two- and four-voice harmonizations.

The Balkan characterization is not exact: it is just the ambiguity of style that allows the listener to perceive the themes of C also as fragments of Italian folk melodies truncated by odd rhythms, and therefore *similar* to Balkan melodies. Trovesi proves to be aware of this twofold reading when, in the middle of the piece, he orchestrates according to the Venetian Renaissance style. In Venice in the sixteenth century sacred and secular musics were mainly performed by choral groups supported by sumptuous ensembles of wind instruments, especially cornetts and trombones, accompanying stringed instruments and organ, and alternating with grandiose antiphonal effects. In the middle of the piece, Trovesi orchestrates C:ab and C':cd first by using two (alto clarinet and contrabass, let alone drums) and then four (alto clarinet, flugelhorn, trombone, cello, plus drums) voices, thus creating a clear Renaissance sonority.

It must be borne in mind that in C's four-voice response not only is the bass part performed by the cello, but also that the flugelhorn gives out a sound which is not dissimilar from the Renaissance cornett: that is why the amalgam sounds typically Venetian. However, there are other aspects short-circuiting the "Balkan" theme with the Renaissance form; both traditions adopt the antiphonal technique and are often based on multiple themes. An example summarizing these stylistic features is Giuseppe Guami's *Canzon XXV a 8*, which goes back to 1608.[3] In any case, the dance rhythms also belong to the Venetian tradition, and are orchestrated according to the patterns analyzed above, such as in the *Canzon XXV a 8* by Giovanni Gabrieli, the greatest maestro of Venetian style. So, Trovesi effectively overlaps the colors and dialogue between sections (which is typical of sixteenth-century Venetian classical music) and Balkan dances. The common stylistic features and the folk character underlying both traditions favor the perfect synthesis of the two worlds, the jazz pronunciation providing the necessary touch of modernization.

The fourth essential—albeit more cryptic—element in *Dance for a King* is the tribute to Eric Dolphy, who was one of the sources of inspiration for young Trovesi's style. Starting from Andrew White's transcriptions, Trovesi used the "Miss Ann" theme and the first notes of Dolphy's solo, ignoring the rhythmic progression of the original and focusing only on pitches. In section B, *Dance for a King* is a first harmonization of "Miss Ann." Dolphy's melody is assigned to the cello, which is not always on top but repeatedly changes its position in between voices, so that the original theme is not clearly recognizable. Trovesi readapts "Miss Ann" as if it were the *cantus firmus* of a Renaissance motet in the style of Josquin de Pres. (The reference to Renaissance polyphony is particularly appropriate if one considers that on *Les Hommes Armés* Trovesi wrote for his octet a series of variations based on *Hommes Armé*'s famous melody, which provided the basis for a number of fifteenth- and sixteenth-century composers' sacred and secular compositions.) Section D presents an even more ingenious solution, though a fluent and natural one. In order to understand its source, it is necessary to divide it into two parts, measures 1–8 and measures 9–15, but the passage is performed by the wind instruments plus the second contrabass in unison and in octave. Measures 1–8 must in turn be divided into two parts, 1–4 and 5–8. Measures 1–4 are the rhythmically free transcription of the first twelve notes of Dolphy's solo in "Miss Ann"; measures 5–8, instead, repeat fourteen notes beginning from the second beat of the solo. Thus, the two segments overlap, creating a sense of familiarity and similarity. Instead, measures 9–15 are taken from the last phrase of the "Miss Ann" theme. So, the whole passage is based on two different sources of the same piece, and one of the two sources—Dolphy's solo—is repeated in a different way.

The same process is adopted in final section F. Measures 1–5 are taken from the two overlapping segments of Dolphy's solo, but now the melody presents a four-voice harmonization, and the contrabass plays short, filling, improvised phrases. Measures 6–15, including the last three notes with fermata signs, come from the last notes of the "Miss Ann" theme. There is a close relationship among the sonorities in section C. Indeed, the orchestration of D and F reproduces the Renaissance sound of section C, with which it is consistently connected. Figure 1 shows the relationships between *Dance for a King*'s different stylistic and linguistic contexts. It is interesting to note that the material related to Dolphy is subjected to more substantial transformations, even though the arrow from "Miss Ann"'s box to the one representing modal harmony refers to Trovesi's solos inspired by Dolphy in section A.

Figure 1 may also be interpreted as an illustration of the tendency to Signifyin(g). The theory of Signifyin(g) has been introduced in African-American literature by Henry Louis Gates (1988) and applied to African-American music by Samuel Floyd (1995). It is the best way to understand how different sources can be blended together and how they influence each other, thus changing their meaning. "To Signify" means to appropriate someone else's speech, words, music, and signify on it, to repeat the same thing in a different way, parodying and changing its meaning. According to this process, the signifier adds new layers of meaning to the discourse,

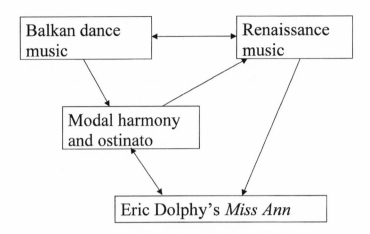

preserves the "old" one and adds his own, discovering links and dynamic exchange between the discourses. In *Dance for a King*, the listener may hear how Trovesi signifies on Renaissance music, Balkan popular music and contemporary jazz. In this way the contemporary composer maintains the original meaning whilst offering his/her personal perspective.

The diagram shows the streams of signifying, that is, how the different sources influence one another. This process is typical of some European jazz: like all African-American music, European jazz too is nourished by an open dialogue with different traditions, which are not only American, though; European musicians use their popular, old, and classical heritage, too. Thus Signifyin(g) short-circuits very distant and different eras and places, discovering and enlightening the most obscure, submerged and surprising links of our culture. The composer rewrites history creatively, shows the central role played by these links in the contemporary world, and enhances the creative ability of the musician as well as of the listener.

LOCAL POLITICS

THE MUSIC OF THE GROSS, 1928-1931

S. Frederick Starr

Excerpted from Chapter 5 in *Red & Hot: The Fate of Jazz in the Soviet Union* (New York: Oxford University Press, 1983; revised edition: New York: Limelight, 1994). Reprinted with permission of the author.

For a form of popular culture to flourish and endure it must meet two conditions. First, it must be genuinely well liked. No amount of promotion or hullabaloo can sustain its vitality if it fails to engage the interest of a large number of ordinary people. If a tune is not whistled in private it will never be popular in public. The tyranny of fashion may briefly cow a few, but never the public at large. Second, when a form of popular culture claims the support of part but not all of the public, as often happens, it must be able to protect itself from the hostility or indifference of the rest. Its supporters may choose to withdraw to avoid conflict, like Bohemian painters in nineteenth-century Paris. Or they may sally forth to conquer the opposition, or at least limit the extent of its damage. But if its proponents can neither build a protective barrier around themselves nor limit the harm their critics can impose, the form of popular culture they espouse will die.

All evidence suggests that Soviet jazz in the years 1928–31 had gained general popularity among the educated public of Russia's cities. But the necessary precondition and sustenance for its success was the relative tolerance fostered by the New Economic Policy, which embraced both musicians and audience. With the onslaught of the First Five-Year Plan, announced in October 1928, this tolerance evaporated. Nor was it possible for the world of jazz to protect itself by seceding into privacy, for the upheaval unleashed by Josef Stalin impinged on the lives of individuals and groups much more deeply than had the Bolsheviks' initial revolution in 1917. Contemporaries called it "The Great Fracture," the dawning of Russia's "Iron Age"; today it is recognized as the first Communist cultural revolution, the progenitor of the later upheavals in China, Cuba, and elsewhere.

CIVIL WAR "FROM ABOVE"

Those who did not live through the turmoil of 1928–31 in Russia can scarcely imagine its extent. What triggered the awful convulsion was the Party's decision to compel peasant farmers—tens of millions of people—to give up their private land and join their poor brethren on collective and state farms. The decision was prompted by the Communists' sustained failure to win over the hostile peasantry by other means, and by what they perceived as their desperate need to gain political control in the countryside. Its effects were devastating. Stalin later confided to Winston Churchill that ten million independent farmers had been "dealt with" in the process, through what was, in effect, a full-scale war in the countryside.[1] Several million more deaths were directly attributed to the famine that followed. Millions of survivors, mostly peasants, were assigned to labor camps, where they were compelled to work on many of the major construction projects of the day.[2] So staggering was the scale of suffering that many people, especially ideologically sympathetic foreigners, simply disbelieved it. Paul Robeson, the black American basso who moved among the same Moscow circles Sam Wooding had touched but who had contact with politicians as well, flatly denied that the tragedy had occurred when he returned to America in 1933. Robeson wrote, "This stuff about starvation is the bunk. What else would you expect Hearst to say? Wherever I went I saw plenty of food."[3]

Robeson's denial must be attributed more to blinders than to blindness, for the results of the social revolution were amply visible in Russian cities. Tens of thousands of homeless waifs, the offspring of murdered or exiled parents, filled the streets of Moscow. A couple walking out to dance at the Hermitage Gardens could not have avoided these gaunt and resourceful children huddling around campfires in the street or curled up asleep in sections of concrete pipe awaiting burial as part of the new sewer system.[4] Such sights touched the public scarcely less profoundly than the rationing of bread, which was begun in 1929.

Soviet news media did their best to shield the urban populace from knowledge of the rural crisis, but each step of the political revolution within the Kremlin was openly proclaimed. Trotsky and his left-wing supporters were purged from the Communist party in 1928, and in January 1929, the great revolutionary was expelled from the country. Before the end of the year Stalin had turned his wrath against his right-wing opponents, seizing them and extracting from them public recantations of past sins against the Revolution and against himself. Though the process was not complete for several more years, the Georgia-born leader had for all purposes consolidated his hold on the apparatus of power by 1931.

Central to Stalin's method of manipulation was terror. As early as 1927 he had whipped up a fraudulent war scare, which he then used to justify his first assault against critics and "class enemies."[5] No sooner had the scare of Western military intervention died down than Stalin announced that an even more insidious threat of economic counterrevolution was being prepared abroad. This time scores of native Russian engineers in the steel industry were charged with being in collusion with Russian emigre capitalists and foreign intelligence services.[6] The government's legal case was preposterously thin, as anyone who had read the newspaper accounts could readily detect. But therein lay its effectiveness. Soviet citizens quickly perceived that no contact with foreigners could be so innocent as to insure their safety, and no flirtation with alien ways so innocuous as to ensure against retribution. The message was clear. Paranoid xenophobia, far from being a psychological aberration, became for the average Soviet citizen the surest and most rational guide to safe conduct during the Cultural Revolution.

Soviet officials who had served abroad or whose families had foreign connections bent over backward to assert their proletarian loyalties, even to the point of exchanging their well-cut suits for the baggier and more proletarian local products.[7] All manifestations of worldliness were abjured so as not to arouse suspicion that one possessed any basis for independence. The tactic did not always work. Eugene Lyons, the politically radical correspondent for the United Press in Moscow, observed that in the larger cities tens of thousands of men and women were rounded up on the mere suspicion of possessing foreign money, silver, gold, or jewels. Many were never seen again.[8]

Linked with this tide of xenophobia was an aggressive and officially sponsored effort to trumpet the uniqueness of all things Soviet. When the League of Nations dared in 1929 to announce plans to built its "capital" in

Geneva, the Soviet government (not yet a member of the League) countered by revealing its intention to build the true world capital, the proletarian capital, in Moscow.[9] The word "Soviet," in its adjectival form, became
associated with an infinite number of phenomena that had previously
remained outside, or at least peripheral to, the ebb and flow of political controversy. To all appearances. Communist internationalism was appropriating the psychology and policies of nineteenth-century chauvinism.

THE IDEOLOGY OF CULTURAL INTERVENTION

Cultural matters were thrust to the center stage of
national policy by these developments. The carefully delineated compro-
mise of 1925, which had permitted a degree of pluralism in the arts, broke
down entirely and was replaced by the slogan "He who is not with us is
against us." Ivan Matsa, an insignificant critic whom the tide of Cultural
Revolution lifted to national prominence, pointed out the new directions
in his essay, "The Lessons of 'Neutralism' in Art."[10] In reviewing a show of
recent works by a painter named Ivan Bogorodsky, who had just returned
from two years' study abroad, Matsa vilified all foreign influences on
Soviet culture. Bogorodsky's political neutrality may have been simple
naivete, but ingenuousness was now a crime. Why paint German peasants
when their native costumes strike Russian peasants as strange? Bogorodsky's error, Matsa said, was to play into the hands of Russia's enemies abroad.
Similar assaults were launched in every field of the arts.[11] Vsevolod Meier-
hold, whose sins in theater had included the patronage of jazz, found his
funding cut by the Main Art Directorate (*Glaviskusstvo*).

Music in general and popular music in particular were singled out for
high-level scrutiny. The campaign, begun in 1928, was conducted with a
greater degree of candor than had existed since 1917. The journal *Soviet Art*,
for example, freely conceded that "Soviet art still lacks a defined style . . .
the creative forces of the proletariat and peasantry which were called forth
by the revolution are still inadequately formed and have not yet led to
anything so celebrated that it could be defined as the prevailing style of
our transitional Soviet epoch."[12] Admitting that the phrase "Soviet art" had
been bandied about indiscriminately in the past, the journal called for its
careful definition. A 1930 decree on popular culture by the Commissariat

of Public Enlightenment made the same admission, pointing out that the so-called revolutionary songs were thoroughly unpopular and largely ignored both by official agencies and by the public.[13] In spite of eleven years of declarations about Soviet culture, musical programming for workers remained much as it had been before the Revolution, the Commissariat claimed. "The phrase 'Soviet music for the Soviet variety theater,' which is so natural and elementary for our circumstances, is not reflected either in the concert bills or in published criticism."[14] Even censorship failed to improve the situation. Glavlit had let the popular music industry do as it pleased, neither criticizing it nor imposing appropriate Soviet goals upon it. Scores of local organizations, most of them private, had perpetuated a chaotic situation which in no way reflected the society's revolutionary objectives. So admitted the Commissariat of Public Enlightenment.[15]

For official organs to admit such failures created a ticklish situation for the regime. Either it had to push forward to create a policy that would revolutionize popular culture or it had to abandon its claims. The pressure of Stalinization made the former course a foregone conclusion. The task at hand was nothing less than "organizing human consciousness," as Commissar Lunacharsky put it.[16]

Curiously, the campaign that was to culminate in 1930 with the call for the suppression of jazz began with an appeal to popular taste. The argument was charming in its simplicity. Soviet popular music had been bad because it reflected the interests of the many small-time, independent profiteers who controlled the booking agencies. If only such people would study public tastes, particularly those of that peasantry, they would change their ways.[17] Whoever proposed such market studies had no way of knowing, of course, that many of the consumers in question—the peasants— would soon be dying by the millions and would scarcely be in a mood to respond to polls on their tastes in popular music.

The consumer-based approach to the music problem was an early fatality of the Cultural Revolution. The discussion did, however, encourage the creation of training programs around the country to develop a new generation of popular artists.[18] But this achievement was trifling in comparison with the success of the alternative approach, which called for the reorientation of all music and art "from above," under the guidance of national organizations of ideologically colorfast "proletarian" artists in every field.

Never mind that most of those seeking to cozy up to the new ideological line were not of proletarian origin. Between 1928 and 1932 these grim zealots pursued a crusade of vilification and intimidation in order to rid Russia of all cultural dross from the past and from the decadent West, pernicious influences the Soviet government had foolishly tolerated for a decade. Like Cromwellians lopping off the heads of sculptured saints in Ely Cathedral, they denounced Tchaikovsky as a feudal lord, Rimsky-Korsakov (a former naval officer) as a militarist, and Chopin as a bourgeois aesthete. In 1929, when Ernst Krenek's jazz operetta *Jonny spielt auf* was performed at the Nemirovich-Danchenko Theater in Moscow, the proletarian ideologues succeeded in closing the show and then launched a campaign to ban the saxophone from the Soviet Union.[19] In this, at least, they failed, although a similar campaign twenty years later was to succeed briefly.

These humorless sectarians had been a growing force in Soviet life for some years before 1928. As early as 1925 they had organized into the Association of Proletarian Musicians. From the day of its foundation, the Association served as a kind of semi-official censorship body, regimenting the ranks of Soviet music. For tactical reasons the Association spoke about the need to respond to market demand, but its consumerist argument had a twist. Invoking the Marxist doctrine of "false consciousness," the Association insisted that public taste had been corrupted by bourgeois propaganda and therefore could not automatically serve as a guide for the culture makers. The Association of Proletarian Musicians, so it claimed, understood what the preferences of the proletariat would be if only it were freed from the effects of corrupting influences. Indeed, the Association contended that it alone was capable of defining the true preferences of the proletarian market.

By December 1928, the Central Committee of the Communist party had moved toward accepting the Association's extravagant claim. Henceforth, it announced, only useful and ideologically correct music and literature would be disseminated through the mass media.[20] The new regimentation rigorously excluded private organizations and amateur groups from a place in the cultural scene. As of December 9, 1910, all amateur musicians and artists were subordinated to the control of official organs, lest they be duped by Russia's ever-present "class enemies."[21] With this stroke, the existing basis for popular initiative in the arts, including popular music, was obliterated.

How did the semi-official Association of Proletarian Musicians manage to wield such staggering power in the face of Stalin's efforts to concentrate all political authority in himself? It succeeded because its members claimed to be acting in the name of the Communist party and because their most frequent targets were those government organs which the Party had never succeeded in subordinating. Government agencies had consistently lagged behind the Party in their zeal for the Communist millennium, preferring instead to curry favor with the populace through cultural programs that responded to the universal desire for diversion. For example, government more than Party patronage had stood behind jazz and other forms of popular culture during the NEP era. The zealots understood this, and condemned it. Like Pascal, who argued that "All great diversions are a threat to the Christian life,"[22] the Communist party and its fervent believers saw the passion for amusement and levity as an impediment to the attainment of their goals. The Association of Proletarian Musicians seemed to be calling the Party back to itself, to its most revolutionary puritanism, and, for the time being at least, the rising forces within the Party represented by Stalin were pushing in precisely the same direction. As long as the Stalinists saw the Association and similar Proletarian Associations in other fields as promoting their own cause, they gave them free rein.

It was a foregone conclusion that the Association of Proletarian Musicians would eventually attack jazz. Its assault did not occur in isolation, however, for many people in Western Europe and in America had also mounted campaigns against jazz in just these years. The relationship between such campaigns and the continuing spread of jazz is both revealing and relevant to the situation in the USSR. Even in the mid-twenties many Americans and Europeans had convinced themselves that jazz was waning in popularity. "Jazz is transitory," violinist Fritz Kreisler declared to an American reporter in 1925.[23] As early as 1922, *The American Musician* gleefully took the view that jazz "was the voice of the Money-Changer in music. Jazz has ceased to be profitable, and hence we shall soon see no more of it." Jazz, and popular music generally, had received its impetus from the strenuous promotional efforts of phonograph dealers and music publishers. With profits off, jazz must die. "The interment of jazz will not be immediate, but it is inevitable."[24]

The Musical Leader, a Chicago journal, reached similar conclusions two years later. Gone were the "discordant and barbarous" jazz bands of the Original Dixieland Jazz Band era. They had been replaced by orchestras such as Paul Whiteman's, whose music bore no more resemblance to jazz than did the music of Victor Herbert, Johann Strauss, or John Philip Sousa.[25]

Such arguments were patently absurd, more wish than reality, but they were soon being voiced across Europe, and especially in Germany. Some German writers even claimed to see the imminent collapse of jazz, a "Jazzdammerung."[26] The facts belied them. Indeed, the impetus behind the "dying jazz" movement seems to have been the awareness that jazz, in a new form, was spreading more rapidly than ever. The director of the Omaha Symphony Orchestra returned from a European trip in 1929 and reported that jazz was being played in the hamlets of the Continent as well as in its great cities.[27] Having long since conquered the popular music scene in England, Belgium, Germany, and France, jazz was now insinuating itself further afield. Vienna had already fallen. The debut of Emmerich Kalman's operetta The Duchess of Chicago had the ancient music capital astir. Viennesse critics asked, "Will American jazz conquer us and force into oblivion our standard operetta forms of decades past, or will some way be found by us to humanize jazz or at least harmonize it with our own musical traditions?"[28] In Turkey the revolutionary government of Kemal Atatürk was licensing jazz bands by 1927, while musicians in Turkey's arch-enemy, Greece, were developing their own style of Hellenic jazz. A Polish dance orchestra scored a dizzying triumph in the same year by performing for thirty-three hours and ten minutes without intermission, a world record.[29]

There was also deepening interest in jazz on the part of the European musical elite. One of the first practical handbooks on jazz for composers and musicians was published in Leipzig in 1929 and included thoughtful essays on rhythm, harmony, improvisation, and jazz aesthetics. Das neue jazzbuch by Alfred Baresel quickly went into a second edition. An even more exhaustive study on jazz, called simply Jazz, appeared the same year in Prague, the work of the Czech bandleader, singer, and musicologist E. S. Burian. By far the most publicized evidence of the deepening hold of jazz in Europe was the decision by Bernard Sekles, director of Frankfurt's

Städtjsches Konservatorium, to open a class for jazz music in his school. Invective was poured on Sekles, but the Herr Direktor coolly responded: "The teaching of jazz is not only the right but the duty of every up-to-date musical institution."[30] He did not cow his critics. Carl Nielsen, the Danish composer, opined that "If it is of vital importance to humanity that men and women, when dancing, press their knees against one another and gyrate with glassy eyes and empty brains, the picture of nonentity, then jazz has a mission. My opinion is that it spoils the young musician's ear and individuality; it is a nasty and death-like music...."[31]

Such tirades anticipate the polemics over jazz which exploded in Russia with the onset of the Cultural Revolution. While direct evidence of influence is lacking—the Association of Proletarian Musicians could hardly admit to having pirated the arguments of "bourgeois" critics—the tone of the Association's campaign against jazz does not rule out the possibility. Certainly, the Association, like critics of jazz in Western Europe, was fighting a rearguard action, trying to regain the initiative in a battle it seemed to be losing.

THE PROLETARIAN CASE AGAINST JAZZ

Until 1928 the Association of Proletarian Musicians did not deign to recognize jazz even by attacking it, preferring instead to whip the ghost of the tsarist musical past. The only serious attempt at a proletarian analysis of jazz had been included in *The Art of Contemporary Europe*, a small book by Ivan Matsa, in 1926. Matsa at that point had been surprisingly receptive to jazz. He acknowledged that neither strict composition nor harmony in the traditional sense was possible with jazz, but considered the "unexpected internal strength and strict rhythmic unity" of a jazz ensemble to be on a par with works of the nineteenth-century classical masters.[32] Of course, Matsa could not have admitted to lounging about in the cafés of Berlin or Paris, and hence he was careful to distinguish "true jazz" from the corrupted form heard in the nightclubs of the fading West.

The decisive moment in the politicization of jazz in the USSR was April 18, 1928, when *Pravda* published an essay by the novelist Maxim Gorky titled "On the Music of the Gross."[33] Gorky's essay defined the

Soviet critique of jazz. The Association of Proletarian Musicians took it as its gospel on the subject, even while recognizing that Gorky himself was quite hostile to their allied Proletarian Association in the field of literature. Long after the Association of Proletarian Musicians had been liquidated and Gorky had died, phrases from the essay appeared time and time again in the press. Over the following half-century, whenever Soviet writers wished to settle scores with this threatening music or simply to contrast the Soviet Union with the degenerate West, they invoked Gorky.[34]

Gorky had lived for many years on the Isle of Capri. Because he was the first Russian novelist to have outsold Tolstoy and because of his earthy style as both man and writer, he had been taken up as an exotic in Western literary circles, a type-cast proletarian from the land of the tsars. After a brief return to Russia at the time of the revolution, he again emigrated in 1919, having discovered that he liked revolution more than revolutionaries. When he wrote "On the Music of the Gross," he was living in a villa near Sorrento. No longer lionized in the West, he found himself increasingly alienated from Western European society. Before the end of 1928 he was to make a return trip to the Soviet Union, and within three more years he would settle there permanently. His bitter ruminations on jazz and modern culture thus have the character of a parting shot at the West that had rejected him. The circumstances could not have been better calculated to produce a tract that would feed Soviet xenophobia.

Gorky wrote from the study in his villa. "It is night," he began, "and the stillness permits the mind to be at rest. . . ." Just then chaos descends.

In the deep stillness resounds the dry knocking of an idiotic hammer. One, two, three, ten, twenty strokes, and after them, like a mud ball splashing into clear water, a wild whistle screeches; and then there are rumblings, wails and howls like the smarting of a metal pig, the shriek of a donkey, or the amorous croaking of a monstrous frog. This insulting chaos of insanity pulses to a throbbing rhythm. Listening for a few minutes to these wails, one involuntarily imagines an orchestra of sexually driven madmen conducted by a man-stallion brandishing a huge genital member.[35]

Jazz, in the form of "a new fox-trot executed by a Negro orchestra," had destroyed the fragile chain of thought of this distinguished writer. This, at least, is where Gorky fixes the blame. It apparently did not cross his mind that he should be railing against the proprietor of the hotel next door who permitted his radio to disturb the neighbors. Nor did he strike out against the radio itself, which he instead generously acknowledges to be "one of the greatest discoveries wrested by science from nature." No, the musicians are at fault for creating vile rhythms that sweep through the ether like birds of prey. Jazz, Gorky proclaims, is "the music of grossness," the music of unbridled sexuality. It is both a cause and a symptom of the collapse of Western civilization. "Degenerates gather in all the magnificent cabarets of a so-called 'cultured' continent and, responding to its rhythms with cynical undulations of their hips, simulate the fecundation of woman by man."

Suddenly the radio, the hotel, and even Sorrento are forgotten. To the accompaniment of a jazz band from the land of the Gold Devil, Gorky philosophizes about sex for the benefit of *Pravda's* readers:

From time immemorial poets of all nations have lavished their creative power to ennoble this act. They have adorned sex so as to make it worthy of man, so that he should be elevated above the level of the goat, the bull, or the boar. Hundreds, nay thousands of beautiful poems have been composed in praise of love. . . . Through the force of love man has become far more social a being than even the cleverest of animals.

What a contrast to the "gross male" for whom women are not friends but "mere tools of pleasure, unless they are as much birds of prey as he himself . . .," in which case there can be no mutual life beyond fox-trotting. Eventually, such people become obese and gross. "The man grown porcine is a poor male. Homosexuality becomes an epidemic in the world of the gross." In the end, jazz and fox-trotting lead to total degeneracy.

Gorky then provides a convenient history of jazz, which he represents as the last step in a process of decline that led from Mozart and Beethoven through the waltz to the fox-trot and finally to the convulsions of the Charleston. But how to reckon with the fact that oppressed Negroes were so prominent among the creators of jazz? Gorky has a ready answer. American Negroes "undoubtedly laugh in their sleeves to see how their white masters are evolving toward a savagery which they themselves are leaving behind." The middle class's infatuation with jazz is a sure sign of its moral collapse, while the American Negro's supposed turn away from it is evidence that only the proletariat possesses the values necessary to save mankind. Meanwhile, the music rolls on:

The monstrous bass belches out English words; a wild horn wails piercingly, calling to mind the cries of a raving camel; a drum pounds monotonously; a nasty little pipe tears at one's ears; a saxophone emits its quacking nasal sound. Fleshy hips sway, and thousands of heavy feet tread and shuffle. The music of the degenerate ends finally with a deafening thud, as though a case of pottery had been flung to earth from the skies. Again limpid stillness reigns around me, and my thoughts return home. . . .

And what is this Russian homeland to which Gorky's thoughts take him? He would have us believe that it is the very embodiment of poetical love, of "active romanticism," and of ennobling relations between the sexes. Strange talk from a man who had written "Twenty-six Men and a Girl," a story based on the widely publicized rape of a young woman by bakers in the south of Russia! Nonetheless, Gorky hit the target where Matsa and most other Russian critics had skirted the main point. Jazz *is* dancing, physicality, emancipation, release. As such, it flew directly in the face of the puritanism of the Cultural Revolution.

Gorky's thoughts on jazz had not come suddenly to the proletarian novelist. Nina Berberova, a young poetess and writer who lived in Gorky's household during these years, remembered a curious event during a Christmas vacation at Marienbad in 1923. Gorky and his entourage of eight emigre Russian artists and writers had descended on the restaurant at the Hotel Minerva near midnight one evening. An eight- or nine-piece jazz band made up of black musicians (probably Louis Mitchell's group) was holding forth. "All of us younger people adored jazz; it was our music," Berberova recalled. "We didn't yet know how to fox-trot or shimmy, but avidly studied all those beautiful girls dancing around us." Gorky loathed it all. After brooding silently for an hour he exploded in rage against jazz, the fox-trot, and modern life generally, and then stomped out of the hall.[36]

Gorky's imprecations fell on receptive soil in Russia. One of the first senior officials of the Soviet state to take up cudgels against jazz was Commissar of Public Enlightenment Lunacharsky, who threw down the gauntlet at the First All-Russian Musical Conference in Leningrad in 1929. Jazz was at the top of the meeting's agenda. Lunacharsky, it will be recalled, had sponsored [Leopold] Teplitsky's jazz sabbatical in America and had bent a receptive ear to the [Sam] Wooding orchestra during its Russian tour. His wife was an actress who went out of her way to find Hollywood-type roles for herself in the Soviet cinema. But times had changed. Following Gorky, Lunacharsky linked jazz with dancing and with the twentieth century's degradation of sexual mores. The fox-trot, he declared, is nothing less than the "extreme mechanization of rhythm, . . . pounding your will into a cutlet."[37] It symbolized blatant eroticism and was a narcotic to true human feelings. In Lunacharsky's view, the fox-trot was nothing less than a frontal attack on Soviet culture. As such, it had to be countered with distinctly proletarian dances free of the aura of eroticism, mechanization, and narcotic stimulation.

At the heart of both Gorky's and Lunacharsky's theses was the notion that jazz and the way of life associated with it were totally bourgeois. They were the instruments of a deliberate capitalist plot to make man live "through his sexual organs, so that during the intervals between work he will be preoccupied with these sides of his existence."[38] Marx had argued that Christianity was the opiate of the masses. Jazz and the fox-trot were now the dominant religion, manipulated by the new capitalist masters in order to secure and extend their dominion.

Lunacharsky praised the Communist party for taking the initiative in determining the policy of the Soviet Union toward "syncopated music" by convening the meeting. The construction of socialism in Russia had its own "vast rhythm of human movement, which, in the end, comes together in a single enormous symphony of motion and labor." There is no task before Soviet culture more urgent than to launch a counterattack against the aggressive, jazzy syncopations of the fox-trot. In place of individual improvisation will be collective, planned forms of expression.[39]

Gorky and Lunacharsky had set down the new line. Other writers picked up the cue and lambasted Russian composers, bandleaders, and publishers for issuing a "musical fix" (*muzykalnyi durman*).[40] Jazz and the fox-trot were tools in the capitalists' conspiracy to control the true forces of liberation. There was no surer proof of this than their intensive dissemination among black Americans. By this hideous means, Wall Street had converted American Negroes from chattel property to "slaves of capitalism, machines of capitalist production."[41] The word was out. Jazz and jazz dancing constituted a capitalist fifth column in Soviet Russia, a key element in the subtle campaign to destroy the USSR from within. They had to be stopped.

The official attack on jazz followed immediately. Leopold Teplitsky was arrested and exiled, doubtless baffled by his patron Lunacharsky's sudden change of heart. Komsomol units in the schools were instructed to organize discussions on the question "Can a young Communist like jazz?" Several girls in the senior class at the International School in Moscow for children of foreign Communists were expelled for admitting their love of jazz. Other children were forced to confess their errors before the entire class.[42] Similar scenes occurred in secondary schools across the country. Foreign jazz and the popular music of Tin Pan Alley were prohibited, and anyone caught importing or playing American jazz records was liable to receive a fine of 100 rubles and imprisonment for six months.[43] The *Small Soviet Encyclopedia*, issued in 1930, failed even to mention the word jazz.

REVERSE GEAR

It was one thing to spin elaborate arguments against jazz but quite another to produce an acceptable alternative. Folk songs were ruled out because they had, as one critic put it, "nothing in common with the tasks, world view, and psychology of the contemporary industrial proletariat."[44] The Association of Proletarian Musicians tried desperately to concoct pop tunes for the masses, but their bland melodies and dogmatic texts held no appeal.[45] In theory, the task could not have been simpler. What was needed were strong melodies with upbeat, positive lyrics. But having been denied the possibility of borrowing from jazz, songwriters produced little that rose beyond the most hackneyed traditions of the past. Eloquent testimony to the depth of the problem was the discovery by the State Publishing House that ideologically acceptable songs accounted for less than one fifth of all tunes sung even by marchers in the parades honoring the anniversary of the October Revolution.[46]

In desperation, popular-song writers began asking if it was impossible for jazz to become Soviet. In 1930, the journal *Worker and Theater* concluded that it was possible, but an entirely new jazz repertoire would have to be created.[47] Left-wing composers in Germany had already come to the same conclusion. "Why should art music barricade itself against such an influence?" asked Kurt Weill in 1929. "It is obvious," he wrote, "that jazz has played a significant role in the rhythmic, harmonic, and formal relaxation that we have now attained and, above all, in the constantly increasing simplicity and comprehensibility of our music."[48] Schoenberg's student Hanns Eisler agreed, and was applying elements of jazz in his socialist "struggle songs" (Kampflieder).[49] Eisler's technique centered on simple lyrics sung to march tempos and to the accompaniment of what he called "Parisian orchestration," which was, in fact, very close to the classical Dixieland idiom. His instrumentation generally called for two trumpets, two trombones, three reeds, a banjo, drums, piano, and a plucked bass.[50]

The head-on conflict between theory and practice, ideology and popular taste, urgently required resolution. Communist doctrine threatened to paint Soviet musicians into a corner, from which they would have to deny the public's and their own liking for the new music. Paradoxically, the Nazis provided the key to escape from this conundrum by declaring their undying hostility to the music. As early as 1925, Siegfried Wagner, Richard Wagner's son, condemned jazz as the barbaric manifestation of "nigger rhythms." "I cannot understand," he declared, "how German youth can dance to vulgar tunes turned out by half-civilized Negroes. . . ."[51] The Hungarian ruler and Fascist sympathizer Admiral Horthy adroitly exploited jazz in songs extolling his regime, but no parallel existed in Hitler's party.[52] The internationalism of jazz music placed it beyond the pale for Fascists, and by the early 1930s it was coming under attack not only by Hitler but by his co-believers in Japan as well.[53] Pro-jazz revisionists in the Soviet Union realized that if the arch-enemies of communism in Germany and Japan were so adamantly opposed to jazz, it could not be all bad. They set to work.

Russians were impressed by the clever fashion in which Hanns Eisler had combined the forms of jazz with the uplifting message of socialism. At the 1930 "Musical Olympiad" in Leningrad, Eisle was a huge success and even drew praise from the Association of Proletarian Musicians, which presumably cheered the message rather than the medium.[54] But the ban on jazz could not be lifted so easily. There were hundreds of practical battles to be fought. Who was in a position to make the decision to reopen the Leningrad Music Hall, closed since 1928, which had earlier welcomed jazz-type orchestras?[55] Who would lift the ban at the radio stations, which had been closed not only to jazz but to every other form of expression anathematized by the Association of Proletarian Musicians?[56]

These operational problems were minor in comparison with the ideological problem posed by the new music. Gorky had stated it succinctly: jazz was bourgeois, the music of the degenerate. With *Pravda's* lead, and egged on by the Association of Proletarian Musicians, this view had gained official status. Unless changed, jazz was doomed to an underground existence in the USSR. Eisler's "solution" may have been clever and even popular, but it was eventually bound to become the victim of the ideologues' wrath, unless the sociological roots of jazz could be redefined in proletarian terms. The very success of jazz in America and Western Europe made this extremely difficult.

SEARCHING FOR PROLETARIAN JAZZ

One American writer observed at the height of the 1930s Depression, "Tin Pan Alley is now paved with profits."[57] And indeed it was: Spencer Williams was doing so well that he could afford to drive a Lincoln; Fats Waller, too, would be buying one in a few years.[58] Swing bands were discovering enthusiastic audiences that were prepared to pay well for their hot music. Sidney Bechet welcomed the prosperity provided by well-heeled clientele. "You hear a lot of folks talk about . . . the way business can't mix with music," he wrote many years later. "But there's no reason for saying a thing like that."[59]

How, then, could jazz be considered a proletarian music? A few American writers had been claiming for some years that jazz was a folk art.[60] Irving Berlin had also argued as much, as had the well-fed and prosperous Paul Whiteman. As Whiteman put it, "Like the folk songs of another age, jazz reflects and satisfies the undeveloped aesthetic and emotional cravings of great masses of people."[61] This notion of jazz as folk art had also been articulated in Western Europe and even in Russia. In 1929, for example, the Leningrad critic Mikhail Druskin argued that "The jazz band has ethnographic roots among those peoples whose music most closely approaches the rhythm of labor."[62]

Such claims, however, did not respond to the overwhelming evidence that the solid burghers of the West had taken jazz into their hearts and that the musicians themselves obviously liked fast cars and clean sheets. If jazz was a proletarian music, how could one account for the blatantly bourgeois aura that surrounded it? The answer revisionist critics proposed was disarmingly simple: there existed not one but two forms of jazz, one proletarian and the other bourgeois. The proletarian variant was rooted in Negro folk life and bore the scars of past oppression. The bourgeois variant derived not from folk blues but from the vulgar commercialism of Tin Pan Alley. Bourgeois jazz was popular culture "from above," devised by capitalist exploiters to lull the masses to sleep and stifle their growing class consciousness.

Elements of this adroit argument had been circulating in Russian jazz criticism for half a decade. After attending a performance by Sam Wooding's polished ensemble in 1926, Marietta Shaginian expounded eloquently on what she believed to be the folk or proletarian origins of jazz.[63] Her conclusions must have been based on sociological rather than musicological research, however, for she was almost completely deaf.[64] Benny Peyton's performance in Moscow moved musicologist Arnold Zukker to extol the virtues of jazz as folk music.[65] Both writers, as well as Ivan Matsa and Commissar Lunacharsky, devoted far more attention to the corrupted bourgeois "salon jazz" they disliked than to the proletarian "true jazz" they claimed to respect. In cafés and fashionable restaurants jazz had become bourgeois and decadent, for, as Zukker put it, it had no other function there than "to be the acoustical background for those bodily movements which have become almost a symbol of a particular class and a particular epoch."[66]

The argument is clever but absurd. If the problem lay with erotic dancing, then the distinction between true proletarian jazz and bourgeois salon jazz vanishes. After all, some of the sensuous dances to which Bolshevik puritans objected had filtered up to the middle classes from the very unbourgeois world of Negro low life, not down from the Plaza ballroom. The distinction between folk jazz and commercial jazz is equally strained. Closely linked with the unfolkish technologies of radio and phonograph, jazz was commercial from the outset. Had it been otherwise, the emigration of New Orleans musicians to Chicago, of Chicagoans to New York, of New Yorkers to Europe, and of all of them to the recording studios never would have occurred.

Such sociological distinctions in jazz had been drawn by critics outside the Soviet Union as well, notably in the United States and in France. In these countries, however, attention was fixed on the juxtaposition of "hot" jazz and the "sweet" style essayed by hotel orchestras. The immense popularity of the smoothly lacquered sound of the Whiteman orchestra had forced the issue. The rise of Guy Lombardo's sweet style in the first years after the American stock market crash in 1929 gave further reason to think that true jazz and popular salon orchestras had reached a parting of the ways.

The youthful and mercurial jazz enthusiast, Frenchman Hugues Panassie, wrote a series of articles that led to his important 1934 publication *Hot Jazz*, which for the first time defined the essence of jazz as its capacity to swing. Panassie found this quality principally in the rollicking polyphonic style of the New Orleans and Chicago pioneers, rather than in the more carefully orchestrated groups that came later during the era of Duke Ellington, Fletcher Henderson, and Glen Gray's Casa Loma band. While superficially appealing, Panassie's distinction can now be seen as too simple to fit the facts. Typical of the data that eludes a hot-sweet division is Louis Armstrong's praise for the work of Vic D' Ippolito on first trumpet in Sam Lanin's sweet band, or his enthusiasm for B. A. Rolfe, a trumpeter with Vincent Lopez's orchestra.[67] Obviously, Panassie's preference for primitive simplicity involved far more than purely musical issues. As the British jazz critic Chris Goddard has put it:

. . . the logic of Panassie's thinking points straight to Arcadia. He seems to have seen the New Orleans era of jazz as an ideal, archaic period, a golden age before the advent of commercialism, peopled by beings of primordial simplicity for whom music was not merely desirable but indispensable.[68]

Much the same could be said of the Russians. For ideological reasons they, too, wanted a jazz that was straight from a proletarian Arcadia. The distinctive feature of their position was that they assigned far more importance to the sociological context of jazz than to its musical identity. However illogically, they searched for a jazz that was uncompromisingly lower class but at the same time purged of all links with eroticism and dancing. It was all but impossible to find. The attempt reveals the heart of the Soviet dilemma; jazz, a genuinely popular form, appealed to the common man precisely because its driving rhythms carried a message of individual and physical liberation that was incompatible with the puritanic morality of communism as it was then defined. . . .

JAZZ AND FOREIGN POLICY

The debates of 1928–32 regarding the sociology of jazz were being held at exactly the same time the Kremlin-sponsored Communist International, or "Comintern," was dramatically revising its policies toward American Negroes. This change of course was to have strongly favorable, if indirect, consequences for the fate of jazz in the USSR. The decisive moment came at the Sixth Congress of the Comintern held in Moscow in the summer of 1928. Prior to this crucial session, the Kremlin had shown scant interest in the racial problem in America or in Negroes generally. The Fourth Congress of the Comintern in 1922 (at which Parnakh had performed) had adopted a "Negro Thesis," which called on black Americans to take up the cause of revolution and spread it back to Africa.[69] This call to arms had had no impact on black Americans or on the American Communist party, which at the end of the twenties still had fewer than one thousand Negro members.[70] Now, in 1928, the need for a bold new policy was fully acknowledged.

The solution proposed by the Sixth Congress of the Comintern was to define the Negro population of the southern Black Belt as an independent nation and to place the Communist party of the United States and the Comintern as a whole at the head of a campaign for their national liberation and political self-determination. This astonishing proposal was embodied in an otherwise turgid document titled "Theses on the Revolutionary Movement in Colonial and Semi-Colonial Countries."[71] Stripped of its sociological claptrap, the new policy called for the establishment of the Black Republic of the South stretching from Virginia to Texas, a kind of Neo-Confederate States of America.

This flabbergasting proposition was the brainchild of Marxist sociologists in Moscow who had been no closer to America than the Lenin Library. None of the four American Negroes who attended the Congress had any knowledge of the South, while the New York-based American Communist party would have been powerless to reverse the policy, even if it had tried to do so.

The proposal was based on the proposition that southern Negroes constituted a distinct nationality. According to Moscow ideologues, these blacks were distinct not only from the white population but also from middle-class Negroes in the northern cities. Since Stalin himself had participated in the commission which had prepared the "Colonial Theses" for the Comintern, it was now necessary to prove the correctness of Comrade Stalin's analysis.[72] The keystone to such proof was to demonstrate the distinctiveness of southern Negro culture in all its aspects.[73]

Enter Jazz. If the "Colonial Theses" were to be sustained, it was imperative that jazz be defined as a proletarian music. Equally important, it had to be presented as a genuine folk music indigenous to the southern Black Belt. But what about its undeniably urban character? Kremlin sociologists could not accept this, so it had be denied. And what about the intimate connection between jazz, modern communication technology, and commercial distribution? This, too, had to be discounted. It is revealing that W. C. Handy, that pioneer businessman-entrepreneur of jazz, emerged as a folk artist steeped in revolutionary consciousness in essays by Michael Gold, Charles Edward Smith, and their Soviet comrades.[74]

Such claims would have seemed even more bizarre had they not been qualified by the doctrine of two jazzes, proletarian and bourgeois. The doctrine itself led to some wild claims, such as Georgi Landsberg's attempt to put forward the urbane Duke Ellington and his sophisticated music as a toiling proletarian struggling in behalf of the political Left.[75] But in the overall defense of jazz in the USSR, the proletarian-bourgeois distinction was a boon. Provided that readers were not too informed on the subject, the juxtaposition enabled Russian apologists to defend the music in terms that were intelligible to the Party and at the same time to sidestep accusations leveled against jazz by its musical and ideological foes. . . .

Begun amid a false war scare and artificially induced xenophobia, the "Great Leap Forward" had at first assumed the character of a full-scale war against those rural and urban elements that refused to yield to Stalinist orthodoxy. As the ideologues prepared to design the new ideals to be proclaimed "from above," they immediately resolved to extirpate from the USSR all bourgeois elements, of which jazz was considered a part. But it proved easier to ban one form of popular culture than to concoct another and get the public to accept it. Some accommodation to jazz was unavoidable by 1930, even without the ideological vindication the Kremlin was forced to mount by the logic of the Comintern's new policy regarding Negroes. The "Colonial Theses" of 1928 were as much a part of the Cultural Revolution as Gorky's fulminations against the degenerate West.

In the end, the demands of foreign policy embodied in those theses took precedence over any purge of domestic culture along the lines of Gorky's dyspeptic essay. . . .

The Cultural Revolution had begun by condemning jazz and concluded by rehabilitating it. What remained to be seen was whether Soviet jazz would continue to develop "from below" with a degree of spontaneity, or whether official vindication of jazz would prompt the regime to take it over and shape its further evolution "from above," along lines more compatible with the recent Communist puritanism.

NATURALIZING THE EXOTIC

The Australian Jazz Convention

—Bruce Johnson

Any attempt to understand Australian jazz history and its relation to the broader national culture must examine, among other things, three events of the 1940s.[1] The first was in 1941, when a jazz band performed for the opening of the Contemporary Art Society's annual exhibition in Melbourne. The third event was in 1947, when an Australian jazz band embarked on a visit to Prague for the International Youth Festival, and went on to tour and perform in Europe and the United Kingdom for a year. Three sectors of interest converge on these events: the jazz and the radical arts communities, and the political left. I have discussed these two elsewhere (Johnson 2000). I wish here to study the event which they bracket, and to tease out some threads which may make intelligible the weave of a significant moment in Australia's larger cultural history.

In December 1946 the first of what has become an annual jazz festival, the Australian Jazz Convention (AJC), was held in Melbourne. This is in many ways a unique event both in Australia and internationally, bringing together from most regions of Australia musicians committed to what, in the context of subsequent developments, has become identified as the traditional style. It is important to emphasize this: in the historical context of this discussion, references to "jazz" are references to what is now more specifically described in such terms as "traditional," "revivalist," or, more problematically, "Dixieland" jazz. When its proponents referred disdainfully to "pseudo" or inauthentic jazz forms in 1946, they were not as a rule referring to what later became known as "modern jazz" such as bop, hard bop or cool West Coast. These had not yet established themselves in the local discourse. As the primary sources cited below suggest, "true jazz" was invoked most frequently in contradistinction to commercial swing.

151

It was in this context that the AJC was inaugurated. The musicians performed gratis primarily for each other's benefit, and were mostly amateurs in every sense excepting their musical proficiency in their chosen style. The AJC has been held every year since, with the same basic format. Apart from continuous informal jam sessions, anyone may ensure programmed performance time simply by registering as a musician. Attendance figures have risen to include increasing numbers of the non-playing public, and the number of musicians has also increased to as many as 520 (in 1998), incorporating amateurs and full professionals. At the fiftieth in 1995, the total attendance of playing and non-playing registered delegates, and the public, was 4500 to 5000 (Haesler 2/18/02; Johnson 1987, 87–90).

The Australian jazz movement has been robust and internationally influential far beyond what the size, location, and history of the country would at first lead anyone to expect. A major international jazz reference work describes it as arguably producing "the most stimulating music outside America" (Carr, Fairweather, and Priestley 1990, 17; Johnson 1995; Johnson 2000, 141–63). The jazz festival movement has been one of many sites at which the music was fostered, with currently around one hundred annual music festivals devoted in whole or in part to jazz. The AJC was not the first jazz festival in Australia, with the once-off "Jazz Week" at the Globe Theatre in Sydney in 1919, presenting film, performance and dance (Johnson 2000, 61). While those responsible for maintaining the democratic and non-commercial character of the AJC avoid the word festival in the generic sense (as used in Grove, for example), the 1946 AJC was the world's first annual jazz festival, and remains the oldest.

My interest is in unraveling the cultural dynamic that produced and was reflected in this event, and this requires as reliable a narrative as possible of what has become tangled by anecdote. It is clear that there had been informal discussions for perhaps a couple of years prior to the earliest reference in print, which appears to have been in the journal *Jazz Notes* (hereafter *JN*) 65 (June 1946, 3). Editor C. Ian Turner suggested an Australian Jazz Convention in Melbourne with a view to establishing a national affiliation which in turn could become part of an "International Jazz Foundation" (Stein 2/15/89; and Graeme Bell 2/16/89). In *JN* 69 (December 1946, 3), the new editor John Rippin announced the forthcoming Jazz Convention to be held in Melbourne December 26–30.

Harry Stein, referred to as President of the AJC, welcomed the delegates at the opening dinner, to a program of performances, including a riverboat excursion on Melbourne's River Yarra, and a concluding public concert. There were also discussion groups on the social background of jazz, on forming record collections, and on organizing jazz events and clubs; and record sessions, results of which were aired by Sydney-based ABC broadcaster Ellis Blain (*JN* 70, January 1947, 22). The event was reported by mainstream press (*Melbourne Herald, Sun*, and *Women's Weekly*, according to Stein 2/15/89), and the professional music press including the Sydney journal *Syncopation* 1.2 (Durbin 1947, 18; Pender 1994). The most comprehensive account was provided by Dave Dallwitz in *JN* 70 (January 1947), 12–16. The general public was served primarily by the riverboat excursion and the final concert held in the main venue, the Eureka Hall in North Melbourne, which accommodated 300, had a gallery, recording equipment and catering facilities (Stein 1994, 86). There were two riverboats "bulging with jazz lovers, mostly in pairs and mostly young, but with a fair sprinkling of middle age (and children)," and for the final concert the hall was "crowded out" (Dallwitz 1947, 14, 16).

The core of the Convention consisted of musicians and committed jazz enthusiasts, estimated at one hundred, with a 1:1 ratio of musicians to non-playing delegates (Haesler 2/18/02). The musicians were ecstatic. "Seventh heaven. Marvelous," recalled Tasmanian reed player Tom Pickering nearly forty years later (Pickering 5/16/84, 19). Graeme Bell (2/16/89) remembered it as "one of the most exciting times of my life . . . we were walking on air." There are four strands in the responses to that event. Beyond the heat of the moment, it inspired further activity. Bruce Gray, clarinettist with Adelaide's Southern Jazz Group (SJG), spoke of "many sleepless nights after that," as it increased commitment and practice activity: "as soon as we got back I can remember Dave [Dallwitz, the leader] saying that we must do so and so . . . for the next convention" (Gray 1/27/82, 16–17). This was a community which had come to the music as something produced by Americans of mythic status, and for the most part mediated non-corporeally, by sound recordings.[2] The AJC conferred agency on those present, moving them further away from the role of consumers to producers. Young Melbourne clarinettist Nick Polites experienced a further reorientation away from his Greek background, with the "watershed" understanding that seeing so many other "ordinary people" actually playing the music confirmed that "it can be done" (Polites 12/28/88). Frank Johnson had experienced the same sense of empowerment, of "revelation," when he first heard live jazz—the Bell band—played by "ordinary people" earlier in the year (Frank Johnson 12/28/88).

The other three strands are woven around the idea of community. The AJC disclosed a national jazz community, a significant matter in a country whose few major centers are separated by thousands of kilometers, and when contact between them was mainly by road, rail, or post. In the souvenir program for the Convention Graeme Bell began:

Six years ago there was but a handful of musicians in Melbourne to play jazz. The pseudo variety of rhythm section supporting soloists had, of course, been operating outside this small circle. When I use the word "jazz" I am not referring to this latter type, but to the collectively improvised music in the negro idiom which is the only music which should be and usually is today referred to as "jazz." It was not long before this music started to spread, until today that handful of musicians sincerely endeavoring to play jazz has grown to an extraordinarily large number considering our small population. (Graeme Bell 1946, 2)

In his report, Dallwitz expressed the belief that the AJC would increase national jazz solidarity (Dallwitz 1947, 14), and in 1982 spoke of his realization "that we had kindred spirits" (Dallwitz 1/25/82, 13; see also Dallwitz 12/28/88; Pender 1994, 23). Bruce Gray recalled it as "indescribable" when he and his Adelaide colleagues, most of whom "hadn't really been further than the front gate . . . meet all these guys, all playing jazz. It really was fantastic" (Gray 1/27/82, 16). Tasmanian musician Ian Pearce spoke of his "excitement that these things had happened quite separately from our activity on a distant island—that they were of a similar mind. . . . It's spontaneous—spontaneous combustion as far as I can tell. Just happening. A mystery" (Pearce 12/28/88). Even for Melbourne musicians, "to see all these other guys playing was a revelation" (Graeme Bell 2/16/89); it "opened our eyes," according to Bell's reed player Don "Pixie" Roberts (Roberts 12/28/88). Musicians also began to discern regional differences. SJG brass bass player Bob Wright found different chord sequences from those evolved in Adelaide (Wright 1/24/82, 11), while for Melbourne musicians, it was the first time they had heard the rhythmic pulse of the SJG, off-beat banjo against on-beat tuba, and the washboard "knitting it all together." The distinctive sound of the SJG "created a storm" (Graeme Bell 2/16/89).

The AJC also gave momentum to an internationalism that went beyond the United States as the only significant site of jazz consciousness. The Program itself reflects this: the co-editor Roskolenko was a U.S. serviceman posted in Australia, and the cover announced articles by "Critics from Three Countries": British writer Charles Fox, U.S. writer Frederick Ramsay, as well as Hobart reed player Tom Pickering. There was an appreciation of Duke Ellington by Inez Cavana[u]gh (Cavana[u]gh 1946), a message of congratulations from (Russian-born) U.S. pianist Art Hodes, and from Alma Hubner, daughter of the Chilean Minister Designate to Australia, who had earlier contributed to *Jazz Notes* an article on the jazz movement in Chile (Hubner 1945). The cover photograph of Roger Bell with African–American corporal "Morris Goode (Harlem, N.Y.)" reinforces the sense of international jazz fraternalism as, wearing each other's hat, they apparently engage in a trumpet "dialogue."[3] The first AJC also inaugurated an unbroken tradition which "gave musicians and devotees a focal point for their continuing involvement in jazz" (Stein 1994, 87), and thus it became a major public workshop for what has become internationally recognized as an "Australian jazz style"(see Johnson 2000, 157–63; and Clunies-Ross 1979).

Present throughout the AJC were also the organizers. Although there is frequent reference to a "committee," it was "very loose" (Graeme Bell 2/16/89). In his report, Dallwitz listed Harry Stein, Graeme Bell, Ade Monsbourgh, John James "and the rest of the Melbourne Committee" (Dallwitz 1947, 12). At the AJC forty-two years later Roger Bell however, recalled that the committee was "spearheaded" by his brother with some input from Stein (Roger Bell 12/22/88), while Graeme remembered a more even balance (Graeme Bell 2/16/89). Trumpeter Frank Johnson's impression was that the committee was made up of members of the Eureka Youth League (EYL): himself, reed player Geoff Kitchen, Stein, Rivka Brilliant, Joe James, and some involvement from Audrey Blake (Frank Johnson 12/28/88), though there is evidence that he may well be confusing this with the second AJC (Graeme Bell 2/16/89). Stein and Blake were senior officials in the EYL, and would later become National President and National Secretary respectively. Stein's own recollection was that the

EYL's most important involvement was logistical: the venue, the catering, cleaning, recording (Stein 2/15/89).

There are three communities of interest which converged in the establishment of the AJC. The Souvenir Program was a special issue of the *Angry Penguins Broadsheet*, edited by Max Harris and Harry Roskolenko. AJC patron Art Hodes congratulated the Eureka Hot Jazz Society, who were often spoken of as the hosts or sponsors of the Convention. And of course there was the broader jazz community. The interwoven interests of these three groups have been recalled in passing from a broader perspective on Australian history by other writers including Ian Turner, who moved in the space shared by artistic and political radicalism and the jazz community, in Melbourne during the 1940s (Turner 1982, 109–10, 124, 206). It is this triangle of interests that frames the inauguration of the world's first and oldest jazz festival.

Of the three, the *Angry Penguins* group, with the radical arts community of which they were largely the center, has attracted the most scholarly attention. *Angry Penguins* itself was established in 1940 by the *enfant terrible* of Australian letters, Max Harris, and financed and generally co-edited by lawyer John Reed. Reed was the country's leading patron of Australian modernism, and his small farm, "Heide," on the outskirts of Melbourne, was a bohemian center which hosted writers, jazz musicians (in particular, the Bell coterie), and leaders of the coming generation of modernist painters, most notably Sidney Nolan, who designed the journal. This group overlapped with other sectors of Australian radicalism, including the Contemporary Art Society, which had been established by modernist painters in Melbourne in 1938 to contest the conservative major arts institutions (Haese 1981, e.g., 43–44). At the center of pivotal debates in the history of Australian modernism, *Angry Penguins* was probably the most significant journal of modernist experimentation in the arts in Australia during its lifetime, 1940–1946 (see Haese 1981; and Heyward 1993). Its political orientation was left-wing; Harris himself was for a period a member of the Communist Part of Australia (CPA) (Heyward 1993, 20). The fourth issue of *AP* carried a piece by Jack Blake, Secretary of the Victorian State Committee of the CPA, and husband of Audrey Blake of the EYL. His essay was an edited version of his speech opening the Anti-Fascist Exhibition of the Contemporary Art Society (Blake 1943).

AP and its network had also had strong connections with the jazz community well before the first AJC. *AP* carried items on jazz, and, in the 1945 issue, announced the inauguration of three regular sections, Music, Film, and Jazz. The first refers clearly to "art music" ("yet to find its proper level in the literature of this community"), and of the latter two it wrote:

... each are [*sic*] of major importance in modern society, both culturally and socially—they are the new art forms of the 20th century, each with infinite potentialities, each surrounded by barriers of commercialism which not only hamper the artists in these mediums but make it almost impossible for the public at large to appreciate their work (3).

Dallwitz's account of being introduced to the Bell band places Max Harris at the point of contact, as someone who knew the emerging jazz scene very well. That connection in turn was through the Contemporary Art Society, of which Dallwitz was also the founding chairman of the Adelaide branch. The Harris "set" followed Dallwitz's band, the SJG, in Adelaide, and Harris himself was present at their first recording session. Parties at Dallwitz's house were attended by both SJG members and radical artists, and Harris would sit on the piano and improvise scurrilous blues lyrics about those present (Dallwitz 12/26/88). The Melbourne *AP* and modernist painters also overlapped both socially and creatively with the jazz scene. Apart from activities at Heide and with the CAS documented elsewhere, Roger Bell recalled jam sessions at Sidney Nolan's studio in Russell Street (Roger Bell 12/28/88; see Haese 1981, 237–36; Johnson 2000, 25–26, 50–52).

The political left also had a longstanding connection with the jazz scene, most conspicuously through the EYL, which in 1945 created the Eureka Hot Jazz Society (EHJS). The Bell band in particular enjoyed a high-profile association with the League and the EHJS until 1948. In 1941 they presented a "History of Jazz" concert co-produced by Harry Stein of the EYL (Bell 1988, 41), and by 1944 the band was "playing for many Eureka Youth League dances, and riverboat trips" (Bell 1988, 54). In June 1946 they rented the EYL premises for their own regular Saturday night cabarets under the name The Uptown Club, though this was entirely run by musicians, spouses, and friends (Bell 1988, 56). In the 1947 May Day March through Melbourne, the EYL contingent, led by the Bell band, won the first prize (Blake 1993, 84). These are not exactly covert associations. The most significant synergy was the Bell band's visit to Prague in 1947 (Bell 1988, 63–118; Stein 1994, 87–98; Johnson 2000, 147–57).

Harry Stein was pivotal in this connection. He had begun playing drums in dance bands in the 1930s, and in particular for dances run by the Young Communist League, of which he was a member. In England from 1937 to 1939 he had attended discussions in the communist community on the social significance of music and its relation to Marxism, "topics I never heard discussed in Australia" (Stein 1994, 44). He had begun presenting talks on the social background of jazz while posted in rural Cowra, New South Wales, during the war, and the foundation of the EHJS was partly to reactivate this project—that is, it was educative as well as recreational. Its aims were: 1) "To encourage the appreciation and playing of hot jazz"; 2) "To study its true history and destroy its myths"; and 3) "To publish material to help these aims" (Stein 1994, 85). Stein's name is as tightly woven into accounts of the first AJC as is that of Graeme Bell.

That there was such overlap in the public sphere is beyond dispute. What is often bitterly debated is what this signifies in terms of a common sociopolitical agenda. In view of that rancor, let us begin with one incontrovertible observation: the convergences signified that jazz was a significant musical preference for individuals who also occupied positions of influence in radical arts and politics. Harry Stein's preference for jazz was a musical one. Frank Johnson remained vigorously socialist all his life, and was eager to play up the left's organizational connection with the jazz movement in the 1940s. Nonetheless, although he did see an affinity between jazz and radicalism in the other arts, he declared unequivocally that for him, playing jazz was apolitical. He played it because he liked it (Johnson 12/28/88). Graeme Bell had socialist sympathies, a member of the EYL, and fully aware of Stein's politics. But the only reason he took the gigs was because they were opportunities to play music he liked (Graeme Bell 2/16/89). Audrey Blake was zealously committed to the CPA through the period under examination, yet she has always been equally clear that her attachment to jazz was visceral before it was ideological. Growing up as a working class girl during the 1930s,

. . . jazz was just the music I liked . . . the pop music of the day didn't satisfy me. I just thought that jazz and blues were [pause] just wonderful, that's all. And it wasn't anything to do with a sort of theoretical working out of anything, because for one thing I didn't have any theory at that time. (8/14/89)

She went on to say very deliberately that the then current understanding of jazz as a non-commercial expression of an oppressed minority enhanced its appeal, but was not the basis of it. These accounts are typical. Blake's final observation resonates with Stein's surprise at what he heard in the U.K., both of which give momentum to the next stage of the discussion. The enthusiasm for jazz was primarily musical, and in fact it survived all later personal and ideological vicissitudes in the relationships between the three communities I have identified.[4] For the EYL in particular, jazz was not a doctrinaire instrument of party policy.

Nor was the EYL in the period under discussion. The perennial question has been to do with what the logistical connections signified regarding ideological overlap (see for example: Johnson 1984; Mitchell 1985; Stein 1985; Johnson 1986). Interpretations range from the assertion that the connection is entirely apolitical, to the claim that the jazz community was highly politicized, and all points in between. At the former end of the spectrum, jazz musicians declare that they didn't know or care what the EYL represented (Roberts 12/28/88; Roger Bell 12/28/88; Dallwitz 12/28/88), while on their side, the EYL members just happened to like jazz. At the other extreme is the claim that there was a party political agenda linking jazz, the EYL, and, explicitly or implicitly, the CPA (Bisset 1987, 125; Pender 1995). Somewhere between these two poles were jazz musicians like Nick Polites and Frank Johnson who were left-leaning, who understood the basic agenda of EYL, but who nonetheless consciously resisted joining the CPA on grounds of its perceived doctrinaire rigidity (Polites 12/28/88; Johnson 12/28/88). Central to the debate is the question of what the EYL represented politically in the 1940s.[5] The matter is by no means simple, and if we examine the history of the EYL more closely we break out of this narrow debate about party affiliations and lay the foundations for a hypothesis that has much broader relevance to Australia's cultural history and the role of jazz in that narrative. Three aspects of the organization are central to this re-assessment.

First, the League was ambivalent about its relationship with the CPA. Throughout the life of EYL there was internal pressure to declare itself a "Marxist or Marxist-Leninist group—in other words, a dedicated revolutionary youth group" (Blears 2002, 2). In the period under discussion the pressure was unsuccessful, but the EYL "constantly had problems of deciding what in fact it actually was, a broadly based and non-aligned body, or broadly based but somehow aligned, or some other position up to an open preference for the Communist Party" (Blears 2002, 2). This ambiguity left open to debate the question regarding CPA alignment which has pervaded discussions of the alliance between the League and the jazz community. This has made it easier for various witnesses to spontaneously (re)construct that identity in whatever way suits them. The ambiguity of the League's position also tends to confirm, however, that it went beyond a doctrinal party line, seeking to tap into and respond progressively to the industrial, recreational and cultural needs of young Australians. Although it "received the benefit, or otherwise, of the CPA's advice and membership support" (Blears 2002, 2), its activities reflected dynamics in the Australian social consciousness rather than implementing detailed Comintern directives: "the League . . . had plenty of latitude on developing its own program and actions" (Blears 2002, 4).

The recruitment of jazz bands by the EYL was, as Stein and Blake have indicated, primarily a manifestation of their own enthusiasms. Other writers in the communist movement such as Paul Mortier condemned the music as decadent, along with modernist art (Mortier 1955) and on at least one (undated) occasion the subject of one of the debates that were part of EYL youth programs, was whether or not jazz was a decadent music, Stein con, Mortier pro (Blears 2002, 90). Given suggestions that EYL was an inflexible instrument of Moscow via the CPA, it is important to recall that in the USSR such a public debate would probably have been impossible. Policy on jazz changed with international politics—during the second front, it was acceptable; after 1946 it "came to a halt" (Starr 1994, 207). In Stalinist Russia, cultural policies might come and go, but at any moment they did not allow for public debate. Likewise, the League's alliance with modernist literati and painters is in sharp conflict with the "socialist realist" Moscow line as enunciated by Andrei Zhdanov in his speech to the 1934 Congress of Soviet Writers (Zhdanov 1934). A rigidly Moscow-oriented Communist organization could not have lined up with such interests in the period we are discussing, nor with the jazz community during much of the time that EYL was publicly sponsoring its activities. This reminds us again of the sparseness of "theoretical direction" from either Moscow or the CPA, and the flexibility exercised by EYL in

adapting youth programs to the local cultural landscape, in concert with
the musical tastes of the local leadership.

A League Leaders study course of about 1943, which Blears attributes
to Audrey Blake, asserted:

Most of our members do not belong to or support any party. Whilst being non-
party, we regard ourselves as part of the labour movement, which is not just the
Labor Party but is made up of all the organizations of the working people, Labor
Party, Communist Party, Trade Unions, Trade Union Youth Organizations, and
the Eureka Youth League. (cited in Blears 2002, 48)[6]

He quotes from the same source that at the first national conference of
the EYL in 1943, changes to the constitution "are evidence of the fact that
the League had developed into an anti-fascist organization rather than a
socialist organization" (49).

This takes us to the second and third aspects of the League's history which
are relevant to this enquiry. Any attempt to investigate the character of the
EYL must also ask: "where, and when?" The largest branches, New South
Wales and Victoria, were more independent of Party interference than those
in other regions (Blears 2002, 8). But even more critical is the period in question. The accounts by Blake (1993) and Blears (2002) disclose a broad trajectory in the history of the EYL and its antecedents, the Young Communist
League (YCL) and the League of Young Democrats (LYD), in which independence from the CPA was at its apogee from the formation of the EYL to
around 1948. Blake had been a member of all of these, and was the founding
President of the Victorian branch of the LYD, which was established in 1939
specifically to give effect to a more broadly based youth agenda and with
diminished Party alignment. In the wake of the banning of the CPA in June
1940 by the government led by Robert Menzies, the LYD was declared an illegal organization and its premises and the homes of its leaders were raided
by the police. With the opening of Hitler's second front, of course, the USSR
suddenly became a valued ally against fascism, and with the advent also of
the Curtin Labor government it was an opportune moment to form a new
socialist-oriented youth organization. Thus, the EYL, formed in December
1941, grew out of a wide-ranging youth movement that had emerged in the
late 1930s, committed to the problem of youth unemployment and the rise
of fascism. Indeed, with the easing of centralized ideological controls marked

by the formation of the LYD, it appears that these two issues of international relevance were at the time more in the foreground than any Moscow-centered communist agenda.

The EYL thus begins to look more like the manifestation of a generalized sea-change in social consciousness than of a rigid party machine. At its first conference it produced a seven-point program (Blake 1993, 44–45) that could hardly be said to be reeking of communist ideology. Apart from the call for the lifting of the ban on the LYD, they might have come from any labor or even church group concerned about working conditions, costs of living, and the need to mobilize in the war against fascism. Although it supported the candidacy of Jack Blake as an Independent Communist (the Party was still illegal) in a by-election, the EYL was allied more generally with youth organizations, including the National Fitness Council, and the National Youth Association, of which Audrey Blake was for a time a member of the Victorian executive (Blake 1993, 54–55). Indeed it received a letter of congratulations from Prime Minister Curtin for its effort on behalf of war production and the military (Blake 1993, 52). The week-to-week activities of the EYL by late 1944 are illustrated by the programs available to the 82 members of the Pacific Youth Club, the Fitzroy branch of the EYL. It rented its own club rooms, had classes in swimming, dancing, a gymnasium, a concert party and discussion group. Saturday was open club night with its library open, table tennis, chess, draughts, and dancing; a social was held on Sunday night. It had representatives on the Auxiliary of the Heidelberg Hospital, the Opportunity Club Committee and the War Loans Committee (Blake 1993, 68).

In the period immediately following the war, the EYL was still carrying much of this agenda, which was primarily anti-fascist and broadly pro-workers' rights, with the emphasis on its youth constituency. At its third National Congress in 1945, the EYL committed itself to a postwar New Deal for Youth campaign, which was entirely directed at the improvement of working conditions and educational and recreational opportunities for youth, with no policies that would not be shared by any organization committed to the interests of young people. Many of its proposals were implemented by the new Labor government (Blake 1993, 70–71).

How, then, did the EYL come to attract the designation of "a communist front" (e.g., Frank Johnson 12/28/88)? There is of course the general problem of trying to retrieve the phenomenology of the past. "They do things differently there." It is important, for example, to remember a circumstance which Audrey Blake has emphasized continually regarding the leisure youth culture of the era, and which is reflected in the program of activities exemplified above. Compared with today there was almost unimaginably less mediated and pre-produced entertainment, less affluence, fewer educational opportunities, less sexually-oriented and commodity-serviced recreation and, it seems, a social life more attuned to collective activity and the family. EYL filled a much larger gap in youthful educational, recreational opportunities than exists today, and at a time of much stronger local and international socialist consciousness.

The perennial difficulties are exacerbated by the special sensitivities associated with the history of communism in Australia, which has erected screens of various traumatic events between then and now. How people remember what it might have signified to be associated with the EYL (say, playing in its street parade or at its cabarets), can be completely transformed, one way or the other, by later Cold War hysteria and the Menzies government's intimidation of the left and the workers. The siege mentality in the EYL also produced a much closer alignment with the CPA, so that by 1952 it identified with the Party perspective (Blears 2002, 54). For a rigid party member of a particular temperament, recollections of EYL membership in the early 1940s may well then take on a more heroically revolutionary complexion. On the other hand, for someone who went on to a career in the public service, looking back through the screen of the late 1940s, it is likely to be useful to remember it just as a youth organization with interests in workers' conditions.

The EYL in 1946 was not the same as the EYL in 1952. The EYL was different, Australia was different, and the nature of the triangular relationship between both of these and the jazz movement also underwent numerous permutations. Arguably, the EYL in 1946 was attuned to the distinctive pitch and timbre of the emerging progressive elements of Australian youth consciousness. By the 1950s, they no longer resonated so closely with each other. What is clear from the foregoing is that the links between jazz and radical arts and politics during the 1940s were not hammered out in the forge of communist ideology and Comintern policy, and in fact were as likely to be in conflict with them as not. Even the activities of the EYL itself during the period under discussion cannot be explained simply in terms of a CPA agenda. Individual tastes in music on the part of key EYL figures are important, but in themselves do not explain the growing jazz following among radicals as well as in the broader community. This alliance reflects the emergence of a larger discourse than that of the Party, or that of a minority group of writers and painters who were often unintelligible to the general public. If we examine the Australian jazz discourse of the time, I believe we can produce a much more ambitious hypothesis. The Australian jazz journals in the mid-1940s were the sites at which the meanings of the word *jazz* were debated (Johnson 1998, 26–37). Certain attitudes emerge from these discussions, which correspond significantly with those which also pervade the EYL and the *AP* groups. Beneath differences of focus and surface differences of opinion, they share a number of very fundamental socio-cultural assumptions and ways of thinking. We don't need theoretical constructs to discover this shared space, though a number of terms suggest themselves as points of departure for its definition: Lukacs' "intellectual physiognomy," Williams' "structure of feeling," Bourdieu's "habitus," or Fish's "interpretive community."

The first AJC was not simply a gathering of performers playing, and audiences listening to, an exotic music, like a gamelan concert in Sydney. They were coming into being as a community, and through this music, extending that community to other sectors. As the witnesses testified, the transition from a textual canon produced elsewhere and by others (sound recordings), to a live social practice, was crucial in this act of "making over" what they regarded as "true" jazz. It was the first time many of those attending had their own activity validated by hearing other Australians play this kind of jazz live, and by the growing sense of emerging local and even national styles. The AJC "naturalized" what was hitherto an exotic, technologically mediated music, through performance and audience rituals, the exchange of opinions in discussion groups, the discovery of shared tastes and "texts," vocabulary and grammar, social practices and attitudes. All this was in spite of the broadest disparities in class, profession, and geography which white Australia accommodated.

The reference to "white Australia" prompts the question, "why jazz?"— a music whose appeal was generally enhanced at this time by virtue of its "black" origins. This invites a study that goes well beyond what is possible here, including a review of the racist and xenophobic strains in the history of the country during the Anglo-European presence. Some lines of enquiry can be sketched, however. One answer is simply that, because of media technology, "it was there," rather than any other foreign provincial "folk" music. And in the late 1930s, the particular version of it of which the emerging jazz community was now becoming aware was not already "spoken for." Unlike classical or other forms of popular music, it was not already compromised by associations with the establishment and its power blocs. It was also haloed with the aura of the new, of the disenfranchised, of folk authenticity, and in relation to other forms of current popular music including commercial swing, it had a "rebellious" (Graeme Bell 2/16/89) unruliness in its energy, which provided a musical articulation of individualism-in-collectivity. And, what must never be forgotten, it provided corporeal and emotional expression of this social transaction in which converged performer, audience, dancer.

The jazz discourse centralized such ideas as "authenticity" in social practice, valorized the "individual statement" over the mass, but sought also to reconcile the individual with the collective—as in the "contrapuntal" (Graeme Bell 2/16/89) model of small band collective improvisation. It held out for artistic and political integrity, against cultural fascism as reflected in regimented and commercialized mass culture—as in the model of orchestrated big bands. Much of the mood is summarized in an article by jazz musician Tom Pickering written in the *AP* program for the first AJC, when he links the jazz movement with modern painting, poetry and prose:

. . . apart from the fact that it is expressive of the age we live in, it has the same freedom of expression and the revolt against the accepted, the respectable, and the conventional. It was born when the period of revolt and experiment in the European art world was in its infancy, although that comparison is one of time only. (*AP Broadsheet* 10, 1946, 21)

This is of course a familiar discourse in the often romanticized jazz aesthetic emerging both locally and internationally from the late 1930s. The overlap with other radicalisms is a sign of something going beyond the aesthetic, however. It is a response also to political conditions—most prominently, the rise of fascism—and to the perceived reifications effected through mass culture. It is a signal of an emerging dissatisfaction that goes well beyond a simple class schema confined to the workers, though inevitably it includes them. The alliance was the manifestation not of any party doctrine. Quite the contrary: it reflects the emergence of a broad-based socially progressive and reformist consciousness, and its chosen music was what was understood as "true" jazz. In the same article Tom Pickering tried to profile its "intellectual physiognomy," writing of younger groups who have modeled their playing on recordings of "authentic" jazz (Pickering 1946, 21). These groups have recognized the "shallowness and worthlessness of swing and all its synthetic offshoots and . . . the truly great possibilities of jazz," and he refers to examples in the U.S., the U.K., Chile, and Australia (Pickering 1946, 23).

The rhetoric is much the same as the international jazz commentary, as for example, in one of the booklets cited by Stein as a source of inspiration, the English publication *The Background to the Blues,* by Ian Lang (Stein 1994, 85n). Stein read it when it was reprinted in part in the local professional show business journal *Tempo.* It is worth reading the original in its entirety as an example of the rhetoric of the time, but what I draw attention to here is that it was published by the Workers' Music Association, founded in 1936, and having as its aim "to encourage music in all its forms and its appreciation among the British people, so as to enrich and develop our musical heritage by giving the widest section of the community the opportunity of participating in musical activity."[7]

There is a rich and provocative convergence of issues here, which provides a springboard for a concluding hypothesis that opens up the next avenue of investigation. It evokes some of the pivotal issues in the study of national cultures: how is a "common culture" defined? Who is included in the idea of "heritage"? Who participates in the creation of "community"? The link with worker education recalls Audrey Blake's summary of the EYL mission. She saw the EYL in the tradition of a "long saga" in the education of the workforce outside the academies: "One thinks of Matthew Arnold, the subsequent experiments in general education . . . the Mechanics Institutes, the 'School of Arts', the Plebs League, the early pamphleteers, the Labour College, the WEA, the Communist Party, the Eureka Youth League—and much more" (Blake 1993, xxiv).

Tom Steele's account of the evolution of British cultural studies traces a transition in the worker and continuing education movements from being (working) class based, to a larger movement which transcended class (Steele 1997). It is suggestive that over the same period, a similar pattern is apparent in the EYL. In 1947 Richard Hoggart identified in this shift a revulsion against mass culture that crossed class lines (cited in Steele 1997, 120–21). At the time Arnold Toynbee saw this as the growth of what he called the "internal proletariat," a "class" that is "defined by its cultural loss or scarcity, rather than sociological position . . . to be found at all levels of society" (Steele 1997, 120–21).

Let us note, then, that the witnesses I have cited regarding the first AJC, where they came together to perform in balances of power largely irrelevant to their professional standing, included an art teacher, professional musician, draughtsman, fitter and turner, insurance clerk, bank clerk, librarian, photographer, research metallurgist, university student in economics, an Oxford graduated solicitor, a future architect. The last-mentioned was Bill Haesler, who opens a further line of enquiry with his recollection that "a lot of us were working class and Roman Catholic, with family affiliations with the union movement" (Haesler 2/15/02). Frank Johnson was struck by the fact that the AJC brought together "a vast spectrum of people filled with good will . . . from all walks of life" (Frank Johnson 12/28/88). It is widely recognized in such fields as ethnomusicology and in popular music studies that all communities define themselves through, among other things, music (see for example Stokes 1994, 1–28). I hypothesize that, with further research, the cultural significance of jazz might be shown to go beyond considerations of local and political identity (though it incorporates these), and that it is the music of the internationally emergent social consciousness recorded by such historians as Toynbee and Hoggart, and more recently Steele, and reflected also in parallel developments in adult education movements and the debates from which emerged cultural studies.

What can we conclude with any certainty? That the first AJC signaled an alliance of interests that constituted a distinctive thread in the social order, and in fact can only be understood by reference to the context from which that thread was spun. That it saw itself to a greater or lesser extent, in the mid-1940s, as a culturally progressive rather than reactionary movement. It was for reform in the name of social justice and welfare, rather than conservative of traditional inequities. It believed in agency against those conservative power blocs, against whom it felt excluded and disaffected. It was

broadly inclined against cultural engineering from the top down. It manifested itself over a range of social practices and sectors: labor, recreation,
ethics, government, the arts. In terms of the international politics of the
time it was anti-fascist; in terms of domestic politics it was left-leaning and
democratic. Its spirit transcended class in its dissatisfaction with mass culture and forces of conservatism. In terms of music, it was drawn towards
jazz, not for reasons of political policy (though they could be harnessed to
that predilection), but because something in its spirit and practice seemed
congenial to the "structure of feeling" that underpinned the alliance. If this
is an example of what Toynbee called at the time the "internal proletariat,"
then the AJC signaled its musical manifestation in Australia.

MUSIC AND EMANCIPATION

The Social Role of Black Jazz and Vaudeville in South Africa Between the 1920s and the Early 1940s

—*Christopher Ballantine*

Excerpted from an article in *Journal of Southern African Studies* 17.1 (March 1991): 129–52. Reprinted with permission of the author and Taylor & Francis Ltd. <http://www.tandf.co.uk>.

As the music culture of black city-dwellers in South Africa grew in breadth and sophistication in the 1920s, 1930s, and 1940s, a great and important question took shape within it. The question was: What could this music accomplish socially? Or, as it was more elaborately framed at the first conference of the South African Bantu Board of Music, held on July 1 and 2 1929: How could this "heavenly gift . . . best be used for the glory of God and the amelioration of our social and cultural conditions?" (*IZ* 2/4/30).[1]

The answers differed—and perhaps nowhere more widely than within the vibrant and virile subculture of jazz and vaudeville fostered by the most profoundly urbanized sectors of the black working class. But the differences here are not mysterious. This nascent, jazzing subculture itself contained somewhat contradictory preoccupations with, on the one hand, styles of jazz and vaudeville derived from the United States, and on the other, musical and performance styles that had developed long ago in the South African countryside or more recently in the towns (see Ballantine 1993; and Erlmann 1988). Nor did these contradictory preoccupations stand alone: they were rooted in, and grew out of, notions of society and of social change that were themselves contradictory. And it is often in the very language of these deeper beliefs about society that the question about music's social role was answered. As this suggests, the answers often lie outside the music itself: in the discourses that surround it, and in the contexts of its performance. The moment at which the music's own content begins substantively to provide the answers, marks (as we shall see) the moment at which the music's own social role begins to be fundamentally redefined.

What then were these beliefs? And what were the corresponding views about a social role for music?

THE LIBERAL VIEW (1): THE MORAL APPEAL

On the one side were a set of beliefs that were essentially liberal and individualistic in character. As such they reflected in microcosm, and were surely in part a consequence of, the basically *petit-bourgeois* outlook and practice of (in particular) the African National Congress for much of the period between the 1920s and the early 1940s. For workers and slum-dwellers, this was a time of relative passivity, the result, it is usually held, of the failure of the ANC to create in the black communities a viable organizational presence which would link up with the lives and struggles of the urban working class. This meant that the oppositional activities of this class were guided by what Gramsci would have called a "corporate" proletarian consciousness—one, that is, which attempts to "define and seek to improve a position within a given order" (in contrast to a "hegemonic" consciousness, which "seeks to perform a transformative work over the whole range of society") (see Koch 1983b).

In particular, two broad assumptions about music's social role stand out here, both concerned with ways in which music might be an aid to improvement within the given order. The first assumption is that the music performed by blacks could demonstrate to whites that blacks were *worthy* of better social, political and economic treatment: in short, it should seek to effect a *moral persuasion*. On the analogy that "God helps those that help themselves," the columnist "Musica" opined in an article on "The Native and Music" in *Umteteli wa Bantu* in 1930, "so will assistance come from either the State or elsewhere if we shew ourselves worthy" (*UWB* 1/25/30). More euphorically, conservative poet and critic B. W. Vilakazi asked the readers of *Ilanga Lase Natal* in 1933 to believe that "[m]usic will induce men of wider aspect to open for us gateways to economic and political liberty" (*ILN* 2/10/33). The argument rested, as so often in the developing South African subculture of jazz and vaudeville, on a presumption about what had happened in the United States. Paul Robeson, Florence Mills, and Layton and Johnstone, were familiar examples: the fate of these and other "descendants of a race that has been under worse oppression," "Musica" argued, proves that "developing our music and singing to the white man will do much better than some of the methods adopted in solving the intricate Bantu problem in South Africa" (*UWB* 1/25/30). And when Robeson himself promised to visit South Africa in 1935 (a visit that ultimately never took place), the argument was put with renewed force. The achievement of men like Robeson, an article in *Bantu World* claimed, "has exploded the theory that the black man is mentally not the equal of the white man"; it is this kind of demonstration, accomplished in Robeson's case through music, that will help deliver local blacks "from the thraldom of European oligarchy" (*BW* 2/2/35).

At home, the musical scene abounded with groups, bands, and individual performers who were embarked upon a similar demonstration, and whose huge and enthusiastic audiences hoped for a similar deliverance. Appropriately—given their assumption about the political efficacy of moral persuasion—their repertoire was overwhelmingly American, learnt from imported gramophone records, or sheet music, or American films (see Ballantine 1993). The best of these local musicians made regular tours of the country, sometimes even venturing into neighboring states. Among vaudeville groups, none was more famous in the early 1930s than the Darktown Strutters. Reporting on a countrywide tour that, by May 1932, was already nine months old, *Bantu World* noted that the Strutters could "boast of being the only Bantu who filled the Durban and Maritzburg town halls with an appreciative audience of Europeans, with turns that are supposed to be associated only with European talents." Better still, they were then "deluged with invitations for private appearances among the elite of Durban European society, not as 'curios' but as 'eye openers' " (*BW* 5/7/32).

Musical performance as an "eye opener": the image is significant—indeed central—to this mythology of moral persuasion, and recurs in countless variations, permutations, and associated analogies. Playing to full houses during a visit to Bechuanaland in 1936, the Darktown Strutters were again "both an education and an eye-opener"; this was because they had showed that, "given the opportunity," blacks were "capable of rising above the ordinary standard of things" (*UWB* 3/14/36). In like fashion the following year, the Johnnesburg-based Merry Blackbirds—already famous as one of the finest dance bands in the land—were an "eye-opener" in Port Elizabeth and a "revelation" in Bloemfontein (*UWB* 4/17/37, and 4/10/37).

On such occasions, what eyes were opened to was not only the performance of the music itself, but a host of associated skills. One of these was the ability of a great many of the bands to read staff-notation, and therefore to play from imported orchestrations. Louis Radebe Petersen, a meticulous observer of the local jazz and vaudeville scene since the 1920s, and once pianist for various groups, makes this point vividly:

> They wanted to prove to the world, I say the world, even: if anybody came from America or London or anywhere, if they put the music sheet in front of them they could read it and do it. . . . It's how they turned the world upside down. . . .
> (Petersen 2/2/84)

If eyes were to be opened, it was obviously not a matter of indifference whose eyes they were. The bands and vaudeville companies played, of course, predominantly to black audiences; but (as is already implicit in the examples cited above) the demonstration of worthiness had ultimately to take place before the eyes of whites. Opportunities for such demonstration were avidly taken up. In 1941, for instance, the Merry Blackbirds, the Jazz Maniacs, the Synco Down Beats Orchestra, and De Pitch Black Follies were linked to performances in Johannesburg for the Blue Lagoon Club, the Log Cabin Club, and the New Paradise Club—events that prompted critic Walter Nhlapo to note approvingly that "these European night clubs are serving a factor to a better South Africa. They are breaking slowly but surely the segregation barrier set up by dirty politics. . . ." (*BW* 12/6/41).

In July of the same year, De Pitch Black Follies made their way to Durban and the south coast of Natal, the holiday playground of white South Africans, for a tour of hotels during the height of the mid-year holiday season. Through this "invasion," as *Umteteli* styled it, black art and talent would be "carried right to the doors of European South Africa," and the Follies would have "the opportunity to 'educate' a not inconsiderable section of Europeans" (*UWB* 6/14/41). And in November, the Follies and the Merry Blackbirds performed at a home in Parktown, one of Johannesburg's most select white suburbs (*UWB* 11/22/41).

These occasions also served as tokens of acceptance, and as signs that headway was being made. Some tokens carried special weight: as on those rare occasions when the *white* press noticed, and made favorable comment about, a performance by a black group; or better (and rarer) still, when a white band played a composition by a black composer. In 1944, the two top white big bands in Johannesburg each gave such a performance— a statistic almost certainly unprecedented at that time. The favored composer was one Henry ("Japie") Mokone: in March, Charles Berman and his Orchestra played his "My Heart is Beating Every Hour For You," and in August, Roy Martin and his Orchestra gave a broadcast performance of his "I'm Blue Without You." *Bantu World* at once supplied the familiar moral interpretation. These events, it proclaimed, were "ample evidence of the composer's untiring efforts to demonstrate the fact that Africans are gifted musicians, not only in the sphere of African classical music, but also in European Jazz Music" (*BW* 8/5/44).

Yet the real reflection on such tokens was made a month later, in *Ilanga Lase Natal*. Alluding to the success of the Follies in winning "the hearts of their white audiences," influential critic Herbert Dhlomo (writing as "Busy Bee") reported what one white observer had said to a member of the cast ("You have done more for your people during these two weeks than many politicians have done for years"), and concluded: "I maintain that Art can, is and will continue to play a great part in solving our problems" (*ILN* 9/9/44).

THE LIBERAL VIEW (2): FAME AND FORTUNE

The first broad assumption about music's social role, then, rested on the belief that whites were racist oppressors because they were ignorant; through music, blacks could help educate their masters and so present a moral claim that the white ruling class would find irresistible. The second assumption was as liberal as the first but more unashamedly individualistic. Its appeal was not to morality but to economics; its logic not that whites would change the system, but that blacks could play the system. It promised not a better deal for all, but a road out of the ghetto for some. Music, it said, could make you rich and famous.

Early support for this view came from an eminent quarter. Benjamin Tyamzashe, the famous Xhosa-speaking choral composer, gave it his blessing at the celebrated 1929 conference referred to earlier. Giving his mundane advice a spiritual touch by reminding his audience that music was "a social as well as a spiritual necessity as in heaven they have nothing else but music," he went on to declare that "the race" possessed "men and women in South Africa who could become millionaires" (*IZ* 2/4/30). *Umteteli*, like other black newspapers, took up the theme on numerous occasions. In 1932, for instance, an editorial noted that "it may be . . . that there are individuals to-day whose voices, unknown to them, may be worth fortunes: just as Robeson's"; and an editorial the following year, alluding to the successes of American jazz musicians and reminding its readers that "[t]he African musician and harmonist has his chance therefore," concluded resoundingly: "the world is waiting" (*UWB* 12/17/32, and 11/11/33).

Though there were not yet any South African Robesons making their fortunes, the local scene seemed pregnant with possibilities. The Natal composer, Reuben Caluza, for instance, had gone to London in 1930 for a series of recordings for the local market (which included many of his ragtime-influenced choral works): the records sold well. And the black press did not omit to report that in 1933, while studying in the U.S., Caluza sang (with a group of fellow students) for both the American and French presidents (*ILN* 6/2/33). Griffiths Motsieloa's two recording sorties to London in 1930 and 1931—both of them also involving other black South African musicians—were other events that aroused similar interest; so that when, in 1932, Motsieloa gave up teaching for a full-time career on the stage, *Bantu World* saw this as a sign that "[t]he Bantu people are on the march" (*BW* 4/9/32). Again the language is revealing. If this was a march, it was, for those lucky enough to be on it, one that was headed upwards, towards greatness, on a route that led out of the slums and into town. In an interview more than forty years later, former vaudeville singer Tommy ("China") Beusen, once a member of the esteemed Africans' Own Entertainers, recalled the excitement of that journey in images that are suggestive:

[We] used to broadcast. Live, live, live, live! That Saturday morning, everybody stayed glued to the radio. Ayi, ayi, ayi! African Entertainers are going to broadcast this morning! When we finish there and we come into town [they] say, "Ayi, man! You chaps were great!" . . . Yes, we are, we are up there now! You see? We up there and we the talk of the town! (Beusen 4/28/86)

Yet on this road from real poverty to promised riches lay a treacherous contradiction: music might be autonomously produced, but it tended quickly to became ensnared in structures of reproduction that were exploitative, were geared towards profit, and were not owned or controlled by those who created the music in the first place. Many experienced this contradiction, but none articulated it as clearly as the remarkable Wilfred Sentso—vaudeville artist, jazz musician, troupe and band leader, composer and educationist. Focusing on the record companies, the institution through which the contradiction was felt most acutely, Sentso gave the typical example of a studio paying a group £4.4s.0d for a double-sided 78 rpm record. That fee would also purchase all rights to the music. Sentso commented:

It is no exaggeration to say that there are music houses which do a large turnover in Bantu recorded music, while the artists themselves go starving. . . . After all the songs are yours; the voices are yours; the work is yours. The firm only comes in to collect the profits! Why, I repeat, sell your songs, your voices, all for £4.4s.0d? Fats Waller gets £400. (*UWB* 1/18/41)

The solution, he concluded, was for blacks to create their own musicians' union (a task which, a few months later, he set about trying to do) (*BW* 11/15/41). Without such a union, he argued, there would be no protection against exploitation, no chance of the musician earning "a living wage," nor—by implication—any possibility of music leading musicians out of the ghetto.

The assumption that music could make one rich and famous—could change the quality of one's life—had unusual resonance for one stratum of performers within the jazz and vaudeville subculture. That stratum was women; and they provide an interesting variant of this assumption. It is remarkable that black women were able to define even the most tentative outlines of a gender-based position here. These women, particularly those now living and working in the cities, were the subject of a relentless discussion about their "proper" roles, as wives, as daughters, as parents, but above all as present or future "mothers of the nation." The patriarchal attitudes and conservative morality of this discussion—conducted *inter alia* through the black press, the schools and the churches—stressed such things as the importance of Christian ethics, dignified behavior at home and an exemplary social demeanor abroad, unblemishable fidelity, devotion to duty, and the virtues of a temperate life. Within the rigid and constricting confines of this discourse, there was little place for the "sinful" and inherently "corrupting" world of jazz, dance and the vaudeville stage. Yet despite this—indeed, in outright contradiction of it—stood the contrasting, and secular, discourse of a developing show-business, which made direct appeals for the incorporation of women, in particular ways and as a special category of performer. In this jazzing subculture, women could at one and the same time make money *and* be exploited for their novelty value and their sex appeal (though, to be sure, the domination of the bands and vaudeville troupes by men meant that women's earnings were largely dependent on the "generosity" of the male leaders or managers).

But there is a dialectic here. The entry of women as wage-earners on to the performing stage, slowly opened up a space which *women themselves* could begin to define in such a way that it started to accord new respectability to women performers, who now even became worthy of emulation; and women themselves could begin tentatively to undermine, or at least extend, the rigid conventions of socially acceptable roles and behavior. For women, then, music could play a role that was at least potentially progressive. It could slowly challenge the stereotypes of oppressed womanhood, deliver a blow to male hegemony, and provide a limited basis for economic autonomy.

Vaudeville troupes provided the primary location for women performers within this subculture. Such troupes proliferated around the country; mixed-gender, and men-only, groups were predominant, but by the mid-1930s troupes consisting only of women, and even managed by women, were not uncommon. . . . In the jazz field, the space for women was restricted—as was the case in the United States—essentially to two roles: vocalists and pianists. Earliest of the pianists was certainly the extraordinary Emily Motsieloa, who was the first pianist of the Merry Blackbirds (in 1930 when it was known as the Motsieloa Band), and held that chair for nearly two decades (Rezant 6/3/84). (She was, as it happens, also wife of Griffiths.) Hope Khumalo was pianist for the Jazz Maniacs for a short period around 1939 or 1940 (Pretorius, 10/18/87), after which she seemed not to play jazz again. (She resurfaces in April 1941, as the "able accompanist" for the Johannesburg African Choral Society's performance of excerpts from Handel's *Messiah*) (*BW* 4/26/41). The first female jazz vocalist—indeed the first black jazz soloist of either sex—was Marjorie Pretorius, who fronted first the Jazz Maniacs and then the Merry Blackbirds between about 1938 and 1961 (Pretorius 10/18/87).[2]

Inevitably, it was the women in the more famous groups who elicited the more public comment. The all-male Darktown Strutters had a well-honed reputation when, in the mid-1930s, and after much debate, they took in a 23-year-old singer by the name of Babsy Oliphant; soon thereafter they also included her sister Eleanor, and Lindi Makhanya, a young singer who had recorded with both Caluza's group in London, and the Bantu Glee Singers at home (Oliphant 5/13/87). "Gossip Pen," *Umteteli*'s critic, commented:

> The Oliphant sisters, notably Babsy, are perhaps best known for their courage. They dared the notions of Bantu conservatism and defied all the conventions which bespoke a less active life for Bantu maidenhood. And they have been a success. (*UWB* 4/30/38)

Lindi Makhanya, too, was hailed as a trend-setter. For *Bantu World* she was "about the only African Lady specially of her age who has enjoyed such an exciting experience in her career as a musician" (*BW* 6/5/37).

But surely no woman made greater impact, or demonstrated greater self-consciousness about the implications of her career, than the brilliant Johanna "Giddy" Phahlane, leader and manager of the celebrated Bloemfontein troupe, the Merry Makers. A pseudonymous letter-writer in *Bantu World*, in January 1936, made the point crisply. Indignant that other centers in the country had not yet produced a female vaudeville performer of Phahlane's calibre, the writer urged that "[o]ur womenfolk have a national gift which if keenly developed would make them stars on the stage" (*BW* 1/25/36). It was a point that Johanna Phahlane herself took up energetically, almost in the manner of a one-woman campaign. Between 1936 and 1938, she wrote an occasional column for *Bantu World*. Using the pen-name, "Lady Porcupine," this became one of her most important forums. Here she joined with the struggle of black women in general; and here she propagated her belief that music could play a significant role in this struggle. Writing in February 1936, for example, she again drew attention to the contradiction between, on the one hand, the abundance of musical talent among black women, and on the other, the virtual absence of women from leadership positions on the musical stage. "Surely," she urged, "I am not the only young woman in this direction. There are others yet unsung: Forward girls!!" (*BW* 2/15/36).

She made similar appeals from the stage. In January 1937, for instance, after two performances at different venues in Port Elizabeth (occasions that struck at least some members of the audience as the "most successful functions ever staged in Port Elizabeth," and in which she impressed as "the best lady we've seen on the stage"), Phahlane gave a closing speech in which she "challenged the Africans to stand up and use their talents" (*BW* 2/6/37). But perhaps her most incisive appeal was made in *Bantu World* in May 1936. In an article entitled "A Modern Woman Struggles for Freedom," she delivered the sort of needle-sharp arguments that must have left her male readers feeling quite stung, and that made her pen-name seem aptly chosen:

Most men have said in all ages: "Woman is stupid; therefore do not waste time and money in educating her much." Let me be frank. Nowadays women are up in arms against this system. I could point to a score of women who really struggle forward for freedom in practical affairs of life. . . . You will realise that a modern woman refuses to spend her time in dressing only for the captivation of gentlemen, as some may think, but will struggle hard to earn her living in many ways as a nurse, teacher, singer, actress, dancer, cook, dressmaker, house-keeper, laundress etc. and is very much anxious to make men comprehend that she can do without them. . . . Now why should she be debarred from serving any state as a maker of laws? Stand in a pulpit and preach? Be a principal of any high school according to her high qualifications? Be a leader for men to follow her? There is no logical answer to these questions. . . . But every silly clown of a fellow begins to cackle when a cultured and capable woman claims the right to take part in the control of a municipality or state. . . .

Do not imagine, O man, that your long supremacy can endure forever. Give a modern woman a chance and work together co-operatively. She also has the right to struggle for freedom.

Woman of the race we all have to march—Forward. (*BW* 5/30/36)

THE RADICAL VIEW (1):
ORGANIZATIONAL LINKS

On what I have called the liberal view, then, the social role of jazz and vaudeville was a question of its being an aid to improvement within the given order. Alongside this, there existed at the same time another view, and another set of practices, on the basis of which this musical subculture might play a role that was at least potentially more challenging—for here it might lend assistance to efforts that *tended* in the direction of more fundamental social change. I shall call this the radical view. As was the case with the liberal view, it is possible here to distinguish between two broad impulses. The first, and chronologically the earlier, is the assumption that music's socio-political role was largely a question of its formal linkage to oppositional organizations; and as a corollary, that issues such as the specific style, content or provenance of the music were of secondary, or even minimal, importance.

One such organization was the Industrial and Commercial Workers' Union (ICU). Founded in 1919 as a trade union, it grew rapidly: by the mid-1920s it was essentially a black protest movement with support in many parts of Southern Africa. The ICU seems to have had a close and ongoing relationship with music. In 1927, for instance, the year it was at its zenith with a claimed membership of 100 000, the organization was hiring jazz bands to play at fancy-dress balls and other events in the ICU-owned Workers' Hall in Johannesburg; the best known of these bands was a "Coloured" group, the Merry Mascots (Erlmann 1983, 199). And in the corresponding venue in Durban, the ICU Hall, the breakaway Natal branch often played host to vaudeville troupes. Performing there in 1932, for example, were Dem Darkies (from Pretoria), the Blue Dams (from Durban), the Midnight Follies and the Dixie Rag Lads (both from Amanzimtoti), as well the Famous Broadway Entertainers, the Sunbeams, and the African Youngsters; the Darktown Strutters themselves performed there at least once (in 1936).[3] The ICU frequently organized large meetings and rallies, at which "The Red Flag" or the ICU Anthem would commonly be sung;[4] and perhaps no association between the union and the jazzing subculture is more suggestive than that in which, at one such rally in 1929, 4000 demonstrators marched through the streets of Johannesburg behind the General Secretary, Clements Kadalie, and a jazz band belting out—and presumably "jamming" to the tune of—"The Red Flag" (Koch 1983a, 172).

A. W. G. Champion, leader of the Natal ICU, seems to have had a special interest in music, and in developing the relationship of the union to music. He was, for example, on the way to meet Caluza and his Double Quartette when the ship bringing them back from their recording sessions in England docked at Cape Town harbor in December 1930; and later that month he organized a concert, at which an ICU choir sang, to welcome them back to Durban. The previous year he had been infuriated by the bad publicity given by the *Natal Mercury* to Durban's African dance halls, as a result of a speech made by the Rev. F. Scogings: he wrote an irate letter to Scogings, promising a public rebuke but demanding to know first whether he had really referred to the halls as "dubious haunts of terpsichorean and alcoholic bliss."[5] (Champion shared this interest in music with at least two ANC presidents: Pixley ka lzaka Seme, who was president from 1930 to 1936, and Dr. A. B. Xuma, his successor. In the late 1930s Seme managed, and gave his name to, a group calling itself Pixley's Mid-Night Follies; Xuma, at the same time, was managing the musical activities of jazz-band and vaudeville-troupe leader, Wilfred Sentso.)[6]

Though they seem to have been the most musically active, the ICU were not the only organization to form links with the jazz and vaudeville subculture. The Communist Party regularly held dances to raise funds; before the late 1920s, the only bands able to provide music suitable for ballroom dancing were those comprising white musicians, and so groups such as Edgar Adeler's Personal Orchestra were engaged (*SAW* 7/23/26, and 9/24/26). But as soon as high-quality "Coloured" groups appeared on the scene—slightly earlier than "African" bands—the Party hired them. Thus in 1928, the Party's newspaper, *The South African Worker*, advertised that Rayner's Big Six were to play at a Grand Carnival Dance in the African Hall in Johannesburg on September 12 (*SAW* 8/22/28). In later years, more famous groups followed—among them Sonny's Jazz Revellers, probably the most celebrated "Coloured" band of all, and the Merry Blackbirds. Various black trade unions, and the ANC, were among other organizations that also called upon the bands and the vaudeville troupes. In 1940, for example, when they were at the peak of their influence and membership with some 21 unions, the Joint Committee of the Non-European Trade Unions engaged the Merry

Blackbirds to play for a dance (*BW* 8/31/40), and the Harmony Kings band played for a function at which "[d]ancing was interspersed by speeches from popular trade unionists" (*BW* 7/20/40). The African Mine Workers' Union was formed in 1941; the following year it held a grand event in the common Concert-and-Dance format, and asked two of the country's top groups perform: they were the Synco Fans (Wilfred Sentso's vaudeville company) and the Jazz Maniacs. . . . (*BW* 11/21/42).

If, through links of this kind, music was entering into oppositional political alignments, this happened for the most part behind the backs of the musicians themselves. With the exception of performers such as James Phillips—the "Coloured" singer with the "Paul Robeson" voice, who frequently appeared with Sonny's Jazz Revellers and who was also a member of the Communist Party (Phillips 4/8/86)—most musicians took a "professional" attitude to such assignments. Merry Blackbirds leader, Peter Rezant, captured this attitude—and began to rationalize it—when he recalled his own band's work for the Communist Party:

I had no political leanings in any way. Anyway, I think that was also the success of the band. I didn't, ah, I didn't discuss politics with them and I didn't show any—; the only thing I was interested in was to entertain them. . . . They were very highly cultured people. Their functions were on a very high plane, very high plane. (Rezant 6/3/84)

Rezant, then, though prepared to have his band provide music that gave functional support to the Communist Party, was not prepared to see his band espouse "political leanings" that would have been detrimental to its "success." On any serious reckoning this is an artificial cleavage—but it would have found extensive support. When asked in a recent interview to comment on Griffiths Motsieloa's political attitudes, or those of his Pitch Black Follies, former star member of the group, Lindi Makhanya retorted: "Oi, Motsieloa! He never wanted to be involved! [Laughs] Never! Ooh! He always wanted to be on the . . . good side of the law. . . ." (Makhanya 2/13/87). Yet there were occasions when musicians explicitly *chose* to identify themselves with a particular oppositional organization, or its work. . . . Late in 1935, the Transvaal section of the ANC set out to raise funds to send delegates to the national meeting of the All-African Convention, summoned to protest about the infamous Herzog Bills which were to remove "Africans" from the common voters' role, set up separate political institutions for them, and fix for all time the unequal distribution of land. Ten days before the meeting, scheduled for Bloemfontein on December 16, a fund-raising dance took place in Johannesburg. The esteemed Rhythm Kings band, led by alto saxophonist John Mavimbela who had previously been with the Merry Blackbirds, considered the event sufficiently important to offer to provide the music free of charge. More than that: the band helped publicize the dance, the convention, the ANC, and the issues at stake, by issuing a strongly worded statement in which they explained their decision:

We feel that it is our bounden duty and that of every true African to assist in every possible way those men who are going to Bloemfontein to consider the Government's Native policy, which in our opinion is detrimental to the future of our race. If there ever was a time when every man and woman of our race should stand shoulder to shoulder this is the time. The passing of the Native Bills by Parliament will seal our doom and condemn us to perpetual servitude. (BW 11/30/35)

And if the general "professionalist" tendency admitted of occasional exceptions, these could take diverse forms. One thinks here again of Merry Makers leader, Johanna Phahlane, who, writing as "Lady Porcupine" in her column in Bantu World, sent from Bloemfontein an enthusiastic and supportive report on Kadalie's "vigorous propaganda tour of the Free State" for the ICU (BW 6/13/36); and of William Mseleku, leader and manager of the famous Royal Amanzimtoti Entertainers, who was personally associated with the "African" trade union movements in the early 1940s, and who not long after became a committee member of the Natal branch of the ANC (Edwards 1989, 41). But for the vast majority of musicians who participated in the extension of music's social role through its organizational linkages, the naive cleavage between professional form and political function remained steadfastly unquestioned.

THE RADICAL VIEW (2): POLITICS IN MUSIC—TOWARDS AN "AFRICAN" STYLE

On the first radical assumption, then, about a more challenging social role for music, it is the links to organizations that were of primary, and virtually exclusive, importance: the politics, in a manner of speaking, was external to the music itself. The second assumption, by contrast, draws this connection much more closely: the politics, though it continues to live outside the music and still seeks to link music to its organizational function, now stands also in much more intimate relationship to the music itself. Politics, that is to say, now invades music, and music in turn now welcomes politics explicitly into its own constitution. Music itself comes to symbolic political character.

This is a shift whose outlines are at first only dimly and intermittently perceived, but whose ultimate impact on the future direction of black South African jazz culture was profound and revolutionary. The content of the shift was to assert the belief that there was intrinsically a value in the adoption or incorporation of musical materials that were "*African*". The precise nature of this value was never adequately spelt out by those who, in this period, were its advocates or its practitioners; but there cannot be any doubt that this belief (and the shift to which it gave rise) was part of a broad groundswell that reached its first culmination in the early 1940s, where it inaugurated a period of militant protest and articulated itself through the social and political philosophy of the New Africanism (see Couzens 1985).

One of those who helped give intellectual shape to this philosophy was the poet, playwright and journalist, Herbert Dhlomo. In an important essay written in 1949, he reviewed the failed strategies of the previous 100 years, in terms that point to the necessity for the rise of the New Africanism. His summary recapitulates some of the tendencies already outlined in the present chapter:

During the period the African did not only admire, but envied and aspired to European ways of life. He thought education and proven ability would solve the question. He strove. He aspired. He was not content with his own as his fathers had been. He was even partly ashamed of his background, and tried to appease and win over the white man by appearing in the best light possible—according to so-called western standards. Rejected and frustrated, despite all his efforts his admiration of the European turned to helpless envy and even to hostility. It was a phase in the long process of evolution. (cited in Couzens 1985, 273–74)

The new, militant period was to stand in striking contrast to the lethargy of the preceding one; yet it was there, in the relatively quiescent decade of the 1930s, that its seeds germinated. The first tokens of the new mood of militancy became visible around the mid-1930s, and occurred in response to the

Herzog Bills and other measures. On the one hand, the new legislation drove younger and more militant activists into leadership positions of the ANC and other organizations; on the other, these bodies, formerly *petit-bourgeois* in their outlook and cautious in their style, now began to perceive that all "Africans" were ultimately subject to a common fate. The results of these changes are most clearly borne out by the ANC itself, which now entered a period of revitalization and began slowly to change into a mass movement.

On top of this, the war produced another set of factors which stimulated the growth of a more militant outlook. Wartime inflation and a huge flow of people from the countryside into the already crowded black city-slums added to the general level of grievance; at the same time, the massive wartime expansion of the African working class led to a sudden development of the African trade union movement which, in turn, affected the ANC, helping to radicalize it still further. Symptoms of the new, militant mood were everywhere to be seen: in the location riots of 1937, 1942 and 1944, the police shootings of 1942, the bus boycotts of 1940, 1942, 1943 and 1944, and the huge squatter movements. Politically, the momentum gathered during these years culminates in two signal developments: the forging of a deeper bond between the ANC and the Communist Party, and the founding of the ANC Youth League in 1944 and its dramatic impact on the leadership of the ANC.

As with politics, so with music: the first tokens of a shift in thinking about music become apparent around the mid-1930s. A headline in *Bantu World* in February 1935 proclaimed the shift in summary form: "Africans Must Not Ape Europeans." The headline stood prominently above a major article written by Paul Robeson, and reprinted from the *Daily Herald*: "I am going back to my people," he had written, "in the sense that for the rest of my life I am going to think and feel as an African—not as a white man. . . . It is not as imitation Europeans, but a Africans, that we have a value. . . ." (*BW* 2/16/35). Robeson was selected as an important symbol, and example, of this early shift: his intended visit to South Africa in 1935 provided occasion for a flurry of articles, editorials and letters in the black press. In February, for instance, a front-page article in *Bantu World* referred to Robeson's "study of African music and life," and argued that his example should:

reveal to our budding artists that there is sufficient material for their calling in the life of their own race, that there is drama, tragedy and comedy in the life of a people who are just emerging from the thraldom of Africa's darkness, and who are being rendered landless and homeless and exploited by an alien race in the land of their birth. This life can be dramatised. (*BW* 2/2/35)

In July, critic Walter Nhlapo took up some of these themes in the form of an impassioned plea:

One often wonders when Africans will learn to help, to be patriotic. . . . We will rather sing the English National Anthem well and blunder with ours. What is wrong with us? . . . Was it not Paul Robeson who condemned the Negroes for trying to sing Brahms, Haydn, Wagner and disregarding their spirituals while Europeans singing them were amassing great fortunes?

Again with African folk lore songs; we, like the Negroes, despise them and laugh and scorn at their singers. (*BW* 7/13/35)

Such appeals, to be sure, were part of a slowly changing cultural climate; and they were followed, soon enough, by audible and visible evidence of this change on the Concert-and-Dance stages of the country. *Umteteli's* critic, Godfrey Kuzwayo, was one of the first to draw attention to it. Writing as "Gossip Pen," the pen-name he used for his regular column, he declared in June 1936 that he had been struck by a new tendency in the productions of vaudeville companies. In the past, these productions had a strongly "European flavour"—but, he said, "there has been a noticeable change in this regard, and concerts and dramatic shows are now being put forward with more and more African background in them." By way of illustration, he cited a forthcoming presentation by the Africans' Own Entertainers: this was to include "an African dramatic love tragedy," "an Abakweta Ceremony," and "a Zulu Witchcraft Dance." (Other kinds of music evidently lagged behind: the following month Kuzwayo referred to the hundreds of Western-style African choirs in existence, and reiterated the widespread criticism that "few, if any, have made any serious attempt to show their interpretative ability of real African music" ([*UWB* 6/13/36]).[7]

By the late 1930s and early 1940s, the clearest embodiment of this new tendency was to be found in the work of a troupe calling itself the Bantu Revue Follies. Their programmes included "sketches, drama, comedy and satire, also sentimental songs, jazz, madrigals and ditties—all of them in the Native vernacular." The experience was of "a real native concert"—the goal, clearly, of the troupe's leader, the extraordinary Toko Khampepe, who "in loincloth and skins only, was a rare spectacle on the piano." They were "premier native music specialists and primitive artists"; it was they, more than perhaps any other group, who "succeeded in reducing the commonplace in Bantu life to a fine art" (*UWB* 7/11/36). Some troupes sought to give expression to an "African" repertoire in less sensational ways. For the Synco Fans—like their stable-companions, the Synco Down Beats Orchestra—this meant a resolve "to play songs composed and orchestrated by Africans" (*UWB* 9/27/41). So too for the newly-formed African Minstrels, who preceded their launch in early 1941 with an announcement of the repertoire they would specialize in. They gave a list of eight categories—including "exclusive novelty numbers," "musical comedies," "old classical jazz songs," "all-round minstrel choruses," "operatic minstrel choruses," "vaudeville revues," and "specialities"—but at the top of the list stood "African numbers composed by Africans" (*BW* 1/11/41).

No one doubted that these changes were significant. Yet for some, and the testy Walter Nhlapo was among them, they still did not go far enough. Spurred on perhaps, by the sharply rising political temperature of the early 1940s, he made bold in 1941 to point precisely to the social and political experiences of blacks that ought to be making an impact on the content and form of vaudeville productions. It was, quite simply, a call for "committed" art:

The theatre of life is so full of incidents which when joined together would form a masterpiece sketch, but because most of these conductors are less imaginative and compositive but merely plagiarists, they fail.

We have, for instance, the drama of pick-ups, the life in the zoo-like locations, the hooliganism and the like, subjects which are full of passion, of sorrow, of strife. We have scores upon scores of daily acts that deserve dramatisation but are passed over. (*BW* 2/22/41)

If for the vaudeville troupes, then, the Africanist impulse might be realized by "not aping the Europeans," by "presenting the commonplace in Bantu life," by staging "songs composed and orchestrated by Africans," or by selecting "subjects which are full of passion, of sorrow, of strife," what—under the sway of the same impulse—were the jazz bands to do? Certainly, they too could play numbers composed by "Africans"; and band- and vaudeville-leader Wilfred Sentso was one of those to pursue this option with particular energy. As Todd Matshikiza was to recall many years later, "Sentso began composing. Swing fever had touched him but he wouldn't touch imported music. He wrote his own numbers" (*Drum*, July 1957).

Furthermore, in the composition of such numbers jazzmen could find new ways to avoid "aping the Europeans." More positively, they could ignore conservative prejudice and instead celebrate and encourage local proletarian music-and-dance styles. Sentso and other composers did precisely this in the early 1940s for the popular *tsaba-tsaba*, a dance that was a successor to the notorious *marabi* dance. . . . (see Ballantine 1993). Alternatively, the jazz bands could give a richly "African" flavor to their renditions of American swing numbers, by finding ways to incorporate elements of the harmonic and rhythmic structure of *marabi*. The Jazz Maniacs were one of the bands who were able to do this—perhaps partly because they were less adept "readers" than, say, the Merry Blackbirds, and were therefore in any case less tied to the printed orchestrations. Former Maniacs trumpeter, Ernest "Palm" Mocumi—himself once a *marabi* pianist—remembered that the band would still play the American charts "straight"; but that "when we played American music mixed with *marabi* style, [the audiences] used to be crazy over it"(6/2/84).

But the most fundamental identification of jazz with the Africanist impulse was yet to come. Between the early and mid-1940s, a number of bands began experimenting with the interaction of a set of musical components now being brought together for the first time. The most readily identifiable of these were the cyclical harmonic structure of *marabi*, a slow, heavy beat probably derived from the traditional (and basically Zulu) secular dance-style known as *indlamu*, and forms and instrumentation adapted from American swing. With these was combined a languorous and syncretic melodic style owing less to the contours of American jazz melody than to those of neo-traditional South African music. The result was nothing less than a new kind of jazz: its practitioners and supporters were eventually to call it African Jazz, or *mbaqanga*.[8]

It had been on the agenda since at least 1941—the year in which Walter Nhlapo expressed the hope that the bands "would play folklores in swing tempo." After all, he declared, "[o]ur folklores are jazzy in tempo, and only require one thing: arranging the brutish rhythm" (*BW* 11/22/41). Yet paradoxically it was this "brutish rhythm" that became one of the defining characteristics of the new style. In a recent interview, Doc Bikitsha—an eminent critic and lifelong observer of the jazz and vaudeville scene— summed this up acutely (11/24/86). In the early 1940s, he said, many black bands—among them the newly-formed Harlem Swingsters as well as the veteran Jazz Maniacs—started playing in what he termed an "African" stomp style: "We call it African stomp because there was this heavy beat. . . . There's more of the beat of Africa in it . . . the heavy beat of the African, the Zulu traditional. . . ." The rhythm of this stomp, as he demonstrated it, is immediately recognizable as the typical *indlamu* rhythm:

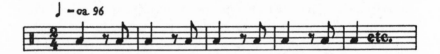

But it was former jazz pianist and composer, the late Todd Matshikiza, who in 1957 left the most evocative description of the new style. For him, what was of supreme importance about this music was that it represented the regeneration of *marabi*, the keyboard or guitar style of the slumyards, that had been on the wane for at least fifteen years. Todd claimed to have been party to its rebirth in a new form. A tour by the Harlem Swingsters had led them to the small Transvaal town of Potchefstroom; and it was there, in this citadel of white Afrikanerdom, that, ironically:

African Jazz was reborn. The original product "Marabi" had died when American swing took over. Gray [Mbau], Taai [Shomang], Gwigwi [Mrwebi], and I recaptured the wonderful mood over an elevating early breakfast of corn bread and black tea in the open air after a heavy drinking bout the previous evening. Gray put the corn bread aside and started blowing something on the five tone scale. We dropped our corn bread and got stuck into Gray's mood. And that is how some of the greatest and unsurpassed African Jazz classics were born. "E-Qonce," "E-Mtata," "Majuba," "Fish and Chips" were born out of that combination of the Harlem Swingsters whose passing remains today's greatest regret.

We invented "Majuba" jazz [as the style was called in a later variant] and gave jive strong competition. We syncopated and displaced accents and gave endless variety to our "native" rhythms. We were longing for the days of the Marabi piano, vital and live. Blues piano, ragtime piano, jazz band piano, swing and modern piano had taken it away from us. And here now we were seedling it again with new blood in its veins. It was [legendary *marabi* keyboard player] Tebejana's original material, but treated freshly with a dash of lime. (*Drum*, August 1957)

After such changes, things could not be the same again. The explicit and conscious acceptance of aspects of a social and political philosophy—in this case the New Africanism—into the very constitution of music, was a turning-point in the history of black South African jazz. Musically as much as socially, the early years of the 1940s were a time of transition. As if to mark and symbolize this transition, two events—each of extraordinary significance in its own right—coincide in February 1944. On February 13, the legendary Solomon "Zuluboy" Cele—former *marabi* pianist, and founder and leader of the Jazz Maniacs—is murdered in mysterious circumstances, and his body is placed across the railway tracks at Nancefield Station in Soweto. Nine days later, on February 24, and at a venue not far away, twelve people sign an attendance sheet as they gather for a small but important meeting. The sheet is headed "A.N.C. Youth League," and the occasion is its inaugural meeting; among the signatories are Nelson Mandela, Oliver Tambo, Walter Sisulu, Anton Lembede, and Jordan Ngubane.[9]

"Zuluboy" Cele was one of the greatest of the first generation of black South African jazz musicians and band-leaders. The ANC Youth League was the political manifestation of the New Africanism, a philosophy that, in turn, had already begun to have a powerful impact on the jazz and vaudeville subculture and on how it understood its social role. The coincidence of these events signals both the end of one era and the beginning of the next.

A JAPANESE STORY ABOUT JAZZ IN RUSSIA

Itsuki Hiroyuki's "Farewell, Moscow Gang"

—Michael Molasky

> Jazz fiction is uniquely American, and the jazz musician, its
> central character, is frequently a distinctively American exam-
> ple of alienated man: the artist as rebel.
>
> —RICHARD N. ALBERT,
> *From Blues to Bop: A Collection of Jazz Fiction*

As any self-respecting jazz buff knows, the Japanese have
long been among the world's most avid consumers of the music, be it
recorded or live. Top American musicians who couldn't *buy* a gig in New
York City during the late 1960s and 1970s traveled to Japan, where they were
invariably greeted with a full house and a reverential audience. During that
time, Tokyo alone was home to dozens of "jazz coffee houses," where, for the
price of a coffee, customers could sit for hours and listen to records from
jazz collections that sometimes numbered in the thousands (Atkins 2001;
Derschmidt 1998). Those jazz fans who bought their own records had access
to what are now considered classic recordings from Blue Note and other
labels, recordings that had long been out-of-print elsewhere in the world.

Japanese have not only been eager consumers of the music but, as
E. Taylor Atkins (2001) demonstrates, they have also been playing jazz since
the 1920s, and their music has ranged from slavishly imitative to strikingly
original. Yet the impact of jazz on Japan cannot be gauged solely by the
nation's consumption and production of the music itself, for jazz has
permeated a wide range of Japanese cultural forms, not the least of which is
literature.

When comparing the number of major literary figures in Japan and the
United States who have written about jazz—particularly from the 1960s
through the 1980s—one might well conclude that jazz has exerted a greater

impact on Japanese writers than on their American counterparts during this period. Poets such as Shiraishi Kazuko (b. 1931) attempted to infuse their poetic language with the rhythms and improvisational qualities of jazz, despite the formidable linguistic challenges of doing so. To this day, Shiraishi occasionally gives public readings of her poetry while accompanied by jazz musicians. And although fewer "jazz novels" have been written in Japanese than in English, many of Japan's leading novelists have paid deference to the music in their works of fiction and social criticism. Acclaimed writers such as Nakagami Kenji (1946–1992), Kurahashi Yumiko (b. 1935), and 1994 Nobel Prize winner Ōe Kenzaburō (b. 1935), have suggested that jazz was a significant force in their intellectual and ideological development. Several bestselling writers have directly stated that jazz has played a salient role in mediating their relationship to American culture, including Murakami Haruki (b. 1949, who ran a jazz bar before becoming a writer) and Murakami Ryū (b. 1952, no relation; he grew up near a large U.S. naval base not far from Nagasaki and has produced jazz CDs). Other popular writers who have written about jazz are Yamada Eimi (b. 1959), Kobayashi Nobuhiko (b. 1932), Ochiai Keiko (b. 1945), Tsutsui Yasutaka (b. 1934), and Itsuki Hiroyuki (b. 1932). Even Ishihara Shintarô (b. 1932), Tokyo's controversial mayor and coauthor of the book *The Japan That Can Say No*, first made his reputation during the mid-1950s as a writer of stories and film scripts, some of which used jazz—as a musical and countercultural icon—to portray a new breed of postwar Japanese youth as rebellious, sexually uninhibited, and thoroughly Americanized in both style and attitude. Among the aforementioned writers, Itsuki, Tsutsui, Nakagami, and Murakami Haruki are perhaps most closely associated with jazz in the Japanese public imagination, due to the number of popular or critically acclaimed works they have written on the subject. In this chapter I concentrate on writer Itsuki Hiroyuki and his debut story, "Farewell, Moscow Gang" ("Saraba Mosukuwa gurentai," 1966).

ITSUKI HIROYUKI

Itsuki Hiroyuki is one of postwar Japan's most popular writers. He has published dozens of books, many of them bestsellers. They include short story collections, multi-volume novels, essays, travel journals, studies of Buddhism, and personal memoirs. He has often appeared on Japanese television, both as a popular subject for interviews and as a narrator for a documentary program on the Hermitage Museum.

Itsuki was born into a middle-class home in the southern Japanese prefecture of Fukuoka in 1932. His mother and father were teachers, and shortly after his birth the family moved to Korea, which had been under Japanese colonial rule since 1910. He was attending a Japanese middle school in P'yŏngyang when Japan surrendered in 1945, and the region was placed under Soviet occupation. The living conditions were harsh for Japanese detainees, and Itsuki's mother died that same year. In 1946, with his father, younger brother and younger sister, he escaped to an American military base south of the 38th Parallel, where he remained until being repatriated to Japan in 1947. Itsuki has written about the stigma of being a "repatriated Japanese" (*hikiage-sha*)—those who returned from the battlefields or Japan's occupied Asian territories after the war. Yet this was not only a stigma but served as a source of strength later in life when, in times of tribulation, he reminded himself that he had survived far worse challenges at the war's end. Itsuki thus grew up as a Japanese citizen in colonial Korea, a child of the colonizers. At the end of the war, he found himself under Soviet occupation, only to escape to a defeated Japan under U.S. occupation. A stable, middle-class childhood, this was not.

In 1952, the year that the American occupation of Japan ended, Itsuki entered Waseda University in Tokyo, one of Japan's most prestigious universities, where he studied Russian literature. After six years he withdrew from the university without a degree and began working in a variety of media-related jobs. As a university student he had worked for a small trade newspaper serving the taxi industry. He later found jobs working in radio, writing lyrics for television commercial jingles, and then signed an exclusive contract as a lyricist for Japan's Crown Records, where he wrote the lyrics to over eighty songs, including many children's songs as well as Japanese popular songs aimed at adult audiences (see Imamura 1990; and Itsuki 1995). In 1965, he quit work and traveled through the Soviet Union and Northern Europe, returning the following year to his wife's hometown of Kanazawa, where he began his career as a fiction writer. His very first published story, "Farewell, Moscow Gang," discussed below, centered on jazz musicians. For this story Itsuki was awarded a New Writer's Prize, and for another story published the following year he received the Naoki Prize, which is the most famous Japanese literary prize awarded for works of "popular fiction." Itsuki quickly established a reputation as an accessible writer with enormous appeal, especially among Japan's youth. (It didn't hurt that he was considered to be quite handsome, in a casual, roguish way.) He continued to write successful stories about jazz, including "G.I. Blues" ("G.I. Burūsu," 1966), "Farewell, My Johnny" ("Umi o mite ita Jonii," 1967), and "Ragtime at Dawn" ("Yoake no ragutaimu," 1970). Despite the enormous popularity of Itsuki's work and his longevity as a bestselling writer, he has received scant attention from English-language translators and scholars.[1]

Japanese literary critics, who are especially fond of assigning writers to qualitative categories, refer to Itsuki's stories as *chūkan shōsetsu* (intermediary fiction), implying that his work falls somewhere in between "pure literature" (*junbungaku*) and "popular literature" (*taishū bungaku*). Itsuki himself, who is well-read in Russian literature, has repeatedly stated that his goal has been to write stories that can be enjoyed as "entertainment" (Itsuki 1982, 256).

Itsuki is known not only for his writing *about* jazz, but has been hailed by critics as among the few Japanese fiction writers who has effectively incorporated musical elements of jazz and blues into his literary style (Hiraoka 1976, 19; Kamiya 1974, 29; Komashaku 1977, 61–62; Mushiake 1976, 34; Saitô 1982, 259; Uekusa 1976, 38–40). Despite the prominence of jazz in his early work, Itsuki does not appear to have been especially knowledgeable about the music itself. In contrast to other postwar Japanese writers such as Tsutsui Yasutaka, Nakagami Kenji, and Murakami Haruki, jazz seems to have played a negligible role in the formation of Itsuki's thought and literature. It is revealing that in his memoir about the years preceding his literary debut, Itsuki hardly even mentions jazz. He does briefly discuss music (as opposed to his work as a lyricist) in the memoir, noting that "my idol at the time was Joan Baez." He also mistakenly attributes "The Girl From Ipanema" to composer Villa-Lobos, and finally notes that "I also listened a lot to Billie Holiday, having already decided to include her song, 'Strange Fruit,' in a story I was writing" (Itsuki 1995, 160–61).[2] The story he refers to is "Farewell, Moscow Gang," Itsuki's very first published work of fiction and among Japan's best-known jazz stories.

ITSUKI HIROYUKI'S "FAREWELL, MOSCOW GANG"

Itsuki published four stories in 1966, all of which centered on music, two of them ("Farewell, Moscow Gang" and "G.I. Blues") on jazz.[3] Both are first-person narratives involving a Japanese jazz pianist-turned-promoter (the narrator) who encounters a younger, foreign jazz musician. These two stories are similarly structured and are both imbued with deep sense of loss. They begin with a narrator who has already abandoned his life as a jazz musician (and thus, his dreams) for the workday world. He then encounters a younger, foreign musician, full of youthful idealism, through whom he vicariously regains his passion, only to see the young man carted off by the authorities, at which point both stories end. "G.I. Blues" is provocative in that the Japanese protagonist serves as a mentor to a young American jazz musician (thereby reversing the teacher-student relationship between the United States and Japan that was codified during the American occupation era), but I have confined my discussion below to "Farewell, Moscow Gang" not only because it is better known but because it launched Itsuki's enormously successful career.

The narrator-protagonist of "Farewell, Moscow Gang" is Mr. Kitami, a successful jazz pianist until quitting his performance career five years earlier. He now runs a music production company that arranges concerts and brings foreign jazz musicians to Japan. The story opens with Kitami on an airplane headed toward Moscow. He had recently run into an old college acquaintance who asked him to arrange a concert in the U.S.S.R. The concert, part of a Japanese-Soviet artist exchange program, would feature Japan's leading jazz musicians. Years ago, while still a struggling jazz musician himself, Kitami lived with a Russian woman in Japan, and he is therefore able to speak some Russian. Kitami is now taking his first trip to the U.S.S.R., to make preliminary arrangements for the concert. He is picked up at the airport by a young man named Shirase, who works for the Japanese Foreign Ministry and who was a big fan of Kitami during the pianist's heyday several years earlier. Shirase himself plays the clarinet and, although he is on the elite course for government bureaucrats and has little time for music, he brought the instrument with him to Moscow, reluctant to completely relinquish his own musical passion. Shirase takes Kitami to meet Danchenko, a large, pompous Russian cultural attaché responsible for approving the arrangements on the Soviet side for the concert. Danchenko promptly embarks on a half-hour monologue, then stands up to leave, pleased that they had such a "productive conversation." Kitami stops him and, having had no opportunity to squeeze in a word until now, asks what kind of jazz Danchenko envisions for the concert, explaining that it could range from a dance band to the avant-garde, from a small group to a big band. The Russian responds tersely:

"Jazz is jazz. That's all there is to it. Your job is simply to bring a jazz group from Japan, isn't that so? Right?"

"Huh?" I thought. Yes, jazz is jazz. There's no doubt about that. Maybe this guy isn't so bad, after all. But as Danchenko continued, it became clear that I was overestimating him.

"There's nothing to get so concerned about. If we were talking about *serious* music, well, that would be a different story."

"Are you saying jazz isn't serious music?" I asked.

"How shall I put it? In other words, stated simply, it's a type of entertainment."

The debate (an old debate about the cultural status of jazz) then moves to a new dimension as Danchenko sits down in front of a piano and, despite his thick fingers, delicately plays a Chopin composition. When he is finished, the Russian triumphantly pronounces, "This is real music. This is art." Kitami, of course, is not to be outdone:

Before I knew it, I was sitting down at the piano and playing the introduction to "Strange Fruit." A black man, lynched, hangs from a tree atop a hill. The body's silhouette, neck extended, sways back and forth in the twilight. It is a pathetic and eerie sight, a "strange fruit."

At that moment, for some reason, I recalled the bare, reddish-brown mountains of the Korean Peninsula as I stood on the deck of our boat and headed back to Japan after the war. Then I heard the squeaking noise of the rusty cart behind us as we traveled down the dusty road. It was a summer day. I was thirteen years old.

I never even thought about tempo or about which sections I should accent, nor did I search for the notes. The music simply came to me. Nervously, I let my fingers trace those sounds across the keys. I played the blues, shaking as if I had been stabbed in the back with a blade of cold steel. Time was fractured; it leapt over the past, and flowed through the crevices. The piano was singing on its own, as if it were part of my body. It was reverberating now with those sounds I had lost five years earlier.

I don't know when I stopped playing. Utterly exhausted, I stared blankly at my fingers, which rested on the keys. The room was silent, and light seeped through the window, forming a pattern of stripes on the floor.

"What's that piece called?" After a while, I heard Danchenko's voice behind me. "It's a Negro blues," I replied. "I wonder. . . . Is this serious music or merely the type of cheap entertainment that you would never permit at the Bolshoi Theater?"

I turned around and stared at Danchenko. And then, I was startled to see tears well up in the eyes of this obstinate man. He clearly was struggling to restrain his emotions.

"So, that's a type of jazz, is it?" he asked, taking out a handkerchief.

"Yes," I nodded.

Danchenko put his handkerchief away and silently walked to the door, standing for a while with his back toward me. Eventually, he straightened up and left the room. Then he suddenly wheeled around and said, "It's entertainment. See you again." (Itsuki 1982a, 32–34)

This scene is clearly intended to be one of the story's dramatic moments. The sudden shift in diction to a lyrical mode in the middle of the passage signals the intensified emotional impact of this moment for the narrator. Especially suggestive, yet perplexing, is the abrupt shift from the image of a lynching in America to the narrator's (and author's) memories of Korea at the war's end. The transition in the text is akin to the antiquated cinematic technique of the "dissolve," in which one scene breaks apart on screen and dissolves into another, usually signifying a relatively seamless change in place, time, or perspective. The story offers no elaboration of its meaning, and it remains unclear how to interpret this scene. Is Itsuki drawing a parallel between the white persecution of black Americans and Japan's colonial domination of Korea from 1910 to 1945? If so, it is but a fleeting analogy never pursued in the story. If indeed this is the implication, when the narrator mentions that he was just thirteen years old at that time, is he absolving himself of responsibility as a member of the colonizing populace and instead identifying with the victim?

Perhaps the key to "unlocking" the meaning of this passage lies in the sound that accompanies the visual image of Kitami's boat leaving Korea decades earlier. The squeaking of the rusty cart not only brings forth another visual image (of a dusty road) but returns the reader to the world of music, specifically to the "Negro blues." The forlorn sound of a rusty cart being pulled along an unpaved road, a boy returning to a childhood home that he has never known—this, Itsuki seems to imply, is the world of the blues. Understood in this way, the narrator's own tribulations as a boy give him special insight into an otherwise distant and distinctly African American musical expression. In other words, this brief passage establishes Kitami's qualifications to play the blues with emotional authenticity, an authenticity that even enables him to wrest tears from the stolid and arrogant Danchenko.

This interpretation is supported by two other passages, one that appears earlier and one later in the text. The first is an internal monologue in which Kitami recalls why he quit working as a professional musician:

I loved jazz too much. My fingers couldn't play the real sounds of the blues like they used to. Whatever it was inside me that enabled me to play real jazz had disappeared. Five years ago, at the end of summer, something broke down, and by the time I noticed, it was already covered in rust. (Itsuki 1982a, 16)

The reference to "rust" and to summer as an end of an era links this passage to the longer one above, implying that Kitami's lost connection to his past (summer) accounts for his inability (rust) to play the blues anymore—and the blues is repeatedly represented in this story as being the essence of jazz.

Kitami underscores this connection later in the story in answer to Shirase's question about why he gave up his jazz career:

"No reason in particular. Well, to tell the truth, I couldn't play anymore. The blues, I mean."
"Why?"
"I don't know. Probably because the world—no, my life—had changed so much. This may sound pretentious, but whatever it was that enabled me to play the blues had disappeared. And by the time I realized this, it was already too late." (Itsuki 1982, 36)

Kitami's trip to the U.S.S.R. thus offers the hope of reclaiming his past, both in terms of his music and those childhood memories that brought his music to life.

It is a young Russian delinquent named Misha who enables Kitami to once again savor his passionate commitment to jazz. Misha first approaches

Kitami on the street, asking him to sell any clothes he can spare, and Kitami soon takes a liking to the spunky teenager and his gang. It turns out that Misha plays jazz trumpet at a hole-in-the-wall restaurant where the boys hang out, and one night Kitami walks in while Misha is trying to impress the girls by shaking his hips and playing "St. Louis Blues" in "a nauseatingly saccharine tone" (Itsuki 1982a, 55). The ensuing melodramatic scene serves as the story's climactic "moment of truth."

"Misha! Stop!" I shouted in English. The boy's eyes opened wide in surprise, and he stopped playing. The room fell silent.

"Misha, don't play like that," I said, more quietly in English. "I said you could become a good player, but obviously I was wrong. What you were just playing isn't jazz. At least it's not the blues."

"Are you sayin' you're gonna teach me how to play the trumpet?" he sneered while tapping on the valves of his horn.

"Jazz is. . . ." I began to speak, but the words wouldn't come. Jazz is a way of life; you can't fake it. That's what I wanted to say. If you don't like to study, you don't have to go to school. If you don't want to work, you can decide not to eat. But just don't play like that. If you hate your mother, go ahead and hate her. If you're jealous of your brother, go ahead and be angry. But do it with your horn. That's what the blues are all about. O.K., Misha?

Yet I couldn't say any of it. That's what I was thinking, but, after all, who am I to be preaching about life? Still, I wanted to do *something*. I couldn't just sit there.

And, of course, he doesn't: Kitami rounds up a few musicians in the room to replace the lame band accompanying Misha. First, he calls up Bill, an American university student who plays bass. Then, he drags the closet clarinetist, Shirase, a Japanese Foreign Ministry bureaucrat, up on stage. Finally, he himself walks over to the piano player, taps him on the shoulder, and sits down at the keyboard—to Misha's astonishment since Kitami had never revealed that he could play. Kitami starts off with the straightforward solo chorus of "St. Louis Blues." The bass joins in, solid but unobtrusive, laying a foundation for the others, who follow one by one. Shirase is nervous and his tone tentative, but Kitami and Bill prod and encourage him, until his sound grows confident. Kitami's thoughts narrate the band's progress: "The music began to swing. It flowed. This was the birth of the blues. Alright! Yeah!"

The emotional temperature rises as each instrument joins in. Finally, Kitami signals to Misha, but "the boy bit his lip and shook his head. I nodded encouragement. C'mon. That's it!" Misha responds and blows his heart out for this final chorus. Although Kitami notes that the band's performance was "nothing special" (which seems disingenuous, following the laudatory two-page blow-by-blow), he does refer to it as "filled with a warm, bluesy feeling" (Itsuki 1982a, 57). For their part, the crowd is stunned into silence for a moment but then erupts into applause. Misha, ecstatic, jumps up and kisses Kitami on the cheek, and Misha's young girlfriend kisses him on the lips. Even Misha's older brother is instantly won over by the sounds he has just heard. His brother is a straightlaced university student and Comintern Youth member who has been worried about Misha's wayward tendencies and musical ambition. The force of the music, however, leads to a sudden but profound conversion, and he admits that he had been wrong in disapproving of Misha's musical pursuits.

Happy endings are not favored in Japanese literature, and Itsuki does not disappoint those readers expecting a less triumphant resolution to the story. The next day Kitami is informed that a Japanese politician who was to supply most of the funding for the cultural exchange has suddenly died. This leads to the cancellation of the entire project, and Kitami is ordered to return home immediately. Before leaving, however, he wants to say goodbye to Misha and heads for the racetrack where he and his gang often hang out. The gang spots Kitami and tells him that Misha has been arrested and put in prison. It seems that after Kitami left the restaurant the previous night, one of the unsavory black marketeers who hung around the restaurant had begun harassing Misha's girlfriend. Misha ended up pulling out a knife and stabbing him in the neck. The narrative ends at the race track, just after Kitami is told about Misha. "I turned around and looked at the stands. But all that I saw was thousands of unfamiliar faces. Then I stood up, turned my back to them, and walked out of the stands, alone" (Itsuki 1982a, 62).

Although "Farewell, Moscow Gang" may not seem compelling to today's English-language readers, it did help launch the career of one of the most popular writers in postwar Japan and remains among the best-known Japanese jazz stories. I wish to argue that part of the story's appeal seems to derive from its status as a fantasy in which Japan assumes authority over the two contemporary superpowers, the United States and Soviet Union. Japan's postwar writers tend to be deeply ambivalent in their attitude toward the United States, and such fantasies are by no means unusual in literary accounts of the occupation era (1945–1952), especially in the case of male authors who came of age during the occupation (Molasky 1999).

General Douglas MacArthur, who ruled over Japan during most of the occupation with the patronizing panache of a king, infamously remarked that if European and American societies were akin to a full-grown adult, then Japan was still at the developmental stage of a twelve-year-old boy. In this formulation, America was the teacher, and occupied Japan its eager pupil. This patronizing attitude permeated the occupation forces in their day-to-day encounters with Japan's occupied populace, so it should come as no surprise that Japanese authors who were, in fact, adolescent boys during MacArthur's reign would later write stories that involved a symbolic reversal of this relationship. When one recalls that Itsuki lived under both Soviet and American occupation following Japan's defeat, it is understandable that his fictional fantasies would extend to the Soviet Union as well. I do not wish to reduce this story to a mere fictional instance of authorial psychotherapy, but rather to emphasize that the particular fantasy articulated by Itsuki is part of a well-established Japanese literary discourse. Accordingly, "Farewell, Moscow Gang" is best understood not only as a Japanese jazz story from the 1960s but as a fictional fantasy of empowerment in response to the experience of Japan's defeat and ensuing foreign occupation.

These fantasies entail a reversal of the usual relationship between occupier and occupied, and this reversal is typically articulated in the following ways:

1) Teacher and pupil—As noted above, in "Farewell, Moscow Gang" it is a Japanese man who assumes the role of teacher, instructing an eager and grateful group of white boys about the essence of jazz, and teaching the arrogant Russian, Danchenko, about the power of the blues.
2) Linguistic mastery—At several points in the narrative, the author draws attention to Kitami's linguistic facility in English, which he uses not to ingratiate himself with those in power but to demonstrate his own knowledge

and authority. Kitami can also speak some Russian, which he learned from a Russian woman he lived with for three years during his early days as a musician.

3) Sexual mastery—Among the most prominent and humiliating images from the American occupation era for Japanese males was that of a Japanese woman clinging to the arms of a G.I. In this story, Kitami gets the prized white girl. Not only did he live with the Russian woman for several years, but when recalling their relationship he casually notes that she was constantly begging him for more sex. And when Misha's pretty girlfriend kisses Kitami on the mouth (as opposed to on the cheek), she further buttresses his virile image. Significantly, this virility is closely linked to his involvement with jazz. Kitami seems to have few such opportunities in his capacity as a music promoter.

The above points help explain how "Farewell, Moscow Gang" resonated with readers (especially men) of Itsuki's generation—not least of all with those publishers, critics, and literary prize committees who brought the work to the attention of a wide readership. Yet most of Itsuki's readers were of the generation born after the Asia-Pacific War, and they were less concerned with that war and the ensuing military occupation than with protesting against the 1960 Security Treaty and the Vietnam War.[4] Their anti-American protests were partly inspired by America's own counterculture and by the U.S. civil rights movement. Jazz—especially recorded jazz and the ubiquitous jazz coffee house—was arguably more integral to Japan's 1960s anti-establishment culture (if not to actual political movements) than it was in the United States at that time, and the image of the iconoclastic jazz musician had broad appeal among university students and other young Japanese, much as it did among the American Beat generation during the 1950s.

During the 1960s and throughout the 1970s, Japanese novelists typically represented jazz musicians as heroic, if tragic, social iconoclasts who pursued their artistic ideals and personal freedom (including sexual freedom) at the cost of financial security and social prestige. Like Jack Kerouac, John Clellon Holmes, and other American Beat writers from the 1950s, they represented jazz as the music of choice for aspiring artists and intellectuals with an anti-authoritarian bent. But as Jon Panish argues in his provocative study, *The Color of Jazz: Race and Representation in Post-war American Culture*, in the case of white American writers this often entailed appropriation of those very African American cultural icons for whom they professed such admiration:

> One of the principal ways black cultural values were transformed in their transmission through white texts was to ratchet up the significance of indi-vidualism. . . . Thus in Norman Mailer's "The White Negro" we get a revolu-tionary program, intended to change the structure of American society, that borrows significant elements from African American culture (or at least Mailer's perception of it) but completely eschews any connection to other Americans— based, for example, on racial or class solidarity—in favor of a radical individualism. (Panish 1997, 20)

In his discussion of Holmes's jazz novel, *The Horn*, Panish points out that the fictional white protagonists are placed "in a long line of alienated white youth who have turned to African American music for meaning" (Panish 1997, 90).

Panish argues in his book that when white writers represent black jazz musicians through the rhetoric of heroic alienation, they are appropriating and transforming a cultural figure understood among African Americans as an individual whose distinctive voice emerges in the adamantly *social* con-text of a musical dialogue. Houston Baker, Henry Louis Gates, and other scholars of African American literature have noted that this dialogical com-ponent is integral to a wide range of African American cultural practices, not least of which are the interrelated realms of music and literature (Baker 1984, Gates 1988).

Itsuki Hiroyuki may not know much about jazz. Certainly, his references to clarinets and to songs such as "Strange Fruit" and "St. Louis Blues" suggest that he was more familiar with swing and Dixieland than with the post-bop music that dominated the jazz coffee house scene in Japan during the mid-1960s.[5] Yet his representation of the improvisational process as a social act aligns him more closely with what Panish, Gates, and others claim is the dominant African American understanding of this music. The jam session with Misha is represented as dialogical, and the emotional intensity that it generates is a direct result of the musical conversation among the players. Kitami directs the conversation, but he is part of it as well—not an alienated genius, oblivious to the world around him and answering the call of his private muse.

I do not wish to imply that Itsuki Hiroyuki necessarily had greater insight into the process of jazz improvisation than did the white Beat writers such as Jack Kerouac (who was no great authority on jazz, either). Instead, I hope that the above discussion has effectively challenged Richard Albert's claim in the epigraph to this essay that "jazz fiction is uniquely American." For if Albert is correct, then "Japanese jazz fiction" is an oxymoron. If the language of jazz must be spoken in an American accent (or, specifically, in an "African American accent"), how can a Japanese ever hope to be more than a skilled mimic, fervently praying that his or her foreign "jazz accent" goes undetected? Atkins (2001) refers to this widespread dilemma in Japan's jazz world as the question of "authenticity," and, as he demonstrates, the obsession with authenticity leads to the insistent refrain, "But can Japanese really play jazz?" (11–12).

Few Japanese writers have confronted this question more directly in their fiction than has Itsuki Hiroyuki. Through his fictional character, Kitami, the author answers with a resounding "Yes!": Kitami is a Japanese musician who, based on his childhood experiences in colonial Korea, is able to understand the essence of jazz—namely, the blues. Kitami proves to his foreign pupils that Japanese musicians can indeed master the language of jazz. Yet those real-life Japanese jazz musicians working in the nation's clubs during the mid-1960s rarely experienced such a facile resolution to this persistent question; in fact, they continued to struggle with the question throughout the late 1960s and 1970s.

In the end, "Farewell, Moscow Gang" is more *symptomatic* of the quest for authenticity than it is an insightful analysis of the problem itself. The narrative's greatest value lies in its success at articulating a fantasy of cultural empowerment that resonated with a wide range of contemporary Japanese readers. As a Japanese story about jazz set in Russia, this is hardly a typical work of jazz fiction. It features just one American character, and he appears only in passing (although, as argued above, General MacArthur and America's occupation soldiers inform the nature of this narrative fantasy). Yet the very way this narrative functions as a fantasy of empowerment, combined with its ambivalent portrayal of interracial harmony through jazz, its swinging linguistic rhythms, and its romantic rejection of dominant social values all combine to make this a classic work of jazz fiction—if, that is, one abandons claims of an American cultural monopoly on the genre and admits the possibility that original and significant works of jazz fiction can emerge from outside the United States.

SWINGING DIFFERENCES

Reconstructed Identities in the Early Swedish
Jazz Age

—*Johan Fornäs*

When jazz was established in Sweden, it was used as an
emblematic symbol for the cultural breakthrough of high modernity, with
its newly established world dominance of the United States of America
and its crucial dependence upon African-American styles.[1] Its early reception in the 1920–1950 period inspired discourses on the modern transformations of identity and difference orders. Different hierarchizing values
clashed in distinguishing the high serious from the low popular, while
prevalent divisions between "us" and "them" were articulated, renegoti-
ated, and mobilized.

It is a common supposition that jazz came to Sweden as something
alien, imported directly from African America, and that it took decades to
finally assimilate and appreciate jazz as the worthy art form it always was. I
question this story. Jazz was never purely "black" but from the very beginning a hybrid genre, created in the encounter between Americans with
African and European roots, being first and foremost an effort to express
the modern feeling of life. It was at first entering Sweden via British versions. The most influential alien aspect of jazz in Sweden was not ultimately its race or ethnicity, but its modernity. And if jazz finally managed
to become an established art form at the price of losing its wide popularity,
this was no late acknowledgement of an originary creativity that other genres allegedly were missing, but a result of a series of elevating strategies.
There was an historical process of emergence, entry, exploration, excitement, and excess, vain efforts of expulsion followed instead by extension,
establishment, and elevation. This process was not driven by white Swedes
meeting, importing, and reproducing an African-American genre, but
rather by their encountering and trying to cope symbolically with *modernity*, of which jazz appeared to be the ultimate expression. This process

took place through a set of interacting discourses through which jazz was connected with race but also with other identity and difference orders.

The ethnic difference of jazz in relation to previously dominant popular music forms in Sweden was surely important, but may nevertheless not actually have been the primary cause behind its intensely though ambivalently charged reception. Its attraction built upon the fact that large groups of musicians and dancing listeners were at the time looking for difference, novelty, and surprise, and for cultural forms capable of expressing the new sensibilities and values of modern urban life. Being itself a multi-ethnic hybrid, developed from mixed roots by black and white musicians, audiences, and critics in the U.S. urban jungles, jazz was able to offer precisely that: the articulation of a modern structure of feelings. This particular modern newness was the important thing that attracted its fans and repelled the moral panics of its time.

A temporal difference between modernity and tradition, itself tending to connect to dimensions of age and generation, where the young came to stand for the new against the old, was acted out and reflected upon in terms of spatial, geocultural contrasts of "us" (white) and "them" (black). These interconnected dichotomies were in their turn mixed or articulated with and complexly projected upon polarities of class and gender as well. This dynamic process produced a flexible structure of crossing differences. The difference of jazz was a kind of key metaphor for the modern, the *new*, attracting and integrating a series of other dimensions of alterity. As a new form of popular music in Sweden, and as a cultural form engaged in aesthetically expressing modern urban life experiences, it repeatedly brought to the fore discussions of modernity. Both jazz-oriented song lyrics and talk or printed texts about this music repeatedly thematized a rupture between the new and the old. When jazz was mentioned, it was at least in the 1920s and 30s in connection with new trends and lifestyles, more than as an old folk or art tradition. These latter aspects grew in importance only after the Second World War.

Popular song lyrics, particularly around the mid 1930s, declared hot and swing to be the sound of the age, and novels about urban life regularly used jazz as a reliable sign of the new time feeling. Cultural essays repeatedly saw jazz as "the most immediate and spontaneous musical expression for its time" (Knut Brodin in *Tidsvittnen* 2/1935, 98), and as "a typical exponent for the new time spirit we experience today" (*Modern ungdom* 1/1936, 9). To depict a modern spirit was almost synonymous with understanding jazz. Hardly ever before or after has one musical style become such a widespread emblem for a whole epoch. Rock and later genres were certainly seen as symbols for new generations, but jazz was at least as much defined as the sound of its time—across generations! The "jazz age" was a considerably more common expression than the "rock age" or the "rap age" were ever to become.

However, the picture was perhaps not quite so straightforward. There were also primitivist efforts to connect back to a pre-modern origin. Both avant-garde authors and popular song texts at the time repeatedly joined explicit references to the absolute newness of jazz with associations to primitive and "childish" states of life. This recalls Walter Benjamin, who in his famous *Arcades Project* defines the modern as "the new in the context of what has always already been there" (Benjamin 1982/1999, 544). He argued that "precisely the modern, *la modernité*, is always citing primal history" (10). This happens in "images in the collective consciousness in which the old and the new interpenetrate;" "wish images" that in a "resolute effort to distance oneself from all that is antiquated—which includes however, the recent past—instead deflect the imagination (which is given impetus by the new) back upon the primal past" (4). These typically modern constellations of ultramodern and archaic were abundant both among aesthetic primitivists and in wider popular discourses between the two European wars. Not only modernist authors but also popular films and songs made similar efforts to bind jazz back to old and traditional practices and ways of life—though then not so much the foreign jungles but rather the rural meadows, forests, and mountains. The goals and effects differ between these examples, but they all tended to bring out something as new and therefore alien, while simultaneously incorporating and assimilating it by associations to something old and traditional. This is a key ambiguity in early jazz discourses.

Like all other epochal concepts, modernity is strongly related to the dimensions of *age* and *generation*. The young always seem to be close to the new. When times change, new generations arise, as the age categories are hit differently and have a diminishing ability to transform. This makes it no surprise that many texts talk of the new jazz fashions and the modern lifestyle as a rejuvenator, as something where living young people were particularly active, and as a dividing factor between past and future generations. At least, the reverse is almost impossible even to imagine. Old people were sometimes depicted as quite as modern as young ones, but the young were never depicted as *more* aesthetically conservative.

However, the age of youth seemed in this period not yet to have evolved into an obvious category of difference. Modern generations were sometimes depicted as carrying different lifestyles, but rarely in terms of age. When youth was mentioned, it was either as a phase of life that everyone passes through and will eventually remember with nostalgia, or in phrases like "young and old together." Expressions of an elaborated generational consciousness are strikingly absent. Such youthful self-consciousness did actually turn up around 1940, but not until rock music in the 1950s and '60s did this identity order seem to gain a more marked importance within popular discourses. Modernity was certainly always youthful, but still in a way that could in principle be shared by all ages.

SOCIAL AND CULTURAL LOWNESS

These discourses inevitably also activated the dimension of high and low, both in social and in cultural terms. While jazz was aligned with modernity and youth (though not always in any exclusionary manner), its links to class and to aesthetic taste hierarchies were more diffuse, and therefore also more debated. Jazz and other genres of popular music had a capacity for forging meeting places between the rich and the poor, in dance halls as well as in radio shows. Musicians and audiences came from diverse class backgrounds, and the jazz genre had its proponents and enemies at both ends of the social scale. When it was attacked, it was either seen as a luxury fad for spoiled dandies, or as a vulgar carnal pleasure for uneducated souls. I will not here go into further details on social class, but instead say some words about cultural taste values, well knowing that they are strongly though not totally related to each other.

Lots of criticism and even moral panics around jazz condemned it as a low culture. "Jazz is an awful infectious disease," and "the poor musician who 'jazzes' 7–8 hours a day will pretty soon lose his artistic capacity, and if he continues for long with this, he will infallibly become an idiot," wrote Hjalmar Meissner, chairman of the Swedish Musicians Union, in the journal *Scenen* (1921). A review of a Louis Armstrong concert, by the composer

Gösta Nystroem in the liberal paper *Göteborgs Handels-och Sjöfartstidning* (1933), argued this was not music at all: "It is an irritating rhythmic throbbing, which in its grotesque ugliness and eccentricity can never be enjoyable and hardly even fun to hear. It is and remains solely and exclusively a coarse instrumental roar." Cultural conservatives from right to left joined that choir, pushing jazz as far down as possible, preferably under the bottom line of civilized culture.

Jazz proponents also argued in terms of high and low. To sum up a very complex field, I propose four main positions, depending on how the new and the low were combined. Some tried to legitimate jazz by associating it with art music, while others instead argued that it was really popular music, but still at least as good or even better than the snobbish sphere of art music. In both these main camps, there were those who saw jazz as part of an old tradition (classical music in the first group, folk music in the second), while others instead emphasized its very newness (as aesthetic avant-gardism or as the latest entertainment fad). I call these four positions *art traditionalists, art modernists, popular traditionalists* and *popular modernists*.

Art traditionalists tried to legitimate jazz by inserting it into a classical canon, inspired by composers like Stravinsky, Milhaud, Gershwin, and Ellington. Art modernists instead preferred to develop jazz into an avant-garde practice, perhaps most clearly in bebop, cool, and free jazz from the late 1940s on. For them jazz was a means of modernizing art and pushing it to the edge of its time. They both joined in trying to escape the degradation of the popular and to get jazz established as a mature art form. This was in opposition to those pro-popular song lyrics and fans hailing the simple pleasures of jazz as widespread entertainment. Popular traditionalists were against high culture but saw the value of jazz primarily in its roots in black folk-cultural history, a position that evolved into the dixieland revival. Popular modernists—particularly strong in the swing era—instead affirmed the latest trends and fashions of the cultural industries, arguing for the right to have fun and follow the stream of time, against arty pretensions and any other boring old farts.

Historical development seems to have gone through some main phases. In the early 1920s, jazz was mainly a modern, popular fad. Towards 1930, some primitivists tried to insert it into a modernist aesthetics, thus elevating it from the sphere of pure entertainment. Artur Lundkvist and his literary circles regarded the more popular jazz styles "with the most profound contempt." His 1940s colleague Gustaf Rune Eriks "protested violently" against "vulgar musics" like the conventional "schlager," and critical voices were heard against the "banalization" and "decadence" of "commercialized" jazz forms. With the advent of swing and the rapidly increasing popularity of the genre in the later 1930s and until the end of the war, the popular modernism seemed again dominant. By the end of the 1940s, however, a deepening split appeared between traditionalist dixieland and modernist bebop. In the 1950s and '60s, this split continued with the decline of jazz as a widely popular genre as it simultaneously was established in concert halls and higher music education as a canonized art form, with its own history, field of criticism, and aesthetic values.

TRANSPOSED ETHNICITIES

It is easy to find openly racist condemnations of jazz throughout the period ending with the Second World War. When Louis Armstrong made his first Swedish concert tour in the autumn of 1933, virtually all reviews used racist arguments, including the one by Gösta Nystroem mentioned above: "Mr jazz-king and cannibal-offspring Louis Armstrong shows his clean-shaven hippopotamusphysiognomy . . ., bares his teeth, snuffles, raises one of the original howls of his wild Negro-African ancestors, now and then alternating with a grave-hoarse gorilla roar from the bush." And the journal of the musicians union, *Musikern*, continued: "Those musical madhouse scenes that were uncovered in Auditorium cannot be desirable phenomena in a cultural nation like Sweden, whereas they naturally are the order of the day for the Negroes in their respective native countries. Let us therefore cease to be bad jazz players and instead devote us to the music that fits ourselves and our cultivated people."

These were no mere ultra-reactionary exceptions, but rather examples of the standard reception of jazz concerts in the mainstream media at that time, from left to right on the political scale. Mainstream popular songs like "Friends of the Polka" ("Polkans vänner," 1940) also attacked "jazz and Negro swing." Similarly, many fans—including primitivist authors like Artur Lundkvist or black musicians themselves—used race arguments in their defense of this genre. They talked about African-Americans as having unique innate abilities to let the music swing, due to their vital connections to allegedly originary, primeval life forms. There is thus no doubt that jazz discourses were heavily coded in terms of race and ethnicity. But, as I have previously suggested, all these racial and ethnic discourses may well basically have been projections of fears that did not actually originate in the combined transcontinental encounters (Africa/America/Europe), even though they might have triggered such fears and gave them a symbolic direction.

African Americans were also far from the only ones involved in these processes. When race and ethnicity were actually thematized in Sweden, blackness was often transposed onto other ethnic differences. In the ad song "I've Got a Little Radiola" ("Jag har en liten Radiola," 1939, lyrics by Jokern a.k.a. Nils Perne), recorded for the twentieth anniversary of a radio company, the fifteen-year-old teen idol Alice Babs gave voice to a modern and youthful openness to the world:

> *I've got a little Radiola*
> *Which I tune in each evening.*
> *"A world in swingtime"*
> *right then is mine.*
> *What's grandfather's pianola*
> *Against the free-standing sound of our time?*
> *To Radiola a toast, live long*
> *And offer the rhythms!*
> *From Harlem's Negroes I hear:*
> *"Baladilidalandalaindudiledulida,"*
> *And London's coming, yes sir,*
> *With a little spleen.*
> *I've got a little Radiola*
> *And it means all to me.*
> *I go from Vienna to Berlin*
> *And from Paris to Tunis and back to you.*

The song can be heard as a celebration of cultural globalization through commodity flows and communication media, with America as the undisputed world vanguard. This opening of the world was all the more attractive as the approaching war actually fenced Sweden off from the surrounding world. It was increasingly hard to travel from Stockholm to New York, London, Vienna, Berlin, Paris, and Tunis, or to meet musicians and other people from there, but this absence of mobility could be compensated by a travel through radio, gramophone, and illustrated magazines. The longing for international contacts accumulated to explode after the end of the war, when the American lead also finally became definitely consolidated.

In the film *Jens Månsson in America*, comedy actor Edvard Persson sang a song called "Sweden-America Hand in Hand" ("Sverige-Amerika hand i hand," 1947, lyrics by Berco). It declared the United States to be more than "jitterbugging and gum-chewing or Hottentot-music," but rather also a country where "real men" worked "in farms and factories." Nylon stockings were okay "if there are Swedish race-legs in them" and the lyrics ended by inviting to "tie firm bonds of friendship" between the two nations that "complement each other very well." Here, a submission to the new U.S. world dominance went hand in hand with a reaffirmation of the kind of racial thinking that used to be associated with German Nazism. In the "Radiola" song, the meeting and hybridizing crossing between races and cultures is instead happily hailed, constructed as enabled by the globalizing commercial currents of the capitalist world order. Its exoticism is contained within a narrative of homecoming: she goes around the world but always ends by returning "back to you." This is a standard theme: most popular adventures start and end at home! In "Aviator Waltz" ("Flygarevalsen," 1927), the pilot travels across an unknown world but moves *from* the foreign shore *home* to his girl who is waiting by the hangar.

A striking detail is that Alice Babs hears the "Harlem Negroes" *yodel!* Her yodeling *might* be interpreted as a personal variant of scat-song, but more obviously connoted Swiss or Austrian Alps to the contemporary domestic audience. Central European mountains had long been familiar exotic ingredients in traditional entertainment, as in the old German "schlager" to which new swing tunes generally were a modern alternative. But Alice Babs and others combined yodel with swing, in songs like "The Yodeler Jazz" ("Joddlar-jazzen"), "Yodel Swing" ("Joddelswing") or "Yodel in Swing." Yodel plus jazz implied not only globalization but also a strategy to mediate and assimilate African American culture into a domestic context. Yodeling was easier to understand, and offered a much more familiar exoticism than trans-Atlantic scat-song.

Just like American urban jungles, the Swedish Alps had the advantage of hosting a distinct ethnic group: the *Sami*. "Lapps," as they were mostly called, did explicitly appear in jazzy tunes from the late 1930s, like "Wooji, Wooji, Wooj," recorded by Harry Brandelius (lyrics by Fritz Gustaf and Ernfrid Ahlin): "All Lapps around / stood singing something / when the Lapp taught them to dance swing." It must have felt easier within a Swedish horizon to depict Sami as those "happy natural children" with whom young urban Swedes liked to identify playfully during a wild evening of dancing. These "Nordic aborigines" were almost totally dominated by the Swedish majority culture and thus a less risky subject than were African Americans, while they could also serve as their less distant analogues. For native Swedes, references to "Lapps" could probably more easily be decoded as ironic images of themselves. The Sami were different but still more comparable to oneself than were the real Harlem inhabitants. Identifying oneself as a "Lapp" could serve as a way to emphasize natural and innocent sides of one's self. A later parallel was the "Rocking Sami" ("den rockande samen") Sven-Gösta Jonsson, with his hit "By the Foot of the Alp" ("Vid foten av fjället," 1959). With a rising awareness of the problems in Sweden's own dealings with domestic minorities, the "happy Lapp" theme has become as taboo within legitimate popular culture as was the "happy Negro" within 1930s jazz.

All this was simultaneously a method for formulating aspects within the "mainstream" Swedish self towards which these tunes were directed. Modern urban life promised to liberate white adult males and females from certain traditional restrictions and let them loose in a new consumption paradise of commercial entertainment. In this carnevalesque utopia, primeval, childish, and primitive levels of the self could again come to the fore, outside of the bounds of old aristocratic and bourgeois etiquette and self-restriction. The new life was not like the boring gray life that had recently passed to history, but the only way to depict this newness was by searching among older images, as Benjamin stated. The black jungle was one road for the aesthetic primitivists, but there were also other primitive roots to choose between. The Austrian yodelers and the joiking Sami were just two such examples. Others could be found everywhere in the rural countryside.

The word *jazz* was first used just to indicate wild dancing, irrespective of musical genre, as in the accordion folk-dance tune "Yokel Jazz"

("Bonnjazz," 1922). It was about a simple old farmer who played his accordion in a lively but unsophisticated manner. Here, the word *jazz* was connected to very old people in traditional settings, but with the intended effect to make their vital joy of living even more strikingly youthful and up-to-date. As the more specific meaning of jazz music was then gradually established, remnants of this more vague use of the term could later be utilized as a means of domesticating foreign jazz into something more familiar. This was partly a defense against the conservative attacks opposing it: partly a way to embrace it and make it one's own.

In tunes like "A Swing on the Grass" ("En swing i det gröna," 1939, lyrics by Sven Paddock), a rural romanticization of jazz assimilates it into a much more innocent traditional countryside culture of local dances for all age groups: "Johnny has said farewell to old-time dance. / He has rehearsed diligently every night, / therefore he has the best swing band in the area." Since most Swedes at that time had firm and still never broken ties to rural life, such a transposition was no pure nostalgic construction. It was as much a strategy to appropriate the music of the absent African Americans and find a place for some of its expressive tools within a local context. The nostalgic aspects were of course already there, and growing in importance as the old rural society gradually faded away, but in the beginning this was more than just nostalgia.

It is noteworthy that even when Swedish provinciality was unfavorably compared to American modernity, it was always painted with a satisfied tone. This is obvious in many of Povel Ramel's songs, including "Our Own Blue Hawaii" ("Vårt eget Blue Hawaii," 1942) or "Johansson's Boogie-Woogie Waltz" ("Johanssons boogie woogie vals," 1944). In the latter, the accordionist Johansson's son has brought a jazz record made in Harlem from the dance halls in Stockholm to his home in the dark rural forests. The father "changed the tune in genuine Swedish fashion" and it became a great hit—which was as true for Ramel's song, with its lovingly and ironically self-reflexive fusion of naive Swedish yokels and the mundane international pop of its time. The fusion is musically enacted through a wonderful amalgamation of rural Swedish waltz with boogie-woogie rhythms!

There are other intriguing images with ethnic dimensions. Trolls turn up as metaphors for nature in opposition to civilization, connected to rural country life and traditional folk tales, and thereby both to certain ethnic roots and to the "underclasses." After all, trolls or goblins are non-educated, horrifyingly dirty, and dark, they live in an underworld and sometimes work in the mountains or perform services for human beings. A popular song called "The Troll Jazz" ("Trolljazzen," 1934, lyrics by S. S. Wilson a.k.a. Anita Halldén) from the cartoon movie *The Taming of a Troll* (*Så tuktas ett troll*) depicts how thousands of trolls swarm forth from within a dark forest to dance some "rumba and jazz." The lazy ones who will not dance will be punished by having their tails tied up or by being "beaten black and blue." "Black and blue" is in Swedish characteristically enough expressed as "yellow and blue"—i.e., the same colors as in our national flag. These jazzing trolls are certainly more Swedish (yellow and blue) than African American (black and blue)—and they have a violently convincing manner of making all join their strange dance! Again, the black element of this "jazz" is hidden, but its combination with Latin American (and thus equally imported) "rumba" and with the sub-human hobgoblins themselves effectively betray an awareness that it is indeed something alien to civilized human beings.

Another popular Swedish folklore figure is Father Christmas or Santa Claus, who is associated with the more ancient brownie or puck, all sharing the Swedish name *tomte*. A Christmas radio medley from 1947 starts with telling to the melody of a traditional Christmas song about Father Christmas, "black as soot," coming with a boat from Harlem to sing a Christmas tree tune. This is then followed by a wild boppy scat-song, with further lines like: "See how the brownies are jazzing, swinging around in a ring / While a brownie band is playing a swing" (lyrics by Gunnar "Siljabloo" Nilson and Povel Ramel).

African American blackness was thus often translated into closer ethnic images like Swiss yodelers, Swedish Lapps, or plain rural nerds, or to mythical figures with a somewhat similar field of association. The effect was to find ways to express how jazz both connected to Swedish life experiences, and contrasted with them, and to assimilate the newness of modernity into the everyday. As this modernity was identified with America, including not least its African American undercurrent, the result was also to fuse white Sweden with black America: "From each curl to each toe I am figuratively speaking yellow and blue. . . . But I know an exception where there is nothing Swedish: / *Yes, yeah, yes* of course I mean *swing*! / I am certainly

Swedish but in every song I become immediately transformed: *One hundred per cent all American!*" (Povel Ramel in "One Hundred per Cent," 1944). The color of this identification was somewhat vague, which made this whole Ramel/Babs intervention double-edged. One possible direction from this universalistic denial of race difference could have been towards a radical alliance with African American culture. This was slowly realized in the more radical currents of the Swedish underground, but the dominant tendency was instead to follow the adverse direction where the effacement of race led to an uncritical acceptance of the dominance of the United States and its cultural exports. This could in fact reinforce rather than challenge white hegemony, as in the Edvard Persson film and tune mentioned above.

GENDERED ALTERITY

Blackness was also always gendered in highly stereotypical ways. The black and the female were repeatedly connected, in Sweden as elsewhere. Moral panics not only attacked "negro noises" but were also particularly sensitive towards the female transgressions of traditional norms that were fuelled by cultural modernization. Many popular songs satirized the cold, hard, self-centered new woman, who no longer cared for husband and home but instead dived into the consumption and entertainment pleasures offered by cities and media.

Those who in popular songs were addicted to excessive jazz dancing were almost invariably modern women. Suffice to mention a few lines from two typical revue hits by the famous Ernst Rolf (lyrics by Herr Dardanell a.k.a. Tor Bergström). First, "So Does the Old Girl" ("De gör gumman me," 1927): "Domesticity and home and hearth is a long past world / Away with femininity and motherhood, for equality and brotherhood. . . . / It is not easy, to be sure, to be born a man / these days when a woman has all that is expected from a guy." Similarly, "In Spare Moments" ("På lediga stunder," 1929):

The modern woman has been blamed these days,
Always in a state of entertainment intoxication.
She is fine and elegant, she is stylish and keen on dancing.
But cooking food and caring for home and house

She only does in small quiet moments,
When she's particularly inclined and in a good mood
[. . .]
She rather goes to jazz at the Moulin Rouge.
But staying in her home and bearing children
She only does in small quiet moments,
When she's particularly inclined and in a good mood.

A series of male literary authors with working-class backgrounds did not share quite such tame ideals, but they also had hard times accepting the increasing independence of modern women. Artur Lundkvist was a leading introducer of African American literature by authors such as Langston Hughes, and later became for many decades the grand old man of the Royal Swedish Academy that chooses the winners of the literary Nobel Prize. He wrote a series of jazz poems in the late 1920s, and wove jazz life into his novels. He also published the jazz essay quoted above, in an avant-garde literary magazine 1935. It was written together with a less famous co-author named Gunnar Eriksson, who had visited the New York jazz scene and brought home a pile of records.

Lundkvist and Eriksson incorporated jazz in a political and social-psychological critique and celebration of modernity. A combination of socialist and psychoanalytic influences made him develop a critique of civilization in which modernism used pre-modern inspiration to cure the maladies of modern life. Jazz was interpreted as a genuine expression of black experience, associated with deeply hidden inner drives, as the opposite of Western civilization and its over-rational subjectivity. They saw jazz as bearing "the stamp of the big city, technology, industrialism," while also emphasizing its "nature side, founded in elementary man." "Machine-song fuses with jungle cacophony, cries of jungle birds: the intricate union of civilization and primitivity" (Eriksson and Lundkvist 1935, 74ff). These formulations strangely echo those of the racist Armstrong reviews that underpinned the moral panic kind of hostility that was here turned upside down.

In a parallel manner, women were idealized as earth-bound pieces of nature. These authors connected both the black and the female to the body, nature, freedom, desire, enjoyment and leisure, implying a Self of the mind, culture, control, discipline, effectiveness, and work. In their writings, "Negroes" and women shared close bonds to nature and to repressed desires deeply within the unconscious, with which modern Western (male, white) civilization needed to reconnect in order to cure its own maladies. In my interview, Lundkvist was very fascinated by the eccentric bravery of his co-author: "Gunnar Eriksson . . . was a pronounced vitalist and eroto-maniac, and he more or less lived on women. He accomplished what I have never seen in Sweden before: he created a veritable harem, living in Gothenburg then, where he had three women who contributed to his maintenance." Lundkvist told me that he actually went out to discover primitivism, and see the race problems on the spot. The trip went to South Africa and was reported in a novel called *Negro Coast* (*Negerkust*, 1933), in which he expressed fascination with African women:

I fall in love with one of them, filled with her image, and I rave against the barrier, the impossible: that we can never reach each other, since we belong to different worlds. . . . I am born in civilization. . . . I belong to culture, I am trapped in it. . . . As contact with nature, as connection to the lost elementary, sexuality has always fascinated me and become my romance. I am a sexual romantic. I have come to live in a time of general sexual liberation, but that is a coincidence, I reside somewhere outside and seek something else: the prodi-gious. Something that bursts the narrow limitation of life. Something that liber-ates me from the ego, my old, petrified, worn ego, of which I am tired to the point of death. A bath in nature. A resurrection to a new life. A world as fresh as on the first day. And I have searched the elementary, the super-individual, in myself and in the woman. As individual I found the woman small and tiresome like myself; I searched her as an element. (116f)

A friend helps him to "get a girl," which then leads to a lyrical reflection upon this combined gender- and race-transgressing transaction: "We can-not talk to each other: our relation is therefore exclusively that of touch and instinctual correspondence. . . . We are representatives of two differ-ent, alien races, but we can meet in one single spot: the condition is the natural drive in our bodies and we are sound enough to temporarily be able to forget the social circumstances" (153). This ingenuous passage says much of how this supposedly radical and critical intellectual allowed him-self to construct an equation between female, black, and nature, and to treat them all as objects accessible for his supreme physical and mental manipulation, aimed solely and egoistically at curing his own civilisatory malady.

In dominating imaginations of Swedish culture, women, Negroes, yodelers, Lapps, and trolls were constructed as completely different, genuinely natural but also particularly responsive to temptations of modern popular culture. Playful identifications with them offered a temporary release from the burden of modern life and release of repressed desires through pre-modern identifications that was itself a typically modern strategy. The swinging, happy Lapp and the modern, free Woman were simultaneously ultra-modern and pre-modern impressionable slaves of modish styles as well as desired embodiments of a lost natural innocence. The interweaving self/other-constructions along different identity/difference-orders such as generation, gender and race were thus intimately related to a hierarchy of high versus low culture, as well as to a polarization of modernity versus tradition.

One of the rare Swedish tunes in which African Americans were actually described was the jazz composition "The Rose of Harlem" ("Harlems ros," 1934, lyrics by Sven Paddock):

> *She's always lived in a world*
> *With love trade and vanity.*
> *In bold types and neon signs,*
> *She has her name on Harlem's program.*
>
> *The eyes promise everything*
> *That the manager has commanded.*
> *She has given her life to a nightclub blues.*
> *She's called the rose of Harlem.*
> *[. . .]*
> *Each night in the Harlem stalls*
> *She catches hearts so easily.*
> *A Negro whispers to a sailor:*
> *"There you have the rose of Harlem!"*

This piece of sentimental social report is unique in my song material, even though it has counterparts among American films and novels. There is a clear ambivalence in how this female entertainer (who could have been inspired by the debated public image of Josephine Baker) is depicted. She uses her erotic powers to make the male customers her slaves—but only in the service of the nightclub manager whose slave *she* is. The depiction of women as both passive objects of male desire and active seducers of male victims was common in popular songs of the time, in particular when they were about *modern* women. A similar ambiguity was often attributed to popular artists in general. There was a long genre stereotype of male musicians and female vocalists (Billie Holiday is a famous case) who were victims of capitalist exploitation but also were ascribed a firm hold over their audiences. The African American as entertainer was also an old tradition, as was the association of mass culture with femininity. All this created a dense conflation of women, blacks, and popular culture, simultaneously despised and desired for being in particular close touch with modernity (see Hall 1992; and Schulze et al., 1993).

It is interesting to notice how this tune was received. The early appearances of the teenage singer Alice Babs in the film *Swing It, Schoolmaster!* (*Swing it, magistern!*, 1940) caused a rage among conservative critics in the press, who called her a "bitch" (*slyna*) and advised that "female swing vocalists ought to get spanked on their bottoms and be put in school." Those words came from Eric Westberg, who was head of the Swedish popular composers' copyright society STIM (equals the PRS in the UK). Her glad, active, and free appearance in the role of a jazz-singing teenage schoolgirl who after much resistance conquered people's hearts with her "natural" skill and innocence, immediately mobilized sexualizing responses that had to be balanced by moralistic condemnations. These responses can certainly be regarded as nasty samples of violent misogyny, but it is hard not also to notice their clearly erotic-sexual charge of an almost sado-masochistic kind, revealing a highly ambiguous desire-abjection play put in motion here.

Alice Babs continued her singing career, became friends with Duke Ellington and thus succeeded in following jazz as it ascended into the realm of high art. But in those early years, this was obviously coded as very popular music, low in the taste hierarchy and mainly defended by those whom I characterized earlier as popular modernists. As for "The Rose of Harlem" six years earlier, it was instead hailed by the leading jazz magazine *OJ* (*Orkesterjournalen*) as being "one of the best Swedish foxtrots that have ever been made in American style." This tune could be enlisted in the art modernist strategy for jazz recognition, due to the seriousness of the musicians and the context. The lyrics fitted that discourse better, since it after all also safely kept the black woman as a victim object, tempting but pitiful, whereas the Alice Babs tune without hesitation celebrated cultural flows and mixing.

AMBIVALENT POTENTIALS

Women were forced to remain pure objects in jazz, regarded as parallel to the sounds and the instruments rather than as creative mates. Entering the world of urban primitivism and taming its brute nature—whether it consisted of musical noises, the Woman or the inner subconscious savage within Man himself—was considered a truly manly task. This was however not quite so simple. Many good men "got lost" on this road, which meant that the step from macho androcentrism to androgynous feminization was never long. There was something "feminine" in abandoning oneself to emotive storms, to corporeal dancing, or to the aesthetic pleasures of style. This "danger" however made real females even more firmly shut out from all dominant positions within these cultural practices.

In spite of the very problematic aspects of those texts that intended to sympathize with the black but actually reproduced racist stereotypes, I do not want to erase the differences between these camps. A white primitivist was not the same as a white racist, and their texts had different social and cultural results. The self-criticism and mobility of the primitivist exoticists might after all have enabled learning processes in actual encounters with blacks and women, making possible a later rejection and at least partial deconstruction of the same cliches. Lundkvist traveled across the globe and encountered literature from all regions, so his stereotypical projections had different effects than those of his racist contemporaries, in spite of their clear parallels. Alice Babs was certainly no radical, but her affirmative opening towards a great variety of music allowed her to become close friends with Duke Ellington. An interviewed old swing fan met and was impressed by the black trumpeter and singer Valaida Snow as she visited Stockholm. Many also remembered female record saleswomen who were well-informed jazz sources for young kids in the 1930s.

Women and blacks thus had an effective presence in Sweden of the 1930s, not only as metaphorical projections but also as acting subjects.

There were instances of both social mingling and cultural hybridization between ethnicities, classes, and genders. Some were quite aware of the fact that we are "strangers to ourselves" (Kristeva 1988/1991). Nazis like Erik Walles, in the journal *The Swedish Folk Socialist* (*Den Svenske Folksocialisten*, 1941), named jazz "a disgusting crossbreeding of depraved Jew mentality and primitive Negro delight." As late as 1946, he published a pamphlet *Jazz Attacks* (*Jazzen anfaller*), in which he feared the spread of immorality by music born out of sex and drugs and Otherness: "You cannot understand jazz without acknowledging three significant facts concerning its origin. It has been created by Negroes. It has been created by drunken Negroes. It has been created by drunken Negroes in a brothel setting." The humorous Povel Ramel immediately replied in the song "Jazz Attacks" that same year, with a definite delight: "Jazz will celebrate a terrible victory: before you know it, you're a Negro!" Jazz provoked and invited a rethinking of identity and difference, along several dimensions. But the male Swedish jazz fan of 1946 would probably have been even more shocked had he been transformed into a woman!

BLACK INTERNATIONALE

Notes on the Chinese Jazz Age

—Andrew F. Jones

The domestic parochialism of much current jazz criticism betrays the resolute internationalism of early twentieth-century African-American critical thinking about the relations between culture and music. The black critic J. A. Rogers' "Jazz at Home," an essay anthologized in Alain Locke's epochal 1929 collection of voices from the Harlem Renaissance, *The New Negro*, is a fascinating case in point. Rogers' essay describes a dialectical movement that has haunted jazz criticism since its inception. Rogers locates the "primal" origins of jazz—"nobody's child of the levee and the city slum"—in the "joyous revolt" of African America against "sordidness and sorrow" (Rogers 1997, 216, 217). And it is precisely by virtue of this spirit, he continues, that jazz has become a globalized balm for the suffering and ennui of "modern machine-ridden and convention bound society" the world over. "Jazz," he writes, "is a marvel of paradox: too fundamentally human, at least as modern humanity goes, to be typically racial, too international to be characteristically national, too much abroad in the world to have a special home" (217).

While Rogers is ultimately unable to resolve this paradoxical movement between the primitive and modern, the native and the international, his intuitive sense of jazz's internationalism points the way toward a revisionist history of jazz in the interwar period, one in which a material account of the global mobility of the music figures as prominently as the frequently mythologizing and myopic narratives of its American origins that characterize so much jazz historiography. That mobility—and the unsettling questions it raises for the study of jazz and global culture in the early twentieth century—was brought home to me when I stumbled upon a dusty gramophone record in a Beijing antique stall in 2001. Entitled "Express Train" (Tebie kuaiche), written by a pioneering Chinese popular music composer named Li Jinhui, and performed by the most

225

famous chanteuse of the era, Zhou Xuan, the song satirizes the breathless pace of modern courtship by way of the story of a couple who are
engaged, marry, and have two children—all within five minutes after having first met![1]

The levity of the scenario belies the importance of the record as an
exceedingly rare material trace of the Chinese fusion of jazz, indigenous
folk melody, and Hollywood "screen songs" called "modern songs" (*shidai
qu*) that flourished in urban China (and particularly in the colonial treaty
port of Shanghai) between the late 1920s and the Communist revolution
in 1949.[2] Derided by its critics on both the socialist left and the nationalist right as "yellow" (or pornographic) music in the 1930s, and tainted by
its association with both the decadence of the Shanghai demimonde and
the hybrid colonial culture of its burgeoning middle classes, the music and
its makers were suppressed in the wake of the revolution (Jones 2001).
Zhou Xuan died under questionable circumstances in a mental asylum
during the Anti-Rightist campaign of 1957; Li Jinhui passed away in
prison at the height of the Cultural Revolution ten years later; and the
recorded legacy of the Shanghai era was either physically destroyed by Red
Guards or subject to disastrous neglect.

What astounded me about the record, however, was not so much its
survival as the musical style in which it was performed. The song begins
with a jazz orchestra delivering a wonderfully inventive rendition of a
train whistle, followed by the sound of a locomotive accelerating down the
tracks, and ends with the train whistling to a shuddering halt. The track
itself bounces jauntily along, propelled by chuffing drums, a duple meter
pounded out on piano, and Zhou Xuan's high-pitched and pentatonic
melodic line. The performance is immediately and undeniably reminiscent of Duke Ellington's "Daybreak Express," a December 1933 recording
lauded by critics for its innovative and "unmatched level of tonal impres-
sionism" (Gaines 2000, 591).

It would be tempting to ascribe the similarity of the two recordings to
the influence of American jazz, which had already begun to circulate
across the Pacific on imported gramophone records and the ocean liners
which carried American musicians to their engagements in high-class
Shanghai cabarets. Tempting—but not entirely accurate. Li Jinhui's song
was first published in 1928, and the record itself was probably released no

later than 1932, over a year before Ellington's groundbreaking effort.[3] In pointing out these dates, I am not arguing that Li Jinhui came first. Such a claim would be both unverifiable and analytically uninteresting. What I do want to assert, however, is that the functional simultaneity of this sort of musical innovation ought to signal to us the extent to which both composers were participating in a globalized musical idiom for which the speed of modern transport (trains and ocean-going vessels) and modern communications (gramophones, radio, cinema) were a fundamental condition of possibility. And interestingly enough, both songs go beyond mere mimesis; they are, instead, self-conscious attempts to represent those conditions in musical terms. Ellington's montage of "metallic variations of sound" (Boyer 1993, 224), sophisticated harmonic effects, and gutbucket vocalization was directly inspired by the band's peregrinations across the nation. The song's title, moreover, frames Ellington's own movements within the larger trajectory of a specifically African American modernity, one in which trains—associated with not only the Underground Railroad, but also migration to the urban North and the romance of the Pullman porter—were powerful "symbols of mobility and opportunity" (Gaines 2000, 591).

The Li Jinhui record is no less expressive of modernist montage aesthetics. First and foremost, Li's pentatonic foxtrot is a collage, composed of sonic fragments drawn from disparate musical traditions and temporalities. And Li's deliberate disjunction of these elements should alert us to the fact that just as Ellington concerns himself with an ineluctably African-American modernity, Li Jinhui's music emerges from a context in which modernity is inescapably tied up with colonial power. As I will discuss in more detail later, the emergence of jazz music in China was a direct result of colonial commerce in the treaty-port milieu. The transpacific traffic in gramophone records and Hollywood sound cinema was one factor, of course. Even more crucial, however, were the contributions of the Shanghai branches of transnational record corporations such as Pathé-EMI and RCA-Victor to the development of a domestic popular music industry in China. The new jazz idiom marketed by these companies, in turn, was bred in the notoriously off-color world of Shanghai's cabaret and dance hall culture. By the early 1930s, that world was vital and varied enough to sustain a sizable contingent of African-American performers from the

United States, Russian émigré musicians, Filipino and East Indian dance bands, aspiring Japanese jazzmen, as well as local Chinese musicians. Jazz in Shanghai was "too international" to belong to anyone in particular and too variously inflected to reflect any single stylistic mode (Rogers 1997, 217). It was less an achieved form than a complex set of musical, racial, and economic transactions conducted in the polyglot crucible of a multiply colonized metropolis.

In this essay, I set out not only to trace some of these transactions, but also to describe the ways in which "jazz" was understood and represented by the Chinese popular press, among serious music critics, and in the modernist fiction of this period. These depictions tend, at least superficially, to oscillate between precisely the same sets of terms—the African-American and the international, the local and the cosmopolitan, the primitive and the modern—that dominate the contemporaneous work of critics such as Rogers. Just as interesting as these affinities, however, are the ways in which the local deployment of these categories speak to the complexity of the colonial hierarchies through which jazz was refracted in Shanghai in particular, and China in general. For Chinese intellectuals dedicated to the creation of a national idiom based on the hegemonic norms of European concert music, a distaste for the "blackness" of jazz becomes a means of foregrounding Chinese aspirations for parity with the West. "Blackness," in other words, becomes an unacknowledged trope for China's own colonization. Similar displacements occur in the writing of a group of modernist writers dedicated to capturing, by way of jazz-inflected prose and literary montage, a sense of the speed, novelty, and cultural hybridity of the colonial metropolis (see Lee 1999, and Shih 2001). In the fiction of authors such as Mu Shiying and Hei Ying, jazz serves both as a stylish emblem of China's participation in the culture of global modernity, and a means of critiquing the colonial exploitation upon which that system feeds. That critique is effected in part through the figure of the black jazz musician, who becomes a proletarian specter haunting the temples of modern consumer culture to which these texts obsessively return. For detractors and enthusiasts alike, finally, jazz is seen not so much as a reified musical form, but rather as an overlapping set of distinctly modern ways of making and consuming music, ways that are intimately bound up with capitalist mobility and mechanization.

SHANGHAI EXPRESS

The ceaseless forward motion of modernity, of course, is what drives the satire of Li Jinhui's "Express Train." But it was also, in a very palpable sense, the very condition of possibility for the creation of such a record in the first place. Indeed, Li's new sinified jazz was the result of a complex convergence of colonial commerce and global migration that had been set in motion by the early years of the twentieth century, when agents of newly established record companies such as the Gramophone Company, Victor Talking Machine, and the Compagnie Phonographique Pathé-Freres first arrived in China, eager to establish offices in the Asian market as well as record examples of native music for manufacture in the metropoles (Gronow 1981; Jones 2001). By the 1930s, the Chinese record market had come to be dominated by Pathé Orient (itself a subsidiary of the much larger British conglomerate EMI) and, to a lesser extent RCA-Victor, both of which maintained recording and manufacturing facilities in Shanghai, and distributed their products (which ranged from traditional Chinese operatic genres to jazzy "modern songs") to customers throughout China and Southeast Asia. In addition, numerous specialty retailers and modern department stores sold Chinese popular music, imported dance numbers, Hollywood "screen songs," and Western classical music to eager listeners in Shanghai and other major cities, as well as mail order customers in the provinces.

The relationship of these entrepreneurial activities to the larger imperialist enterprise—one which saw the establishment of no fewer than 7000 foreign companies in China by 1918, many based in Shanghai (Spence 1990, 329)—is succinctly (if unintentionally) captured by Josef Von Sternberg's celebrated Marlene Dietrich vehicle, *Shanghai Express*. The film opened in one of Shanghai's many first-run cinemas in 1932, and its derisive tale of colonial adventure in a war-torn and hopelessly backward China was greeted with vociferous protests on the part of Chinese nationalists. The train in question is quite clearly both a symbol for and an agent of Western colonial domination: populated by an appropriately motley crew of British soldiers, American speculators, French missionaries, and a half-breed Chinese revolutionary whose dastardly plot to hijack the train is ultimately foiled, the locomotive is filmed (on a Hollywood stage set) steaming through an impossibly chaotic and congested byways, and is at one point even delayed by the presence of a sacred cow lying across the tracks. (Never mind that eastern China is not exactly known for the density of its Hindu population!) Midway through the film, Dietrich (playing an adventuress known only as Shanghai Lily) sets up a portable gramophone in her compartment, lights a cigarette, and dreamily places the needle on a record. The wail of a clarinet and the insistent hot jazz rhythms that emerge from the machine quickly merge with those of the train itself, and a close-up of the spinning phonograph record yields to a match shot of churning locomotive wheels. The mutual complicity of these technologies in the work of imperial domination could hardly be clearer: the gramophone and its alluring new culture of musical consumption quite literally ride into town on wheels of colonial steel.

BLACK SHANGHAI

The diversity of the multinational cast of characters composing Shanghai's jazz scene, however, far exceeded the narrow boundaries of a Hollywood soundstage. By the early 1930s, a small but vital African-American jazz community had been established in Shanghai, fueled by transpacific steamship lines (on which many musicians initially secured employment as entertainers and waiters [Atkins 2001, 53]) and the city's impressive array of nightclubs and cabarets. Indeed, as Langston Hughes noted in an account of his own 1933 visit to what he termed the "neon-lighted Dragon city of the East," Shanghai "seemed to have a weakness for American negro performers" (Hughes 1956, 251). Sources vary as to exactly how many American acts performed in Shanghai. Paul de Barros estimates that "scores" of American bands, including jazz orchestras led by the legendary Chicago pianist Teddy Weatherford, Buck Clayton (who went on to enduring fame in the Count Basie Orchestra upon his return from Asia), Earl Whaley, and Tommy Foy, either took up residence or passed through Shanghai on an Asian circuit that originated on the West Coast and included cities such as Kōbe, Yokohama, Nagasaki, Manila, Hong Kong, Singapore, Penang, Bombay, and Calcutta (de Barros 1993, 47). Even the musician S. James Staley, in a dispatch written from Shanghai to *Metronome* in 1936—debunking an earlier article praising Shanghai as a "Seventh Heaven for the jazz musician" (Lapham 1936, 39)—states that elegant clubs such as the Canidrome, the Lido, the Paradise, the

Ambassador, St. Anna's Ballroom, and the Casa Nova were supporting no fewer than six complete "all-American" orchestras by 1933 (Staley 1936, 17). The scene was well enough established, as both Hughes' and Buck Clayton's anecdotal accounts suggest, that many musicians brought their families along with them, and were even catered to by Chinese cooks who had mastered the art of "real soul food" (Clayton 1986, 67). This state of affairs persisted until 1937, when the outbreak of hostilities between Japan and China led to the ultimate dissolution of the community.[4]

ÉMIGRÉS AND ENTERTAINERS

Black musicians in Shanghai, while sometimes subject to racial harassment at the hands of their Euro-American compatriots, were also beneficiaries of the city's colonial hierarchy.[5] Their remuneration far exceeded that of the "Filipino bands, Russian bands, East Indian bands, and of course the oriental bands" who played jazz and other hybrid musics in lesser venues (Clayton 1986, 68). Indeed, Russian musicians played a pivotal role in the dissemination and indigenization of jazz music in China. While African-Americans seldom left the multinational confines of Shanghai's cabaret culture—an interesting exception being Clayton's stint at the relatively downmarket Casa Nova, where he was compelled to learn and play Chinese "modern songs" by the likes of Li Jinhui for local audiences (Clayton 1986, 76)—Russian bands dominated the Chinese club and hotel scene in cities as far-flung as Beijing (where no fewer than ten jazz orchestras were active as early as 1927 [Ke 1927, 20]), Tianjin, and the German colonial resort of Qingdao. Importantly, they also tended to play at Shanghai clubs such as the Lido and the Paramount, whose patronage was predominantly Chinese (Staley 1936, 17). Many of these musicians were czarist refugees who had flocked to émigré communities in both Shanghai and the northeastern city of Harbin in the wake of the Bolshevik revolution and then established themselves in the entertainment industry in the 1920s.[6] Oleg Lundstrem, a band leader who emerged as maverick proponent of Soviet jazz in the postwar years, is a representative example. Born in Siberia and raised in Harbin, Lundstrem learned his craft from Ellington and Louis Armstrong recordings, and had established a nine-piece orchestra with his brother Igor by 1936. Securing employment first in Harbin, then in Qingdao, and finally at Shanghai's Paramount, Lundstrem remained in Shanghai until the eve of the revolution in 1948, when he elected to repatriate to the Soviet Union.

Perhaps even more pivotal to the development of a distinctly Chinese jazz idiom were the contributions of the house band at the Pathé Orient studios in Shanghai, some of whom were classically trained "white" Russian and Jewish émigrés (see Wong 2000). Perhaps the most notable of these musicians was the composer Aaron Avshalomov (1895–1964), who grew up in northern China, and is noted for his efforts to incorporate elements of traditional Chinese musical aesthetics into European art music. Avshalomov directed the Pathé band alongside Chinese colleagues such as Li Jinguang (Li Jinhui's younger brother) until his departure from China for the United States in 1947, and in that capacity was responsible for many of the sophisticated arrangements still audible in the classic "modern songs" of the late 1930s and 1940s. Between 1939 and 1941, finally, an estimated fifteen to eighteen thousand Jewish refugees from Germany and Eastern Europe arrived in Shanghai, some of whom secured employment in the city's cabarets and its after-hours cafes as interpreters not only of jazz and Hollywood standards, but also klezmer and Hasidic music as well (Tang 1998, 8). One performer, violinist Eddy Weber, was famous for singing popular songs in ten different languages in order to cater to the diversity of his audiences (Tang 1998, 7).

The lowest levels of this multinational musical pyramid, however, were reserved for Filipino, Japanese, and Chinese popular musicians. By all accounts, Filipino musicians were quite common on the Asian steamship line and hotel circuit, a fact attributed by Staley to their excellence at "faking" (playing from charts) and their willingness to work at low wages in Shanghainese "dance mills" where songs were ground out "ruthlessly, with an inhuman disregard for the feelings of the unfortunate musician . . . bereft of any sort of labor union or society" (Staley 1936, 17). They were, in short, musical proletarians, relentlessly churning out product, usually in the taxi-dance halls (in which male patrons, having bought a clutch of dance tickets at the door, would redeem them by "hailing" the female taxi-dancers inside) that characterized the lower echelons of Shanghai nightlife. Dance halls sometimes employed local musicians as well, but it would have been highly unusual for Chinese musicians to work relatively prestigious nightclubs and hotel ballrooms.

The unspoken colonial politics of this sort of exclusion are made explicit by an interesting anecdote. When Li Jinhui was asked in 1935 by a prominent underworld figure to assemble an all-Chinese jazz band for the ballroom of the posh Yangtze River Hotel as a patriotic gesture, he deliberately hand-picked a group of "tall Northern Chinese so that they wouldn't be mistaken for Filipinos" (Li 1985, 240–41). Japanese musicians, finally, many of whom had been drawn to Shanghai because of its reputation as an adventurous Asian jazz mecca, also tended to command lower salaries and less respect, and often restricted themselves to working in cafés and cabarets catering to the Japanese community that had grown up in and around the Hongkew (Hongqiao) district (Atkins 2001, 85–90).

JAZZ IN PRINT
The extent to which musicians and entertainers of different national origins fraternized with each other is uncertain; there are few textual records and almost no oral histories of the period on which to rely. Buck Clayton, for one, was an enthusiastic (if by his own admission, sometimes uncomprehending) consumer of this musical multiplicity, and we know that he also took pains to learn and transcribe Chinese popular songs (Clayton 1986, 68–69, 76). What is clear, however, is that this dense underbrush of musical cultures, fertilized by the ready availability of gramophone records from all over the world, was the necessary breeding ground for the (sadly fragmentary) recorded legacy of this period. That legacy, of which Li Jinhui's "Express Train" is only one example, reveals in aggregate an urban music of almost stunning stylistic variety: Hawaiian steel guitar embellishing melodies drawn from the surrounding southeastern Chinese countryside, Soviet-style accordion accompanied by Chinese clappers, scat singing crossed with the melismatic vocal production typical of late Qing dynasty courtesan houses. There are blues vamps, Cuban rhythms, and episodes of New Orleans-style polyphony as well as European waltzes. Some of the orchestral arrangements produced in the Pathé studios, finally, are redolent of both Hollywood screen songs and the "sweet music" of major American figures such as Paul Whiteman and Bing Crosby (see CD accompanying Wong 2000).

What united these disparate musical practices under the sign of "jazz" was not only their participation in an irrevocably globalized commercial culture, but also the way they were understood by contemporary listeners. As Nicholas Evans reminds us, "discourses about jazz can never be separated from jazz music, for they impact the way we experience the music's sounds" (Evans 2000, 21). For the remainder of the essay, I discuss the ways in which jazz in China—as an intellectual category, a socio-cultural phenomenon, and a site for ideological contention—was also a product of discursive transactions conducted in the vibrant print culture of the period. I begin the discussion with an introductory article which appeared in 1932 in what was then China's premier general interest magazine, the *Eastern Miscellany* (Dongfang zazhi). Titled "Jazz Music is All the Rage the World Over," and translated from an English text by the progressive Italian composer Alfred Casella, the piece is quite literally a discursive transaction in which the translator's introduction frames and quite openly contradicts Casella's eloquent defense of the artistic value of popular and folk forms for Chinese readers. Whereas Casella lauds jazz as a worthy successor to Beethoven in its "total lyricism" and ability to "represent the spirit of modern art" (Casella 1932, 94), the interests of the translator, Anna, lie elsewhere. Her introduction begins with an orthographic bang, energetically invoking the English word for "jazz!" rather than its Chinese transliteration: "Jazz! Jazz! A freak of modern times. Even in our own Chinese cities you hear its decadent and infectious melodies wherever you go. Jazz was originally the music black people in America played in the jungle, yet it has now become a fashionable commodity circulating among civilized humanity" (Casella 1932, 93).

What is immediately apparent here is the way in which Anna rehearses familiar binary oppositions: between the primitive and the emphatically modern, between the jungle and the global. The invocation of the "infectious" quality of jazz also partakes of the "figurations of contagion" which Radano (2000) has linked to the construction of racial difference in nineteenth- and early twentieth-century American discourse on music (474). But the distressing similarity of this account to the "primitivist myth" of early jazz criticism (Gioia 1988, 19) should not blind us to the significance of its deployment in this particular time and locale. For what is being positioned here is not so much jazz as China itself.[7] The appearance of the phrase "civilized humanity" (*wenming renlei*)—and China's implicit inclusion in this category by virtue of the ubiquity of jazz within its borders—is key to this rhetoric. The discourse of *wenming* in China has its historical roots in the late nineteenth-century encounter with the Imperial West, a West whose success in colonizing an as yet "backward" China was often imputed by reformist intellectuals to the cultural superiority of "civilized" nations such as Britain, France, and the United States. What we witness here, then, is a form of rhetorical decolonization effected by way of China's implicit inclusion in a modern circuit of civilized commodity consumption. Blackness becomes a kind of rhetorical sleight of hand which functions to include China in the company of colonizers rather than the colonized. This inclusion, in turn, necessitates a parallel exclusion (and recolonization): jazz is relegated to the realm of the primitive, to a "jungle" space which can only exist at the margins of culture and outside of history.

"PITIFUL JAZZ"

The hostility to jazz implied by Anna's bemused tone ("a freak of modern times") is amplified many times over in the writings of many serious music critics and educators of this period. This generation of music professionals, many of whom were trained abroad and committed to the modernization of Chinese musical life along Western lines, shared a common faith in the "evolutionary" superiority of European concert music vis-a-vis traditional musical forms (Jones 2001, 21–52). For these reformers, Chinese music came to be seen primarily in terms of what it lacked (functional harmony, equal temperament, standardized notation, counterpoint), and they advocated its wholesale supplantation by Western modes of musical education and practice (with allowances made for the retention of local tone color and the occasional pentatonic marker of national identity). As I have discussed elsewhere in great detail, adherents to this particular vision of musical probity led the charge against Li Jinhui's attempts to fuse Chinese folk music with American jazz (Jones 2001, 114–19), a form which the influential founder of the Shanghai Conservatory of Music, Xiao Youmei, succinctly summed up as "a bad kind of Western music" (Xiao 1934, 13). Indeed, Li Jinhui's music, castigated for its ostensible decadence and indiscipline, was banned (if only ineffectually) by the ruling Nationalist Party in 1934, and repeatedly came under attack from the socialist left because of its association with the colonial, petit-bourgeois culture of urban Shanghai.

Music educators were equally outraged by both the imprecations of American popular musicians against classical standards of musical propriety, and the frank commercialism of the popular music industry. A 1934 article called "Pitiful Jazz" by Ou Manlang, a critic associated with the Canton Conservatory of Music, is an illuminating case in point. Ou ascribes the rise of jazz to the empty materialism of American life, likening its temporary triumph over "pure music" to one of the magical, if illusory, transformations wrought by the simian trickster Sun Wukong in the beloved Ming dynasty adventure novel, *Journey to the West* (Ou 1934, 1). Beethoven, Schubert, and Chopin are similarly naturalized, for rather than turning in their graves upon being informed of having been "jazzed," they gnash their teeth in the Chinese purgatory "beneath the Nine Springs." This vein of humor is mined further when Ou, mocking the impurities of tone deliberately introduced into the music by jazzmen, disingenuously suggests that if "having come to China, [one of them] came to realize the benefits of using our domestically manufactured ceramic chamber pots or wooden toilet seats as mutes for their trombones or trumpets, they would be sure to find imitators back home in America." But perhaps the most telling moment of the essay is when Ou discusses what he sees as the deficiencies of untutored jazz vocalists: "Their lack of vocal substance, the unloveliness of their voices, the unctuous quality of their crooning are reminiscent of the masters of Cantonese opera, who these days not only make me nauseous, but give me a headache as well" (1). The rhetorical interchangeability of the indigenous and the global here is precisely what enables Ou himself to rise above the fray, identifying himself neither as Chinese, nor with a modern West already degraded by commercial considerations, but instead with the apparently timeless and universal values of an idealized Romantic past.

The contemporaneous writings of the Taiwanese-born scholar and composer Ke Zhenghe (1889–1979) are a refreshing counterpoint to this sort of critical venom. In a series of articles introducing jazz and dance music to Chinese readers in the late 1920s and early 1930s, Ke attributes the worldwide popularity of jazz to the innovative practices of mass musical production developed in Hollywood and Tin Pan Alley, as well as the global reach of their global distribution networks (Ke 1932, 1–2). Unlike Ou Manlang, who attributes the popularity of jazz to "the infection of rhythm" (Ou 1934, 2), Ke Zhenghe posits the existence of an "industrial organization" composed of "jazz composers, performers, music publishers, and dance instructors" jointly dedicated to the mechanized production of the music. Ke is also astute enough to realize that what this industry produces is not only the music itself, but also an urban culture centered around the consumption of style, and it is for this reason that he also includes "café managers and waiters, cosmeticians, tailors, shoe stores, and beauty salons" as cogs in this industrial mechanism (Ke 1932, 1). While Ke's historical objectivity is sometimes called into question—he credits an apparently apocryphal "Charleston Promotion Corporation" with the rise of the Charleston from humble origins in African-American South Carolina to global sensation (Ke 1932, 2)—his multifaceted emphasis on the material aspects of the production of the music is nonetheless instructive.

FROM PRIMITIVE TO PROLETARIAN

In much of the modernist literature produced in Shanghai in the late 1920s and early 1930s, however, it is the consumption rather than the production of jazz that becomes a favored means of signifying Shanghai's colonial modernity. Influenced by Japanese avant-garde and proletarian fiction (Kawabata Yasunari, Kataoka Teppei), European and American modernism (Paul Morand, John DosPassos), and dedicated to representing the exhilarating speed, commodity-driven alienation, and exotic cultural multiplicity of their immediate urban surroundings, writers of what has come to be known as New Sensationist fiction (*Xin ganjue pai xiaoshuo*) return almost obsessively to a space which seemed to best exemplify these prototypically modern conditions: the jazz dancehall. In a technologized idiom that exploits the novel possibilities of cinematic form (montage, close-ups, narrative cross-cutting) and endeavors through synaesthesia and fractured syntax to convey an unmediated and fragmentary sense of the experience of the city, the works of authors such as Liu Na'ou, Mu Shiying, and Hei Ying often follow fashionable "modern boys" as they pursue desirable "modern girls" through the streets, cafés, and cabarets of the International Settlement. As Shu-mei Shih has argued, these women often function as stand-ins for the thoroughly fetishized and commodified "seductions" of the city itself (Shih 2001, 292), seductions

which are at once material (Hollywood cinema, sex, brand name cigarettes, coffee, liquor, late-model automobiles) and spiritual (the allure of
aesthetic experimentation and cosmopolitan philosophical *flânerie*).[8]

Not surprisingly, then, this brand of fiction sometimes elicited the dis-
pleasure of leftist critics committed to an agenda of anti-colonial and anti-
capitalist critique (Shih 2001, 264–65). And indeed, the self-consciously
syncopated prose with which these authors portray the sensual abandon
of the dance hall world is often merely celebratory. A story entitled "Games"
(Youxi) by the Japanese-educated New Sensationist and film critic Liu
Na'ou (1900–1939) begins in just such a mode:

> Everything here in this Tango Palace is in melodic motion—male and female
> limbs, colored lights and glowing drinks, red and green liquids enfolded by
> slender fingers, lips the color of persimmon, smoldering eyes. The lustrous cen-
> ter of the dance floor mirrors the tables and chairs and the tangled tableaux of
> the people around its perimeters, so that it seems one is inside an enchanted
> palace and one's soul has come under the influence of a powerful spell. Amidst
> this scene, the most delicate and agile movements are those of the white-jacketed
> waiters, who flit from here to there with the liveliness of butterflies among blos-
> soms, without a trace of coarseness. . . .
>   . . . Suddenly the air shudders with a wave of music, and a startling cry begins
> to sound. A musician in the middle of the bandstand holds that demon of jazz,
> the saxophone, and begins to blow crazily toward the crowd. And with that
> comes the palpitating cries of cymbals, drums, piano, strings. This is Black
> African memory, the sacrificial rite before the hunt, a rumble of blood in the
> veins, the discovery of the primitive, cymbals, drums, piano, strings, boom
> chucka chucka boom. . . .
>   And with the music his recent melancholy is cast beyond the clouds.
>   "Let's dance!" (Liu 1930, 3–6)

What kind of ideological work does such an evocation achieve?
Through a series of interesting displacements, Liu's reiteration of the
primitivist myth—by which the melancholia of modern civilization is cast
off by way of the liberating energies of primal African "savagery"—serves
to validate the ethos of capitalist modernity. Consumption is celebrated as
a series of aestheticized "tableaux," labor is assimilated to the realm of the
pastoral ("butterflies among blossoms"), while the savagery of economic
competition ("the hunt") is banished to a timeless and distant world of

African memory. The world of the Tango Palace itself, finally, also represents a kind of displacement. This is a space without geographical specificity, a temple to the enchantments of a globally circulating culture that is everywhere and nowhere, a space which ultimately signifies Shanghai's cosmopolitanism, that is, its functional equivalence with the world of the colonial metropole.

Not all of the New Sensationists are quite as sanguine in their invocation of black music as a figure for modernity. The work of colleagues such as Mu Shiying (1912–1940) and Hei Ying are also densely populated with black musicians. Indeed, jazz musicians in these tales are exclusively black, and almost invariably subject to miserable mistreatment at the hands of the clubs where they work. These representations, of course, fly in the face of what we know to be true of the Shanghai jazz world, in which African-Americans were not only outnumbered by Russians, Filipinos, and other Asians, but also better paid. To what can we attribute this rather anxious insistence on the blackness of these fictional figures? One illuminating example of the uses of racialized representation can be found in Mu Shiying's 1932 story "Five in a Nightclub" (Wuge ren zai yezonghui li). Mu, whose first collection of short stories, *Poles Apart* (Nanbei ji), was an exercise in the application of Marxist class analysis to the urban-rural divide in Chinese life, focuses here on the intersecting lives of five urban Chinese (a stock speculator, a socialite, a professor, a college student, and a bureaucrat), each of whom has been driven more or less to ruin by the cruel exigencies of capital, as they encounter one another one Saturday night at the Empress Nightclub. This exotic space is described by way of a series of binary oppositions:

Tablecloths: white linen, white linen, white linen—whiteness. . . .
   On the white tablecloths: dark beer and black coffee—blackness, blackness. . . .
   By the white tablecloths sit men in formal evening wear: strata of black and white: black hair, white faces, black eyes, white collars, black bow ties, white starched shirts, black jackets, white vests, black pants . . . black and white. . . .
   Beyond the tablecloths stand the waiters in their white suits and black caps. Black piping runs down their white pants. . . .
   White man's joy, black man's misery. Music of the cannibal rituals of Africa; the loud thunder and low rumble of drums, the wa-wa wail of a trumpet, and in

the center of the dance floor a row of hard luck Slavic princesses performing the black man's tap dance; scores of white legs kick below black-clad trunks:
Got-got-got-got-got-cha!
More strata of black and white! . . . Everyone contracts this malaria! Malarial music! There are poisonous mosquitoes in the jungles of Africa. (Mu 1932, 75–76)

As William Schaefer (2003) has pointed out, Mu's racist conflation of "African Americans with black Africans under the sign of the savage" is an all too common characteristic not only of New Sensationist texts, but also of the global mass culture of this era. Perhaps even more significant here is what is missing from Mu Shiying's reiteration of such representations. Throughout Mu's breathless recital of racial signifiers—during which racial injustice and colonial inequality are simultaneously critiqued and reproduced—fragments of blackness and whiteness construct an unsettled, oscillating sense of space, and yet "Chineseness" as such is never foregrounded. What remains unspoken and implicit is this: in the "jungles" of Shanghai, no one (and not least the Chinese spectators of such dazzling scenes) is immune from the "malaria" of racialized ways of thinking, seeing, and listening.

This plot thickens when our cast of affluent Chinese club-goers are shown to fraternize with the band's drummer, a man named Johnny whose "black misery" is made complete when he is denied permission by the club manager to leave his post and look after his pregnant wife at home. The child is stillborn, his wife falls into a coma, and yet Johnny is still forced to mount the bandstand and rally the assembled revelers ("Cheer up, ladies and gentlemen") for one last round of frenzied dancing. What this awkward and rather cruelly contrived subplot seems to suggest, of course, is another displacement, one in which blackness becomes a pathetic figure for proletarian abjection. Johnny, that is, shadows the brilliantly neon-lit world of the cabaret, disclosing the economic exploitation upon which its fevered consumption is predicated.

"SHANGHAI SONATA"
Nor is Mu Shiying's the only instance of this particular textual strategy in the literature of the period. In the fiction of Hei Ying

(Zhang Bingwen, 1915–?)—a New Sensationist prodigy whose intriguing pen name, "Black Baby," seems to play on both on his boyhood in Indonesia and his obvious affinity for jazz culture—we see an even more explicit deployment of the black musician as a displaced figure of colonial power and capitalist exploitation. Hei Ying's first short story collection, *Daughter of Empire* (Diguo de nu'er), published in 1934 at the age of eighteen, is saturated with the varied sounds that collectively composed Shanghai's dance hall culture: blues, Hawaiian steel guitar, Hollywood screen songs, Cuban mambo, foxtrots, the waltz. Indeed, the very words that describe these genres, rendered in English, rise like exotic isles from the surrounding sea of Chinese characters. The thrilling "otherness" of this archipelago of sounds notwithstanding, Hei Ying alone among Shanghai modernists never succumbs to the "primitivist myth" and its racially stereotyped rhetorical gestures. His depictions of the dance hall world, although tinged with modernist touches, are often grittily realistic, and evince a naturalistic interest in the varied ethnic groups and social types who fill the polyglot space of the aptly named Ambassador Dancehall:

Jazz tunes, Cuban love songs, yes, and so many men and women dancing, dancing. The smell of alcohol, the reek of tobacco, that mixes with the scent wafting from women's bodies. A bank manager holds the yielding waist of his mistress, sentimental taxi-dancers pinch the cheeks of a pretty pale-faced teenager. There's a mob of college students in one corner, faces contorted in merriment; one slip and the black coffee spilled all over someone's shirt. Fat, sharp, triangular, and thin: hundreds of laughing faces. The eyes of the taxi-dancers enchant. Eyes and more eyes, slanted eyes, eyes the shape of longan fruits in the South. Blue jewels adorning someone's head, a row of them, cutting across the dancefloor, emitting a blue glow. The mingled sounds of Shanghai-nese, Cantonese, Russian . . . and only if you lean close to someone's ear can you make yourself heard. (Hei 1934, 143)

What Hei Ying endeavors to make heard above this international Babel of sounds and voices is his own "Shanghai Sonata" (as this particular novella is titled)—a sonata in which the contrapuntal colonial power relations informing even the most mundane activities in the metropolis are rendered painfully clear. At the Ambassador, even the "tables are as neatly arrayed as imperial armies, row after row" (162).

The novella follows the fortunes of one Wang Ke, a naive young man who comes to Shanghai from the provinces and is both seduced and repelled by the cosmopolitan pleasures of its consumer culture. Indeed, upon Wang Ke's entrance into town, which not incidentally takes place aboard an express train, he is literally consumed by the city: "Ahead of [the train] was Shanghai. The maw of this brilliant and exotic metropolis opened in a smile, and soon they would all be swallowed. . . ." (Hei 1934, 133) Wang Ke soon takes up with a group of modish young clubgoers and becomes a regular at the Ambassador, where he encounters and befriends Benny, a saxophonist who seems to represent a self-conscious attempt on Hei Ying's part to steal some of Mu Shiying's black fire. Like Johnny, Benny is a victim of the capitalist mechanization of musical life whose misery serves as a pointed reminder of the decadence of the dance hall:

Blowing, blowing, blowing that tune which plays on men's souls. Benny stretched out his neck yesterday, was stretching out his neck today, song after song, until he'd blown all the wind from his belly, and yet blow he must, stretch out his neck he must, until the break of dawn.

Blowing, blowing, until the tears came to his eyes. The crowd was smiling so happily as they waltzed, and yet he had a sick wife at home to whom he was unable to return. Poor lonely Sally! Blowing, blowing, blowing a downhearted tune: *Sally, I love you! But I leave you alone!* (Hei 1934, 144; italicized portions originally in English)

Benny's blackness, no less than that of Mu Shiying's Johnny, figures the powerlessness of the proletariat (at one point his drummer tells him that "There's nothing we can do about it. We have no freedom, Benny" [Hei 1934, 146]) as well as the vulnerability of the colonized, for the story concludes with the harassment of his wife Sally at the hands of a group of drunken English sailors. But perhaps the most ideologically charged and syntactically daring depiction of this jazzman comes in a jarring sequence midway through the story:

He gazed at the saxophone player performing under the klieg lights on the stage in front of him. His neck was stretching forward like a white crane, blowing, cheeks reddened with the effort, a little like the Chairman's speech today, he was stretching his neck out as well, droning on in a loud voice quarter of an hour after quarter of an hour, from China to the world, laborers beyond number. And yet there were so many people in a place like this tonight. (Hei 1934, 144–45)

Through free association, satirical juxtaposition, and deliberate ambiguity of reference, the black jazzman is apotheosized. No longer is he "merely" black—he stands in for the workers of the world. Nor yet is he simply an unambiguously racialized emblem for the Internationale—in the mind of the observer he is likened to a "white crane." This image, in turn, yields suddenly and almost surrealistically to a final and distinctly parodic portrait of Generalissimo Chiang Kai-shek, the dictatorial Chairman of the ruling Nationalist Party and President of the Republic of China. He becomes, in other words, a "marvel of paradox": at once the oppressor and the oppressed; black, international, and Chinese; a montage-man who in his very incoherence reflects the homelessness of jazz in an age of global mobility.

NOTES

Toward a Global History of Jazz

1. See Hughes 1974; Ogren 1989; Radano 1993; Kenney 1993; Berliner 1994; Gabbard 1995; Collier 1996; Monson 1996; Panish 1997; DeVeaux 1997; Gerard 1998; Erenberg 1998; Lock 1999; and Tucker 2001.

2. There are variants of this general narrative pattern. Black nationalist jazz discourse typically maintains that jazz exemplifies the exceptional creative ingenuity of *African* Americans rather than of *all* Americans. The acceptance and appropriation of jazz by non-African Americans as a *national* music is thus depicted as a neo-colonialist gesture.

3. On National Public Radio's *Morning Edition* (April 3, 2002), Cynthia Schneider, former U.S. ambassador to the Netherlands, bemoaned cuts in funding for cultural exchange programs and the United States Information Agency. She praised Cold War policies for being "proactive in the use of culture as a vehicle for diplomacy" and for "explaining America." She specifically mentioned jazz as a "universally accepted symbol of freedom": "Jazz has represented freedom all over the world, [it] gives voice to freedom. . . ."

"Si no tiene swing no vaya' a la rumba": Cuban Musicians and Jazz

1. Editor's note: see Joe Boyd's liner notes to ¡Cubanismo! 2000.

2. On the Gabici story, see liner notes to *The Cuban Danzon*.

Django Reinhardt's Left Hand

I thank Todd Millstein and Ramon Satyendra for their comments on earlier drafts. A version of this essay was presented at the 46th Annual Meeting of the Society for Ethnomusicology in Detroit, October 2001.

1. Delaunay 1961 reports that Reinhardt was first introduced to the records of jazz violinist Joe Venuti (and probably Venuti's frequent collaborator Eddie Lang) by Emile Savitry around 1930 (47). Stéphane Grappelli later recalled that when he first became acquainted with Reinhardt in the early 1930s, "we decided every day to do like Eddie Lang and Joe Venuti to amuse ourselves" (quoted in Sudhalter 1999, 534).

2. Hoefer gives no precise citation for this source. The writers' claim that, by playing octaves on two strings with a damped intervening string, Reinhardt avoided "rushing up and down the fingerboard," seems misplaced, since this fingering would still require a good deal of such movement.

3. Both Peters and Balliett may base their accounts on a reading of Grappelli's description, cited here, since it appears in Delaunay 1961, which (in translation) remains the most widely circulated biography of Reinhardt in English. Another source is the American guitarist Art

Ryerson, who states that "[Reinhardt's] third finger wasn't a hundred percent, but he could use it about two-thirds of the time, and he could even use the damaged fourth once in a while" (quoted in Sudhalter 1999, 534).

4. "Supination" describes the rotation of the wrist in the direction that brings the palm uppermost; its antonym is "pronation," in which the wrist is rotated in the direction bringing the palm face-down (and beyond). See Galamian 1962, 50; and Tubiana 2000, 13. I would like to thank the British violin pedagogue Harry A. Cawood for bringing this terminology to my attention.

5. The tablature assumes that, as most sources suggest, the strings of the banjo-guitar are tuned identically to conventional guitar tuning (E2-A2-D3-G3-B3-E4) (see Odell and Winans 2001, 662). The usual conventions of guitar tablature are observed. The numerals used here refer to specific registers; by convention middle C and the notes within the octave above it are described as C4, C#4, D4 etc.. The pitches one octave higher are indicated by the number 5, the octave below middle C by the number 3, and so forth.

6. Again, the tablature and fingering are speculative, and in many cases alternatives exist. The left-hand fingering is displayed between the guitar staff and tablature as follows: the index finger through the pinkie are numbered 1–4, and the thumb is indicated by "T." When two or more notes are struck simultaneously, the fingering numbers are arranged vertically, with the highest sounding string (usually also the highest sounding pitch) at the top, and the others in order beneath it.

7. Both this, and the performance represented by the following transcription (Example 4), are extremely free glosses on Silèsu's theme as originally published, and in both cases their rubato tempi are difficult to capture in musical notation. This difficulty has no ramifications for the present discussion, however.

8. Lang frequently arpeggiates four-, five-, and six-note chords. When these are played slowly, the pitches are notated with individual rhythmic values. When a note within any such chord continues to sound (i.e. the string continues to be depressed by the left hand), this is indicated in the left-hand fingering notation with the use of a horizontal line (e.g. m. 2). (In a few, mostly self-evident, cases I have omitted these lines in the interest of visual clarity.)

9. Schmitz 1997 points out that Reinhardt's technique of playing octaves by stretching a distance of three frets between two strings with one (damped) intervening string, later adopted by Montgomery, differs from the octave fingering often favored by classical guitarists whereby there are two intervening strings between the sounding strings, and the fingering (e.g. first and third fingers) involves a heavily supinated wrist (34).

Brazilian Jazz and Friction of Musicalities

1. Charles Keil recounted via e-mail that when Brazilian percussionist Airto Moreira played with salsa bands in New York, he was criticized because the band wanted each beat and conga slap in its exact place, whereas Airto improvised too much. Keil told me about a Brazilian looseness or openness, contrary to the perfectionism of Puerto Rican music, linked to the specific characteristics of its African roots.

2. For example, in addition to the aforementioned *chorinho* revival, the natives are referring currently to a Jabour school, related to the disciples of Hermeto Pascoal who are developing their solo careers, such as Itiberí Zwarg, the group *Curupira*, Nenê, Carlos Malta, and others. There are also several instrumental groups connected to the *Mangue beat* movement in Pernambuco.

3. See the *Rumos Itaú cultural Música* Project (http://www.itaucultural.org.br).

Jazz in India: Perspectives on Historical Development and Musical Acculturation

1. In the liner notes to *Jazz and Hot Dance in India—1926–1944*, Lötz indicates that various forms of Afro-American music—"coon songs, spirituals, cakewalk, ragtime, hot dance music and jazz"—appealed to European colonists but had no effect on the local population. This study will show that, contrary to Lötz's assessment, jazz did influence some members of the indigenous population.

2. Braz Gonsalves, Chick Chocolate's son-in-law, showed me Chocolate's portfolio, which contained newspaper clippings, reviews and photographs of Chocolate and his band at various venues. According to Gonsalves, Chocolate did not record commercially.

3. Cotton is generally regarded as one of India's foremost jazz musicians. He is also one of the pioneers of *raga*-based soloing in jazz music in India. A band led by Cotton played the first notes at the inaugural Jazz Yatra in 1978.

4. The term "Anglo-Indian" means individuals of both English and Indian ancestry.

5. The other members of the band were: Ramesh Shottam, *thavil* and assorted Indian percussion; Ranjit Barot, drums and *khanjira*; Karl Peters, bass; and Rajagopalan, *ghatam* and *mridangam*.

6. The Dagar family is best known for performing this tradition; there are also many Hindu singers who perform Dhrupad.

Interpreting the Creative Process of Jazz in Zimbabwe

1. Occasionally, for example, children stretch plastic (reinforced by rubber) over the top of cans to make drums or to imitate the drum's sound. Similarly, they make tiny guitars using tin cans as the sound box. The addition of wood planks (as the fingerboard) and fish twine (for the strings) transforms the tiny sound box into a small guitar (Sasikwa 3/13/92).

2. Although these compositional rules direct the structure of many songs, creativity emerges as musicians extend the rules beyond the imposed limits. By manipulating the undercurrent rhythm, for example, African American jazz musicians in the past have appropriated Broadway show tunes into their musical vocabulary. John Coltrane's version of "My Favorite Things" and Miles Davis' version of "My Funny Valentine" demonstrate how tonal progressions within traditional melodies remain standard while the rhythm changes.

3. All transcriptions are by the author. Written music is limited in its ability to represent what is heard. The harmonics in the bass line of Figure 1 are achieved by sliding from C# to E, as demonstrated in the notation, while muting the strings and not allowing them to vibrate.

4. Marumahoko described the effect of what he classifies as "alternating suspensions" in an audio recording of one of his pieces (transcribed by the author, 4/16/94).

Musical Transculturation: From African American Avant-Garde Jazz to European Creative Improvisation, 1962–1981

1. I appreciate inspiring feedback received in seminars and conferences at institutions in California, Pennsylvania, Michigan, New York, Paris, Prague, and Leeds. This essay is adapted from my dissertation "African American Musical Avant-Gardism," completed at York University in January, 2001.

2. Bill Dixon (Bennington College, University of Wisconsin Madison), Arthur Brooks, Milford Graves, Charles Gayle, Raphe Malik (Bennington College), George Russell (New England Conservatory), George Lewis (University of California-San Diego, New York University), Clifford Thornton (Wesleyan), Charlie Haden (Cal Arts), Bobby Bradford (Pomona College, UCLA), Archie Shepp (University of Massachusetts-Amherst), Yusef Lateef (University of Massachusetts-Amherst, Hampshire College), Ishmail Wadada Leo Smith (Bard College, Cal Arts), Makanda Ken McIntyre (Smith College, CUNY, SUNY-Old Westlary), William Shadrack Cole (Wesleyan University, Dartmouth College), Cecil Taylor, Andrew Cyrille (Antioch College, Glassboro State College, University of Wisconsin Madison), Anthony Braxton (Mills College, Wesleyan University), Reggie Workman (New School for Social Research), Marion Brown (Bowdoin College), Anthony Davis (Yale University, University of California-San Diego).

3. This musical adherence to locale contains a feedback loop to American musicians like Dave Liebman who, under Coltrane's influence and following his tenure with Miles Davis, began talking about being able to feel his Jewishness (Williams 1981, 165). New York-based musicians John Zorn and Marc Ribot coined the phrase "radical new Jewish culture," which appears in the program notes of the Art Projekt Festival that took place in Munich in September, 1992. Zorn remarks that, "no one has ever disclosed the evidence of the Jewish presence in the new music, which is largely superior in proportion to that of Jews in the overall population. And hardly ever has there been an intimation of its influence. . . . Among the musicians involved in Munich, some have an articulate knowledge of traditions, some are totally secular. . . . There are participants who want to celebrate their own Jewish identity, others who want to perform a political act, in order not to remain silent in a moment when anti-Semitism is mounting" (quoted in Minganti 1996, 2).

Gianluigi Trovesi's Music: An Historical and Geographic Short-Circuit

1. Tangos appear regularly in Trovesi's music: in *Les Hommes Armés* the piece *Tango* undergoes four radical variations scattered throughout the record like interludes.

2. Although the Trovesi-Coscia duo records completely fail to render the energy and humor of their live shows, in the present discussion of their work reference is made to their first record *Radici*, as in my opinion it is much better than the next—and more famous—*In Cerca di Cibo*, which is somewhat artificial and affected.

3. It is available from the group Hesperion XX on the CD *Canzoni da Sonare* (EMI 63141), with compositions by Giovanni Gabrieli, Andrea Gabrieli, and Giuseppe Guami.

The Music of the Gross, 1928–1931

1. Robert Conquest, *The Great Terror: Stalin's Purge of the Thirties* (New York: Macmillan, 1973), 46; Winston S. Churchill, *The Hinge of Fate* (Boston: Houghton Mifflin, 1950), 498. See also R. W. Davies, *The Industrialization of Soviet Russia, the Socialist Offensive: The Collectivization of Agriculture 1929–1930* (Cambridge: Harvard University Press, 1980); Frank Lorimer, *The Population of the Soviet Union: History and Prospects* (Geneva, 1946), 133–37.

2. See Alexander I. Soizhenitsyn, *The Gulag Archipelago*, trans. Thomas P. Whitney (New York: Harper & Rowe, 1974) vol. I, chap. 2.

3. Paul Robeson, *Paul Robeson Speaks: Writings, Speeches, Interviews, 1918–1974*, ed. Philip S. Foner (New York: Citadel Press, 1978), 106.

4. Hans von Herwarth with S. Frederick Starr, *Against Two Evils* (London: Rawson, Wade, 1981), 37–38.

5. Alfred G. Meyer, "The War Scare of 1927," *Soviet Union/Union Sovietique* 1 (1978), 1–25.

6. Sheila Fitzpatrick, "The Foreign Threat During the First Five-Year Plan," *Soviet Union/Union Sovietique* 1 (1978), 26–35.

7. Herwarth and Starr, 1981, 53–54.

8. Eugene Lyons, "To Tell or Not To Tell," *Harper's* June 1935: 100ff.

9. See Anatole Senkevitch, Jr., *Soviet Architecture, 1917–1961: A Bibliographic Guide to Source Material* (Charlottesville: University Press of Virginia, 1974), 166–73.

10. I. Matsa, "Uroki 'neitralizma' v iskusstve," *Literatura i iskusstvo* 2–3 (1931): 151–57.

11. Sheila Fitzpatrick, "The Emergence of Glaviskusstvo," *Soviet Studies* Oct. 1971: 249.

12. S. Korev, "Sovetskoe iskusstvo i ego potrebitel," *Sovetskoe iskusstvo* 3 (1918): 36.

13. Dec. 9, 1930, reprinted in *Sovetskoe iskusstvo za 15 let: Materialy i dokumenty*, I. Matsa, L. Rempel, and L. Reingardt, eds. (Moscow, Leningrad, 1933), 450.

14. Korev 1918, 39.

15. S. Voskresenskii, "Organizanonnye voprosy estrady," *Sovetskoe iskusitvo* 16 (1928): 47.

16. A. Lunacharskii, "Kultumaia revoliutsiia i iskusstvo," *Sovetskoe iskusstuo* 4 (1928): 9.

17. Korev 1918, 37–39.

18. Vosicresenskii 1928, 47.

19. Volkov-Lannit, *Iskusstvo zapechatlennogo ivuka*, 177–78.

20. For the theory of proletarian culture see Edward J. Brown, *The Proletarian Episode in Russian Literature, 1918–1931* (New York: Columbia University Press, 1953), 64ff.

21. *Sovetskoe iskusstvo za 15 let*, 449.

22. Blaise Pascal, *Pensees* (New York: E.P. Dutton, 1931), 44. See the interesting discussion of this issue in Leo Lowenthal, *Literature, Popular Culture, and Society* (Englewood Cliffs: Prentice-Hall, 1961), 15.

23. "Fritz Kreisler Returns," *New York Times* (hereafter *NYT*), Jan. 11, 1925: 31; see also "Says Jazz Will Play Itself Out," *NYT,* Nov. 11, 1924: 16.

24. "The Decline of Jazz," *American Musician* May 1922: 1.

25. "Jazz Not What It Once Was," *Musical Leader* July 24, 1924: 26–27.

26. Karol Rathaus, "Jazzdammening?" *Die Musik* Feb. 1927: 333–36.

27. "Jazz All Over Europe," *NYT* Apr. 30, 1929: 14.

28. "Vienna Is Alarmed by Inroads of Jazz," *NYT* Apr. 15, 1928; see also Ernst Decsey, "Jazz in Vienna," *Living Age* Mar. 1, 1928: 441–45.

29. "Jazz Bands Popular in Turkey; Kemal Enjoys Western Music," *NYT* Oct. 12, 1927: 7; H. H. Stuckenschmidt, "Hellenic Jazz," *Modern Music* Apr.-May 1934: 22–24; "Orchestra Plays Jazz Thirty-three Hours," *NYT* Dec. 14, 1927: 8.

30. "Jazz Bitterly Opposed in Germany," *NYT* Mar. 11, 1928. See also Alfred Einstein, "Some Berlin Novelties," *NYT* Feb. 19, 1928; Fritz Stege, "Gibt es eine 'Deutsche Jazzkapelle'?" *Zeitschrift für Instrumentenbau*, July 1929: 410–11; Paul Schwers, "Die FrankfurterJass-Akademie im Spiegel der Kritik," *Allgemeine Musikzeitung*, Dec. 2, 1927: 1246–48.

31. "Jazz Bitterly Opposed in Germany," 10.

32. I.L. Matsa, *Iskusstvo sovremennoi Evropy* (Moscow, Leningrad, 1926), 120.

33. M. Gorkii, "O muzyke tolstykh," *Pravda*, Apr. 18, 1928: 4. An authorized translation by Marie Budberg, "The Music of the Degenerate," appeared in *Dial*, Dec. 1928: 480–84.

34. Utesov, *Pesnia po zhizni*, 129.

35. Gorkii 1928. All quotations are from this source.

36. Interview with Nina Berberova, Aug. 19, 1979.

37. A. V. Lunacharskii, "Sotsialnye istoki muzykalnogo iskusstva," *Proletarskii muzykant*, 4 (1929): 12–20.

38. *Ibid.*, 18.

39. *Ibid.*, 19.

40. N. Briusova, "Na borbu s muzykalnym durmanom," *Zaproletarskuiu muzyku* 1 (1930): 3–5.

41. L. Lebedinskii, "Nash massovyi muzykalnyi byt," *Literatura i iskusstvo* 1 (1931): 76–77

42. Interview with Konstantin Simis, May 4, 1979.

43. I. N. "The Soviet Cult," *NYT* Jan. 8, 1928.

44. Iu. I. Laane, "Musykalnaia rabota sredi natsmen zapada," *Sovetskoe iskusstvo* 1 (1917): 41.

45. *Istoriia russkoi sovetskoi muxyki*, ed. A. D. Alekseev (Moscow, 1956), vol. 1, 137.

46. Robert A. Rothstein, "The Quiet Rehabilitation of the Brick Factory: Early Soviet Popular Music," *Slavic Review* (Sept. 1980): 374.

47. "Mozhet li dzhaz stat sovetskim?" *Rabochii i teatr* 43 (1930): 7.

48. Kurt Weill, "Notiz zum Jazz," trans. in Kowalke, *Kurt Weill in Europe*, 477.

49. Hanns Eisler, *Reden und Aufsätze* (Leipzig, 1961).

50. Albrecht Betz, *Hanns Eisler—Musik, eine Zeit die sich eben bildet* (Munich: Edition Text u. Kritik, 1976), 87; also Hanns Eisler, "Musik im Klassenkampf," *Sozialistische Zeitschrift für Kunst und Gesellschaft* Nov. 1973: 93ff.

51. "S. Wagner Attacks Jazz," *NYT* Dec. 7, 1925: 19.

52. F. Sabo, "Put fashizma v nemetskoi muzyke," *Sovetskaia muzyka* 1 (1934): 108.

53. Richard Litterscheid, "Das Ende des Jazz in Deutschland," *Die Musik* Dec. 1935: 236–37; Ludwig Altmann, "Untergang der Jazzmusik," *Die Musik* July 1933: 744–49; also "Nazis Reject Jazz," *NYT* Mar. 18, 1933: 12; and "Hitler Frowns on Jazz," *Literary Digest* Mar. 24, 1934: 24. On Japan see M. S. Druskin, *Ocherki po istorii tantsovalnoi muzyki* (Leningrad, 1936), 66.

54. E. Stepanov, *Kulturnaia zhizn Leningrada 20-kh-nachala 3o-kh godov* (Leningrad, 1976), 159.

55. *Ibid.*, 103.

56. In 1932, Association composers got thirty-two radio hours per week in Leningrad; others got only three or four. *Ibid.*, 223.

57. Lewis Nichols, "Tin Pan Alley Now Paved with Profits," *NYT* Mar. 17, 1932: 10.

58. Maurice Waller and Anthony Calabrese, *Fats Waller* (New York: Schirmer, 1977), 113.

59. Sidney Bechet, *Treat It Gentle* (New York: Hill & Wang, 1960), 112.

60. Waldo Frank, "Jazz and Folk Art," *New Republic* Dec. 1, 1926: 42–43.

61. "Berlin Calls Jazz American Folk Music; Composer Predicts It Will Eventually Be Sung in Metropolitan Opera House," *NYT* Jan. 10, 1925: 2; Paul Whiteman, "In Defense of Jazz and Its Makers," *NYT* Mar. 13, 1927: 4, 22.

62. M. Dr. (Druskin), "Muzyka zhizni," *Leningradskii student* 5 (1929): 14.

63. M. S. Shaginian, "Dzhaz-band," *Izvestiia* (Odessa), June 3, 1926.

64. Tatiana Tchernavin, *We Soviet Women* (New York: E.P. Dutton, 1936), 172.

65. A. S. Tsukker, "Dzhaz-band," *Novyi zrtel* 10 (1926): 5.

66. *Ibid.*, 5.

67. Richard Hadlock, *Jazz Masters of the '20s* (New York: Macmillan, 1961), 16–17.

68. Goddard 1979, 13.

69. Edward Thomas Wilson, *Russia and Black Africa Before World War II* (New York, London: Holmes & Meier, 1974), 133–34.

70. Wilson Record, *The Negro and the Communist Party* (New York: Atheneum, 1971), 62.

71. Wilson 1974, 168–69; Record 1971, chap. 3.

72. Adam B. Ulam, *Stalin, the Man and His Era* (New York: Beacon Press, 1973), 367.

73. Record 1971, 67ff.

74. Michael Gold, "What a World!" *The Daily Worker* Jan. 1, 1934; Charles Edward Smith, "Class Content of Jazz Music," *The Daily Worker* Oct. 21, 1933; "Diskussiia o dzhaze," *Sovetskaia muzyka* 2 (1934): 67.

75. Cf. G. Landsberg, "Na putiakh k dzhazovoi kultury," *Rabochii i teatr* 22 (1935): 22–23.

Naturalizing the Exotic: The Australian Jazz Convention

1. I wish to acknowledge the generous assistance provided by Graeme Bell, Roger Bell, Audrey Blake, Ian Collinson, Eric Myers, Peter Newton, Mike Sutcliffe. I take full responsibility for the arguments.

2. The early specialist jazz journals were largely devoted to recordings, which also constituted the most usual introduction to jazz for this generation; see for example Blake 1984, 17.

3. Cavanaugh is described in *AP* July 1945, 62, as "Noted Negress jazz critic; lyric writer for Duke Ellington; only woman on "*Esquire*'s Jazz poll." Roger Bell's recollection was that she was a singer, and I thank him also for information on Morris Goode, in a telephone conversation 2/11/02. Roger recalls that they met through Roger's band's residency at the Melbourne Palais Royal on Thursday nights, and that Goode, alone and far from home, "spoke the same language as we did," and became particularly attached to Bill Miller. While Roger recalls that Goode's playing was not particularly impressive, the Graeme Bell band appear to have recorded two sides with him on 6/22/1944, but which were unissued (Mitchell 1988, 24).

4. See for example the exchanges between Max Harris and Bill Miller, in *Australian Jazz Quarterly* No. 2 (August 1946) and *JN* 71 (February 1947) and 73 (misnumbered on front cover as 72) (April-May 1947). Likewise the ideological falling out between the Bell band and the EYL in 1948 did not diminish the enthusiasm of either Stein or Blake for jazz.

5. The word "Eureka" in this context refers to a brief armed insurrection by miners ("diggers") near the Victorian town of Ballarat in 1854. Resentful of the manner of policing of miners' licenses, they built the "Eureka" stockade and declared themselves an independent republic. The word has since been appropriated by a range of reformist, revolutionary, and republican movements.

6. For the period up to 1956, much of Blears' information, and indeed sections of text, duplicate Audrey Blake's document originally of that year, revised in 1993 (Blake 1993). In his Appendices Blears cites a version of Blake's document from "c. 1960" (227). I have tended to use the Blake ms, simply as being the prior account, and the one I initially worked from. There are, however, discrepancies between the ms cited by Blears, and the one given me by Blake, which is a version privately circulated in 1993. There are therefore points at which I cite text from the Blears transcript rather than the one in my possession. I have raised these discrepancies with Audrey, but as Blears's book was launched in Sydney just a few days ago as I write, she has not been able to throw light on the puzzle.

7. Lang [1943], [57]. My thanks to Sydney collector and archivist Mike Sutcliffe for making his copy available.

Music and Emancipation: The Social Role of Black Jazz and Vaudeville in South Africa Between the 1920s and the Early 1940s

1. Editor's note: the following abbreviations are used in the text: *Bantu World: BW*; *Ilanga Lase Natal: ILN*; *Imvo Zabantsundu: IZ*; *The South African Worker: SAW*; *Umteteli wa Bantu: UWB*.

2. I have been unable to find any corroboration for Henry Nxumalo's assertion that "Miss Nomvila, and Dolly Matsabe . . . helped give birth to the African blues" (presumably while Griffiths Motsieloa was recording in London?): see his "How African Music-Makers Made the First Gramophone Record," *Umlindi we Nyanga*, May 1949.

3. Erlmann 1987, 23; ICU handbills ("Isaziso"), Forman Papers, University of Cape Town Library, BC 581 (B22.7 to B22.11); *BW* 1/16/37.

4. H. Bradford, " 'A Taste of Freedom': Capitalist Development and Response to the ICU in the Transvaal Countryside," in Bozzoli 1983, 135.

5. See *ILN* 12/26/30; Champion's letter is in the University of Cape Town Library, BC 581 (A 1.32).

6. See for instance the Minutes of the Executive Committee of the Bantu Men's Social Centre, Johannesburg, held on November 10, 1938 (South African Institute of Race Relations Records, Library of the Church of the Province of South Africa, University of the Witwatersrand, AD843.B73.1); and *BW* 1/29/38.

7. It is important not to confuse this new tendency to create what one might call an African vaudeville, with the apparently similar—but differently motivated—ethnic vaudeville that had, for some four or five years already, enjoyed considerable success in Natal. The ideological underpinnings of Mtethwa's Lucky Stars and William Mseleku's Amanzimtoti Royal Entertainers—to mention the most famous of Natal troupes—lay in what Erlmann (1991) has described as "the gradual shift of liberal position urban reform projects towards an acceptance of territorial segregation and African reserves as viable repositories of black development." Citing the work of Paul Rich, he attributes this to "an ideological alliance" in Natal, which "exerted a strong influence on African thinking about ethnic tradition" (76–77).

8. The term *mbaqanga*—Zulu for "African maize bread"—has designated different kinds of music during the course of the last fifty-odd years; but its first musical usage was as a synonym for African Jazz.

9. The Champion Papers, Library of the Church of the Province of South Africa, University of the Witwatersrand, A922.

A Japanese Story About Jazz in Russia: Itsuki Hiroyuki's "Farewell, Moscow Gang"

1. Itsuki and another popular writer known for his jazz stories, Tsutsui Yasutaka, have each published dozens of books, yet have been all but ignored by English-language translators and scholars of Japanese literature. Perhaps one reason is that Japanese "popular writers" did not begin receiving attention from English-language translators and scholars until the 1980s, by which time those interested in popular literature were chasing after the latest "new face." These two writers continue to publish bestsellers to this day, but they are generally associated with the late 1960s and 1970s, whereas Murakami Haruki, Murakami Ryū, Yamada Eimi (Amy), and Yoshimoto Banana are post-1980s writers who appear to have greater contemporary appeal for readers and publishers.

2. Itsuki has published a collection of essays on music entitled "Furimukeba tango," which, as the title suggests, focuses on his love of tango, both music and dance. He draws parallels between the origins of jazz and tango that are provocative but seem to derive more from popular mythology than from serious research. See Itsuki 1992.

3. Japanese music critics have argued that although "Farewell, Moscow Gang" revolves around jazz musicians, it is not a "jazz story" in the strict sense (Aikura 1976, 88; Uekusa 1976, 44). According to one of these critics, it was Itsuki's 1967 story, "Farewell, My Johnny"

("Umi o mite ita Jonii") that is the first true work of jazz fiction written in Japanese, although this critic never clarifies why he makes such a distinction (Uekusa 1976, 44). A literal translation of the Japanese title would be "Johnny, Who Was Staring at the Sea." To my knowledge, none of Itsuki's "jazz stories" has been published in English translation, and few of his other works are available in English, either.

4. The revised Japan-U.S. Security Treaty, or *Anpo*, as it was commonly known, permitted American troops to remain on Japanese soil, and, in the minds of many Japanese, sanctioned America's ongoing political and military hegemony long after the U.S. occupation of Japan's main islands had officially ended in 1952. Opposition to the Treaty led to Japan's largest protests in decades, with hundreds of thousands taking to the streets in 1960. This was followed on June 22 by a nationwide general strike involving an estimated 6.2 million workers. Ultimately, these protests failed to turn the political tide and became a lingering source of disillusion for many Japanese students and intellectuals. On Japan's protests against the Vietnam War, see Havens 1987.

5. By the mid-1970s, however, Itsuki had developed an appreciation for "free jazz" saxophonist Abe Kaoru (1949–1978). In December 1991 he presided over a TV Asahi roundtable discussion on Abe's life and musical legacy with various musicians, critics, and friends of Abe (transcript published in Morita 1994, 240–55).

Swinging Differences: Reconstructed Identities in the Early Swedish Jazz Age

1. This is a revised version of Fornäs (2001 and 2002a), and permission for the overlaps has been generously granted by the respective publishers. It is based on themes developed in Fornäs (2002a), making use of songs, films, literary works, interviews and other sources that thematize jazz and popular music in relation to media, modernity and identity. Theoretical foundations are outlined in Fornäs (1995a). When no published source is given, quotations are from my own interview material. The reprinted song lyrics are the author's translation, with words originally sung in English italicized. They are printed with permission of the publishers (Harlems ros © 1934 AB Nordiska Musikförlaget / Ehrlingförlagen AB, Stockholm).

Black Internationale: Notes on the Chinese Jazz Age

1. Zhou Xuan is accompanied by the Kaikai Band (*Kaikai yinyue hui*), released on the Victor (*Meiguo shengli*) label (matrix number 54690-A).

2. "Treaty port" refers to cities (Hong Kong, Canton, Shanghai, and Tianjin, among others) forced open to Western military and economic encroachment in the wake of China's defeat in the Opium Wars of 1839–1842.

3. Records from this period are extremely difficult to date due to the destruction of record company archives and masters attendant upon years of war and revolution. My dating of this particular record is based on the informed judgement of Edwin Loui, a noted discographer of early Chinese popular music.

4. Several of these musicians, including Earl West and pianist Earl Whaley, who failed to heed the warning signs and stayed on in Shanghai after the war began, were eventually interned by the Japanese. West apparently died in Shanghai, while de Barros quotes one source who asserts that Whaley's fingers were broken by his Japanese captors (de Barros 1993, 49).

5. Buck Clayton, for instance, provides several interesting accounts of racist run-ins with American marines and "southern crackers" in his memoir of his two years in Shanghai (Clayton 1986, 71, 75). Langston Hughes, in turn, is quick to note that "I was more afraid of going into the world-famous Cathay Hotel than I was of going into any public place in the Chinese quarters. Colored people were not welcomed at the Cathay. But beyond the gates of the International Settlement, color was no barrier" (Hughes 1956, 250–51).

6. White Russian women in the entertainment business are often depicted in accounts of Shanghai nightlife as low-class cabaret dancers and prostitutes (Greene 1923, 25), but also worked as dance school instructors, music teachers, and cafe waitresses.

7. Here I draw on Schaefer's (2003) argument that the pervasive representation of savagery in the Shanghai media culture of this era "aimed to negotiate Shanghai's own uneasy temporal and spatial location . . . on the margins of global modernity" (92–93).

8. An example of these uneasy conjunctions is Mu Shiying's short story "Of Camels, A Devotee of Nietzsche, and a Woman," in which the male protagonist's exposition of a parable from *Thus Spake Zarathustra* about a camel merges seamlessly with a discourse on the merits of Camel cigarettes, all in an effort to seduce a beautiful young woman drinking at a café (Mu 1988, 191–97).

BIBLIOGRAPHY

Books and Articles

Abdulgani, Roeslan. 1981. *The Bandung Connection: The Asia-Africa Conference in Bandung in 1955.* Trans. Molly Bondan. Singapore: Gunung Agung.

Acosta, Leonardo. 1996. "La Habana: capital del jazz latino?" In Radamés Giro, ed., *Panorama de la Música Popular Cubana.* Colombia: Universidad del Valle. 245–53.

———. 2001a. *Raíces del jazz latino: un siglo de jazz en Cuba.* Barranquilla, Colombia: Editorial La Iguana Ciega.

———. 2001b. "Raíces y Desarrollo del Jazz Afrocubano y afrolatino." Unpublished ms.

Adas, Michael. 2001. "From Settler Colony to Global Hegemon: Integrating the Exceptionalist Narrative of the American Experience in World History." *American Historical Review* 106.5 (December): 1692–720.

Adorno, Theodor W. 1981 [1967]. "Perennial Fashion—Jazz." In *Prisms.* Trans. Samuel and Shierry Weber. Cambridge: MIT Press. 119–32.

Agawu, V. Kofi. 1991. *Playing with Signs: A Semiotic Interpretation of Classic Music.* Princeton: Princeton University Press.

Aikura, Hisato. 1976. "Senaka awase no dōjidai." In Bungei Shunjū, eds., *Itsuki Hiroyuki no sekai.* Tokyo: Bungei Shunjūsha. 82–94.

Albert, Richard N. 1990. *From Blues to Bop: A Collection of Jazz Fiction.* Louisiana State University Press.

Andriessen, Louis. 1996. "Notes Towards Anarchy." *Border Crossings* 15.1 (Winter): 32–38.

Appadurai, Arjun. 1996. *Modernity at Large: Cultural Dimensions of Globalization.* Minneapolis: University of Minnesota Press.

Araújo, Samuel. 1999. "The Politics of Passion: The Impact of *Bolero* on Brazilian Musical Expressions." *Yearbook for Traditional Music* 31: 42–56.

Atkins, Chet, with Bill Neely. 1974. *Country Gentleman.* Chicago: Henry Regnery.

Atkins, E. Taylor. 2001. *Blue Nippon: Authenticating Jazz in Japan.* Durham: Duke University Press.

———. Forthcoming. "Multicultural Jazz: Expanding the Borders of Jazz History." In Sherrie B. Tucker and Jeffrey Belnap, eds., *Musics of the Americas: Studies in National and Transnational Formations.*

Attali, Jacques. 1987. *Noise: The Political Economy of Music.* Translated by Brian Massumi. Minneapolis: University of Minnesota Press.

Awosusi, Anita, ed. 1997. *Die Musik der Sinti und Roma, Band 2: Der Sinti-Jazz.* Heidelberg: Schriftenreihe des Dokumentations-und Kulturzentrums Deutscher Sinti und Roma.

Ayala, Cristóbal Díaz. 1998. *Cuando Salí de La Habana, 1898–1997: Cien años de música cubana por el mundo.* Puerto Rico: Fundación Musicalia.

Backlund, Stefan. 1989. "Swing i Skuggan Av Krigs-Och Kristider: Jazzmusikens Genombrott i 1940-Talets Helsingfors." *Historik Tidskrift for Finland* 74.4: 623–45.

Baker, Houston A., Jr. 1984. *Blues, Ideology, and Afro-American Literature: A Vernacular Theory*. Chicago: University of Chicago Press.

Bakhtin, Mikhail M. 1986. "The Problem of Speech Genres." In C. Emerson and M. Holquist, eds., *Speech Genres and Other Later Essays*. Austin: University of Texas Press. 60–102.

Baldwin, James. 1963. *Notes of a Native Son*. Boston: Beacon Press.

Ballantine, Christopher. 1993. *Marabi Nights: Early South African Jazz and Vaudeville*. Johannesburg: Ravan Press.

Balliett, Whitney. 2000. "Seeing Music." *The New Yorker* (September 11): 98–100.

Baraka, Amiri (LeRoi Jones). 1999 [1963]. *Blues People: Negro Music in White America*. New York: Quill.

Barlow, Tani, ed. 1997. *Formations of Colonial Modernity in East Asia*. Durham: Duke University Press.

Bell, Graeme. 1946. "Introduction: Jazz in Australia." In Harris and Roskolenko 1946: [2].

———. 1988. *Australian Jazzman*. Frenchs Forest NSW: Child & Associates.

Bell, Roger. "Reply to Inez Cavana[u]gh." In Harris and Roskolenko 1946: 8.

Benjamin, Walter. 1969 [1936]. "The Work of Art in the Age of Mechanical Reproduction." In *Illuminations*. Ed. Hannah Arendt. New York: Schoken. 217–52.

———. 1999 [1982]. *The Arcades Project*. Cambridge/London: Belknap Press.

Berendt, Joachim Ernst. 1984. "Jazz and World Music." *Jazz Educators Journal* 16.4 (April/May): 12–16.

———. 1987. *Nada Brahma: The World is Sound*. Vermont: Destiny Books.

Bergerot, Frank, and Arnaud Merlin. 1993. *The Story of Jazz: Bop and Beyond*. New York: Harry N. Abrams, Inc.

Berliner, Paul. 1994. *Thinking in Jazz: The Infinite Art of Improvisation*. Chicago: University of Chicago Press.

Billard, François. 1993. *Django Reinhardt: Un géant sur son nuage*. Paris: Lieu Commun.

Bisset, Andrew. 1987. *Black Roots White Flowers: A History of Jazz in Australia*. 2d ed. Sydney: ABC Enterprises.

Blake, Audrey. 1984. *A Proletarian Life*. Victoria: Kibble Books.

———. 1993 [1956]. *Notes on the Development of the Eureka Youth League and Its Predecessors*. Unpublished ms, originally written 1956, revised May 1993.

Blake, Jack. 1943. "One of 'Three Views on Art.'" In Max Harris, ed. *Angry Penguins* 4: 47–48.

Blake, Jody. 1999. *Le Tumulte noir: Modernist Art and Popular Entertainment in Jazz-Age Paris, 1900–1930*. University Park, PA: Pennsylvania State University Press.

Blears, Barrie. 2002. *Together with Us: A Personal Glimpse of the Eureka Youth League and Its Origins: 1920–1970*. Marrickville NSW: Southwood Press.

Bose, Shantanu. 1988. "From Dambar Bahadur to Louis Banks: A Jazz Wizard's Success Story." *Filmfare* (January 16–31): 44–49.

Boswick, John A. Jr. 1974. "Rehabilitation of the Burned Hand." *Clinical Orthopaedics* 104: 162–74.

Bourne, Michael. 1980. "Global Jazz Boosters Demand More U.S. Music." *Down Beat* (January): 25–27.

Boyer, Richard O. 1993. "The Hot Bach." In Mark Tucker, ed. *The Duke Ellington Reader.* New York: Oxford University Press. 214–45.

Breakey, Basil, and Steve Gordon. 1997. *Beyond the Blues: Township Jazz of the '60s and '70s.* Cape Town and Johannesburg: David Philip.

Brokensha, David, and Michael Crowder, eds. 1974. *Africa in the Wider World: The Inter-Relationship of Area and Comparative Studies.* London: Pergamon Press.

Brown, Lee B. 1991. "The Theory of Jazz Music—'It Don't Mean a Thing . . .'" *Journal of Aesthetics and Art Criticism* 49: 115–27.

Budds, Michael J. 1990. *Jazz in the Sixties: The Expansion of Musical Resources and Techniques.* Rev. ed. Iowa City: University of Iowa Press.

Calado, Carlos. 1997. *Tropicália: A história de uma revolução musical* [History of a musical revolution]. São Paulo: Editora 34.

Cameron, William Bruce. 1954. "Sociological Notes on the Jam Session." *Social Forces* (December): 177–82.

Campos, Augusto de. 1974. *O balanço da bossa e outras bossas.* São Paulo: Perspectiva.

Cardoso de Oliveira, Roberto. 1964. *O Índio e o Mundo dos Brancos.* São Paulo: Difusão européia do livro.

———. 1972. *A Sociologia do Brasil Indígena.* Rio de Janeiro: Editora da Universidade de São Paulo/Tempo Brasileiro.

Carr, Ian, Digby Fairweather, and Brian Priestley. 1990. *Jazz: The Essential Companion.* London: Paladin, Grafton Books.

Casella, Alfredo. 1932. "Fengmi shijie de jueshi yinyue." Trans. Anna. *Dongfang zazhi* 29.4: 93–94.

Castro, Ruy. 1990. *Chega de Saudade: a história e as histórias da bossa-nova.* São Paulo: Companhia das Letras.

Cavanaugh, Inez. 1945. "American Jazz Scene: 1945." In Harris and Reed 1945: 35–37.

Cavana[u]gh, Inez. [1946]. "A Day with the Duke." In Harris & Roskolenko 1946: [3]–8.

Cazes, Henrique. 1998. *Choro: do quintal ao Municipal.* São Paulo: Editora 34.

Chilton, John. 1997. *Who's Who of British Jazz.* London: Cassell.

Ching, Leo. 2000. "Globalizing the Regional, Regionalizing the Global: Culture and Asianism in the Age of Late Capital." *Public Culture* 12.1: 233–57.

Clayton, Buck. 1986. *Buck Clayton's Jazz World.* New York: Oxford University Press.

Clunies-Ross, Bruce. 1979. "An Australian Sound: Jazz in Melbourne and Adelaide 1941–1951." In P. Spearitt and D. Walker, eds., *Australian Popular Culture.* North Sydney: George Allen & Unwin. 62–80.

Collier, James Lincoln. 1993. *Jazz: The American Theme Song.* New York: Oxford University Press.

————. 1996. "Local Jazz Scene." In Robert Gottlieb, ed., *Reading Jazz: A Gathering of Auto-biography, Reportage, and Criticism from 1919 to Now.* New York: Pantheon. 997–1005.

Collins, John. 1987. "Jazz Feedback to Africa." *American Music* 5.2: 176–93.

Connel, Andrew M. 2001. "Cosmopolitan Identities: Aquarela Carioca, *Música Instrumental Brasileira,* and the (Re)imagination of Place." Presented at the Annual Meeting of the Society of Ethnomusicology, Detroit, October 27.

Couzens, T. 1985. *The New African: A Study of the Life and Work of H.I.E. Dhlomo.* Johannesburg: Ravan Press.

Crowdy, Denis, and Michael Goddard. 1999. "The Pedagogy, Culture and Appropriation of Jazz in Papua New Guinea." *Perfect Beat* 4.3 (July): 48–65.

Cruickshank, Ian. 1989. *The Guitar Style of Django Reinhardt and the Gypsies.* London: Wise Publications.

Da Matta, Roberto. 1979. *Carnavais, malandros e heróis: para uma sociologia do dilema brasileiro.* Rio de Janeiro: Jorge Zahar.

Dallwitz, Dave. 1947. "The Australian Jazz Convention." *Jazz Notes* 70 (January): 12–16.

Dapieve, Arthur. 1995. *BRock: rock brasileiro dos anos 80.* São Paulo: Editora 34.

Davenport, Lisa. 1999. "Jazz and the Cold War: Black Culture as an Instrument of American Foreign Policy." In Darlene Clarke Hine and Jacqueline McLeod, eds., *Crossing Boundaries: Comparative History of Black People in Diaspora.* Bloomington: Indiana University Press. 282–315.

Dean, Roger T. 1992. *New Structures in Jazz and Improvised Music Since 1960.* Buckingham and Bristol, PA: Open University Press.

de Barros, Paul. 1993. *Jackson Street After Hours: The Roots of Jazz in Seattle.* Seattle: Sasquatch Press.

Delaunay, Charles. 1961. *Django Reinhardt.* Trans. Michael James. New York: Da Capo Press.

Derschmidt, Eckhart. 1998. "The Disappearance of the 'Jazu-Kissa': Some Considerations about Japanese 'Jazz-Cafés' and Jazz-Listeners." In Sepp Linhart and Sabine Frühstück, eds., *The Culture of Japan as Seen Through its Leisure.* Albany: SUNY Press. 303–15.

DeVeaux, Scott. 1991. "Constructing the Jazz Tradition: Jazz Historiography." *Black American Literature Forum* 25.3: 525–60.

————. 1997. *The Birth of Bebop.* Berkeley: University of California Press.

Dodds, Baby. 1959. *The Baby Dodds Story, As Told to Larry Gara.* Los Angeles: Contemporary Press.

Ducrot, Oswald e Todorov, Tzvetan. 1972. *Dicionário Enciclopédio das Ciências da Linguagem.* São Paulo: Perspectiva.

Dunn, Christopher. 2001. *Brutality Garden: Tropicália and the Emergence of a Brazilian Counterculture.* Chapel Hill: University of North Carolina Press.

Durbin, Wal. 1947. "Jazz Convention." *Syncopation* 1.2 (January): 18.

Dutton, Denis, and Michael Krausz. 1991. *The Concept of Creativity in Science and Art.* London: Marinus Nijhoff Publishers.

Edwards, I. 1989. "Umkhumbane Our Home: African Shantytown Society in Cato Manor Farm, 1946–1960." Ph.D. thesis, University of Natal.

"11 Leaders on Down Beat's All-American 1939 Band." 1940. *Down Beat* (January 1): 12–13.

Erenberg, Lewis A. 1998. *Swingin' the Dream: Big Band Jazz and the Rebirth of American Culture.* Chicago: University of Chicago Press.

Eriksson, Gunnar, and Artur Lundkvist. 1935. "Hot-Jazz." *Karavan* 2: 73–91.

Erlmann, Veit. 1983. "Black Political Song in South Africa—Some Research Perspectives," *Popular Music Perspectives 2: Papers from The Second International Conference On Popular Music Studies,* Reggio Emilia, September 19–24 (IASPM, 1985).

———. 1987. "Singing Brings Joy to the Distressed." Paper given at the History Workshop, University of the Witwatersrand, February 1–14.

———. 1988. " 'A Feeling of Prejudice': Orpheus McAdoo and the Virginia Jubilee Singers in South Africa 1890–1898." *Journal of Southern African Studies* 14.3: 331–50.

———. 1991. *African Stars: Studies in Black South African Performance.* Chicago: University of Chicago Press.

———. 1993. "The Politics and Aesthetics of Transnational Musics." *The World of Music* 35.2: 3–15.

———. 1996. "The Aesthetics of the Global Imagination: Reflections on World Music in the 1990s." *Public Culture* 8.3: 467–87.

Evans, Nicholas. 2000. *Writing Jazz: Race, Nationalism, and Modern Culture in the 1920s.* New York and London: Garland.

Farrell, Gerry. 1988. "Reflecting Surfaces: The Use of Elements from Indian Music in Popular Music in Jazz." *Popular Music* 7: 189–205.

Feather, Leonard. 1996. *The Encyclopedia of Jazz in the Sixties.* New York: Horizon.

Fehrenbach, Heide, and Uta G. Poiger, eds. 2000. *Transactions, Transgressions, Transformations: American Culture in Western Europe and Japan.* New York: Berghahn Books.

Feld, S., and C. Keil, eds. 1994. *Music Grooves.* Chicago: University of Chicago Press.

Ferris, Leonard. 1975. "Mary Osborne: A Unique Roll [*sic*] in Jazz Guitar History." In *Jazz Guitarists: Collected Interviews From Guitar Player Magazine.* Saratoga, CA: Guitar Player Productions. 78–79.

"Final Results of Band Contest." 1939. *Down Beat* (January): 16–17.

Floyd, Samuel A., Jr. 1995. *The Power of Black Music: Interpreting Its History from Africa to the United States.* New York: Oxford University Press.

Fornäs, Johan. 1995. *Cultural Theory and Late Modernity.* London: Sage.

Fornäs, Johan. 2001/2002a. "Yokel Jazz with Yodeling Negroes and Swinging Lapps: Swedish Others 1920–1950." *Black Renaissance* 3.2: 27–47; and in Jostein Gripsrud, ed., *The Aesthetics of Popular Art.* Bergen: Senter for kulturstudier/Program for kulturstudier vid Norges forskningsråd. 175–198.

Fornäs, Johan. 2002b. *Moderna människor. I den svenska jazzens ungdom.*

Gabbard, Krin, ed. 1995a. *Jazz Among the Discourses.* Durham, NC: Duke University Press.

———. 1995b. *Representing Jazz.* Durham, NC: Duke University Press.

Gaines, Kevin. 2000. "Duke Ellington, *Black, Brown, and Beige,* and the Cultural Politics of Race." In Ronald Radano and Philip V. Bohlman, *Music and the Racial Imagination.* Chicago: University of Chicago. 585–602.

Galamian, Ivan. 1962. *Principles of Violin Playing and Teaching*. Englewood Cliffs, NJ: Prentice-Hall.

Garcia, Walter. 1999. *Bim-bom: a contradição sem conflitos de João Gilberto*. São Paulo: Paze Terra.

Garofalo, Reebee. 1993. "Whose World, What Beat: The Transnational Music Industry, Identity, and Cultural Imperialism." *The World of Music* 35.2: 16–32.

Gates, Henry Louis, Jr. 1988. *The Signifying Monkey: A Theory of African-American Literary Criticism*. New York: Oxford University Press.

Geertz, Clifford. 1973. *The Interpretation of Cultures*. New York: Basic Books.

Gennari, John. "Jazz Criticism: Its Development and Ideologies." *Black American Literature Forum* 25.3: 449–521.

Gendron, Bernard. 1989–90. "Jamming at Le Boeuf: Jazz and the Paris Avant-Garde." *Discourse* 12.1: 3–27.

Gerard, Charley. 1998. *Jazz in Black and White: Race, Culture, and Identity in the Jazz Community*. Westport: Praeger.

Giddens, Anthony. 1991. *As consequíncias da modernidade*. São Paulo: Editora da Unesp.

Gioia, Ted. 1988. *The Imperfect Art: Reflections on Jazz and Modern Culture*. New York: Oxford University Press.

———. 1997. *The History of Jazz*. New York and Oxford: Oxford University Press.

Godbolt, Jim. 1985. *A History of Jazz in Britain 1919–50*. London: Quartet.

Goddard, Chris. 1979. *Jazz Away From Home*. New York: Paddington.

Goldblatt, Burt. 1977. *Newport Jazz Festival: The Illustrated History*. New York: Dial Press.

Greene, Marc T. 1923. "Shanghai Cabaret Girl." *Literary Digest* October 23: 25.

Gronow, Pekka. 1981. "The Record Industry Comes to the Orient." *Ethnomusicology* 25.2: 251–84.

Gronow, Pekka, and Ilpo Saunio. 1998. *An International History of the Recording Industry*. Trans. Christopher Moseley. London/New York: Cassell.

Gross, Joan, David McMurray, and Ted Swedenburg. 1994. "Arab Noise and Ramadan Nights: Rai, Rap, and Franco-Maghrebi Identity." *Diaspora: A Journal of Transnational Studies* 3.1 (Spring): 3–37.

Gutstein, Michael H. 1978. *Charlie Parker Omnibook for E Flat Instruments*. Atlantic Music Corp.

Haese, Richard. 1981. *Rebels and Precursors: The Revolutionary Years of Australian Art*. London and Ringwood Victoria: Allen Lane.

Hall, Stuart. 1991. "The Local and the Global: Globalization and Ethnicity." In Anthony D. King, ed., *Culture, Globalization and the World-System*. Binghamton, NY: SUNY-Binghamton. 19–39.

———. 1992. "The West and the Rest: Discourse and Power." In Stuart Hall and Bram Gieben, eds. *Formations of Modernity. Understanding Modern Societies: An Introduction*. Book 1. Cambridge/Milton Keynes: Polity Press/Open University Press. 275–331.

Hamm, Charles. 1995. *Putting Popular Music in Its Place*. Cambridge: Cambridge University Press.

Hannerz, Ulf. 1991. "Scenarios for Peripheral Cultures." In Anthony D. King, ed., *Culture, Globalization and the World-System*. London: The Macmillan Press, 107–28.

Harootunian, Harry. 2000. *Overcome by Modernity: History, Culture, and Community in Interwar Japan*. Princeton: Princeton University Press.

Harris, Max, and John Reed, eds. 1945. *Angry Penguins 1945* (July).

Harris, Max, and Harry Roskolenko, eds. 1946. *Angry Penguins Broadsheet #10—Jazz: Australia. Souvenir Program of Australia's First Jazz Convention* (December).

Harvey, Mark S. 1991. "Jazz and Modernism: Changing Conceptions of Innovation and Tradition." In Reginald T. Buckner and Steven Weiland, eds., *Jazz in Mind: Essays on the History and Meanings of Jazz*. Detroit: Wayne State University Press. 128–47.

Hasse, John Edward. 2000. *Jazz: The First Century*. New York: Harper Collins.

Havens, Thomas R.H. 1987. *Fire Across the Sea: The Vietnam War and Japan 1965–1975*. Princeton: Princeton University Press.

Hei, Ying. 1934. *Diguo de Nu'er*. Shanghai: Kaihua.

Heyward, Michael. 1993. *The Ern Malley Affair*. St Lucia Qld: University of Queensland Press.

Hiraoka, Masaaki. 1976. "Ongakuteki sakka toshite no Fukuzawa Shichirō to Itsuki Hiroyuki." *Kokubungaku—kaishaku to kyōzai no kenkyū* 21.8: 16–20.

Hobsbawm, Eric J. 1993. *The Jazz Scene*. Rev. ed. New York: Pantheon.

———. 1998. "Jazz Comes to Europe." In *Uncommon People: Resistance, Rebellion and Jazz*. New York: The New Press. 265–73.

Hobsbawm, Eric J., and Terence Ranger, eds. 1982. *The Invention of Tradition*. Cambridge: Cambridge University Press.

Hoefer, George. 1966. "Django Reinhardt: The Magnificent Gypsy." *Down Beat* (July 14): 21–25, 60–61.

Holmes, John Clellon. [1953] 1988. *The Horn*. New York: Thunder's Mouth Press.

Hood, Mantle. 1960. "The Challenge of Bi-musicality." *Ethnomusicology* 4: 55–59.

Horricks, Raymond. 1983. *Stéphane Grappelli*. New York: Da Capo Press.

Hubner, Alma. 1945. "Chile Peppers." *Jazz Notes* 57 (October): [1–3]; and 58 (November): [5].

Hughes, Langston. 1956. *I Wonder as I Wander: An Autobiographical Journey*. New York: Rinehart.

Hughes, Phillip S. 1974. "Jazz Appreciation and the Sociology of Jazz." *Journal of Jazz Studies* 1.2 (June): 79–96.

Imamura, Tadasumi. 1990. "Itsuki Hiroyuki." In Kokubungaku henshūbu, eds., *Gendai sakka benran*. Tokyo: Gakutōsha. 22–23.

Itsuki, Hiroyuki. [1966] 1981. *Umi o mite ita Jonii*. Tokyo: Shinchō Bunko.

———. [1966] 1982a. *Saraba Mosukuwa gurentai*. Tokyo: Shinchō Bunko. 8–62.

———. [1966] 1982b. "G.I. Burūsu." In *Saraba Mosukuwa gurentai*. Tokyo: Shinchō Bunko. 64–106.

———. 1972. "Yoake no raugtaimu." In *Hato o utsu*. Tokyo: Shinchō Bunko.

———. 1992. *Furimukeba tango*. Tokyo: Bunshun Bunko.

———. 1995. *Debyū no koro*. Tokyo: Shūeisha.

Jalard, Michel-Claude. 1959. "Django et l'école tsigane du jazz." *Les Cahiers du Jazz* 1: 54–73.

James, Michael, with Howard Rye and Barry Kernfeld. 2002. "Django Reinhardt." In Barry Kernfeld, ed., *The New Grove Dictionary of Jazz*, 2d ed., Vol. 3. New York: MacMillan. 396–97.

Jameson, Fredric, and Masao Miyoshi, eds. 1998. *The Cultures of Globalization.* Durham: Duke University Press.

Jarab, Joseph. 1993. "The Story of the Jazz Section in Czechoslovakia." In Rob Kroes, Robert W. Rydell, and Doeko F.J. Bosscher, eds., *Cultural Transmissions and Receptions: American Mass Culture in Europe.* European Contributions to American Studies 25. Amsterdam: VU University Press. 209–15.

Jazz Yatra Festival. 1982; 1986; 1988. *Jazz Yatra Program Guide.*

Jhaveri, Niranjan. 1985. "Jazz India and Jazz Yatra." *Jazz Educators Journal* 17.3: 18–20.

Johnson, Bruce. 1984. "Graeme Bell at Seventy." *Jazz: The Australasian Contemporary Music Magazine* (Winter/Spring): 8–11.

———. 1986. "Bruce Johnson Comments." *Jazz: The Australasian Contemporary Music Magazine* (Summer/Autumn): 26–27.

———. 1987. *The Oxford Companion to Australian Jazz.* Melbourne: Oxford University Press.

———. 1995. "The Production and Consumption of Jazz in Live Performance in Australia." *Jazzchord* (June/July): 9.

———. 1998. "Doctored Jazz: Early Australian Jazz Journals." *Perfect Beat* 3.4 (January): 26–37.

———. 2000. *The Inaudible Music: Jazz, Gender and Australian Modernity.* Sydney: Currency Press.

Jones, Andrew F. 2001. *Yellow Music: Media Culture and Colonial Modernity in the Chinese Jazz Age.* Durham: Duke University Press.

Jorgensen, John. 1996. "Gypsy Guitar Primer." *Acoustic Guitar* 6 (February): 40–42.

Jost, Ekkehard. 1974. *Free Jazz.* Graz: Universal Edition.

———. 1982. *Jazzmusiker: Materialien zur Soziologie der afro-amerikanischen Musik.* Berlin: Ulstein.

———. 1987. "Europas Jazz 1960–80." *Beitrage zur Jazzforschung* 4. Frankfurt/Main: Fischer.

———. 1993. "Uber das Europaische im europaischen Jazz." *Jazz in Europa: Darmstader Beitrage zur Jazzforschung*, Band 3. Ed. Wolfgang Knauer. Darmstadt: Jazz-Institut Darmstadt.

———. 1997. "Jazz, Musette und Cante Flamenco: Traditionslinien in der Musik der französischen Gitans und Manouches." In *Awosusi 1997*, 15–27.

Kaemmer, John. 1980. "Between the Event and the Tradition: A New Look at Music in Socio-cultural Systems." *Ethnomusicology* 24. 1: 61–74.

Kamiya, Tadataka. 1974. "Saraba Mosukuwa gurentai." In Ōkubo Norio and Kasahara Nobuo, eds., *Gendai shōsetsu jiten.* Tokyo: Shibundō. 28–29.

Kartomi, Margaret. 1981. "The Process and Results of Musical Culture Contact: A Discussion of Terminology and Concepts." *Ethnomusicology* 25: 227–49.

Kartomi, Margaret, and Stephen Blum, eds. 1994. *Music Cultures in Contact: Convergences and Collisions.* Australia Pty. Limited.

Kater, Michael. 1989. "Forbidden Fruit? Jazz in the Third Reich." *American Historical Review* 94 (February): 11–43.

———. 1992. *Different Drummers: Jazz in the Culture of Nazi Germany.* New York: Oxford University Press.

Ke, Zhenghe. 1927. "Zhazi yinyue." *Xin yuechao* 1.5 (December): 16–20.

———. 1932. "Zhazi yinyue de chanye hua." *Yinyue zazhi* 1.10 (February): 1–3.

Keil, Charles. 1994. "Participatory Discrepancies and the Power of Music." In S. Feld and C. Keil, eds., *Music Grooves.* Chicago: University of Chicago Press. 96–108.

Kennedy, Rick. 1994. *Jelly Roll, Bix, and Hoagy: Gennett Studios and the Birth of Recorded Jazz.* Bloomington: Indiana University Press.

Kenney, William Howland. 1993. *Chicago Jazz: A Cultural History.* New York: Oxford University Press.

———. 1999. *Recorded Music in American Life: The Phonograph and Popular Memory, 1890–1945.* New York: Oxford University Press.

Kernfeld, Barry, ed. 2002. *The New Grove Dictionary of Jazz,* 2d ed. 3 vols. New York: Grove's Dictionaries, Inc.

Kiefer, Bruno. 1979. *Música e Dança popular: sua influéncia na música erudita.* Porto Alegre: Editora Movimento.

Kienzle, Rich. 1985. *Great Guitarists.* Facts on File.

Knauer, Wolfram. 1993. *Jazz in Europa: Darmstader Beitrage zur Jazzforschung,* Band 3. Darmstadt: Jazz-Institut Darmstadt.

Koch, E. 1983a. "Doornfontein and Its African Working Class, 1914 to 1935: A Study of Popular Culture in Johannesburg." M.A. thesis. University of the Witwatersrand.

———. 1983b. " 'Without Visible Means of Subsistence': Slumyard Culture in Johannesburg 1918–1940." In B. Bozzoli, ed., *Town and Countryside in the Transvaal.* Johannesburg: Ravan Press. 151–175.

Koepke, George H., Barbara Feallock, and Irving Feller. 1963. "Splinting the Severely Burned Hand." *American Journal of Occupational Therapy* 17: 147–50.

Komashaku, Kimi. 1977. *Zatsumin no tamashi: Itsuki Hiroyuki o dô yomu ka.* Tokyo: Kôdansha.

Koopmans, Rudy. 1975. "The Retarded Clockmaker." *Key Notes: Musical Life in the Netherlands.* Donemus Foundation 1.1: 19–31.

———. 1976. "The Netherlands in the Inter-War Years: Society, Culture and the Arts." *Key Notes: Musical Life in the Netherlands.* Donemus Foundation 3.1: 4–9.

———. 1982. "Composers Voice Special—Misha Mengelberg." *Key Notes: Musical Life in the Netherlands.* Donemus Foundation 16.2: 34–35.

Kraus, Richard C. 1989. *Pianos and Politics in China: Middle-Class Ambitions and the Struggle Over Western Music.* New York: Oxford University Press.

Kristeva, Julia. 1991 [1988]. *Strangers to Ourselves.* New York: Harvester.

"Label Watch: Mosaic Records." 2001. *Jazz Times* (March): 22.

Lang, Ian. [1943?]. *The Background to the Blues.* London: Workers Music Association.

Lapham, Claude. 1936. "China Needs American Bands." *Metronome* July: 13, 39.

Lee, Bill. 1975. "Barney Kessel." In *Jazz Guitarists: Collected Interviews From Guitar Player Magazine.* Saratoga, CA: Guitar Player Productions. 56–59.

Lee, Leo Ou-fan. 1999. *Shanghai Modern: The Flowering of a New Urban Culture in China, 1930–1945.* Cambridge: Harvard University Press.

Levi, Erik. 1994. *Music in the Third Reich.* New York: St. Martin's Press.

Levine, Lawrence. 1993. "Jazz and American Culture." *The Unpredictable Past: Explorations in American Cultural History.* New York: Oxford University Press. 172–88.

Li, Jinhui. 1985. "Wo he Mingyue she." *Wenhua shiliao* 3.4.

Litweiler, John. 1984. *The Freedom Principle: Jazz After 1958.* New York: William Morrow.

Liu, Na'ou. 1930. *Dushi fengjing xian.* Shanghai: Shuimo shudian.

Lock, Graham. 1999. *Blutopia: Visions of the Future and Revisions of the Past in the Work of Sun Ra, Duke Ellington, and Anthony Braxton.* Durham: Duke University Press.

Lomax, Alan. 1950. *Mister Jelly Roll.* New York: Grove.

Lucas, Maria Elizabeth. 2000. "Gaucho Musical Regionalism." *British Journal of Ethnomusicology* 9.1: 41–60.

Lundkvist, Artur. 1933. *Negerkust.* Stockholm: Bonniers.

Mackenzie, Andy. 1999. "The Legacy of Django." In Charles Alexander, ed., *Masters of Jazz Guitar.* London: Balafon Books. 154–61.

Manuel, Peter. 1988. "Popular Music in India: 1901–1986." *Popular Music* 7: 157–76.

Mayer, Günter. 1984. "Popular Music in the GDR." *Journal of Popular Culture* 18.3: 145–58.

Maylam, Paul, and Iain Edwards, eds. 1996. *The People's City: African life in Twentieth-Century Durban.* Portsmouth: Heinemann.

McGregor, Maxine. 1995. *Chris McGregor and the Brotherhood of Breath: My Life with a South African Jazz Pioneer.* Flint, MI: Bamberger Books.

Mello, Maria Ignez. 2000. "Música, Mídia e Novas Identidades." In Rafael J. de Menezes Bastos e Maria Elizabeth Lucas, eds., *Pesquisas Recentes em Estudos Musicais no Mercosul.* Porto Alegre: PPGMUS/UFRGS. 141–51.

Menezes Bastos, Rafael José de. 1999a. "The Origin of Samba as the Invention of Brazil (Why do Songs Have Music?)." *British Journal of Ethnomusicology* 8: 67–96.

———. 1999b. "Músicas latino-americanas, hoje: musicalidade e novas fronteiras." In Rodrigo Torres, ed., *Música Popular en América Latina: Actas del Ilo. Congresso Latinoamericano del IASPM.* Santiago de Chile: FONDART. 17–39.

———. 2000. "Brazilian Popular Music: An Anthropological Introduction." *Antropologia em Primeira-mão* (Social Anthropology Graduate Program of the Federal University of Santa Catarina), vol 40.

Menn, Don, ed. 1992. *Secrets from the Masters: Conversations with Forty Great Guitar Players.* San Francisco: Miller Freeman.

Merriam, Alan P. 1964. *The Anthropology of Music.* Evanston: Northwestern University Press.

Merriam, Alan P., and Raymond Mack. 1960. "The Jazz Community." *Social Forces* (March): 211–22.

Meyer, Leonard. 1967. *Music, the Arts, and Ideas*. Chicago: Chicago University Press.

Middleton, Richard. 1990. *Studying Popular Music*. Milton Keynes: Open University Press.

Miller, Manfred. 1966. "Free Jazz: Eine New Thing Analyse." *Jazz Podium* 15.7: 182–84.

Miller, Mark. 1998. *Such Melodious Racket: The Lost History of Jazz in Canada, 1914–1949*. Toronto: Mercury Press.

Minganti, Franco. 1996. "Intimations on Radical New Jewish Culture: An Agenda to the Music of John Zorn and Don Byron." Paper delivered at the April in Paris Conference: Legacy of African Americans in Europe, Sorbonne, Paris.

Minor, William. 1995. *Unzipped Souls: A Jazz Journey Through the Soviet Union*. Philadelphia: Temple University Press.

Mitchell, Jack. 1985. "Jazz, Art and the Communist Party." *Jazz: The Australasian Contemporary Music Magazine* (Winter/Spring): 16–18.

———. 1988. *Australian Jazz on Record 1925–1980*. Canberra: Australian Government Publishing Service.

Molasky, Michael S. 1999. *The American Occupation of Japan and Okinawa*. London: Routledge.

Monson, Ingrid. 1996. *Saying Something: Jazz Improvisation and Interaction*. Chicago: University of Chicago Press.

Moody, Bill. 1993. *The Jazz Exiles: American Musicians Abroad*. Reno: University of Nevada Press.

Morita, Yuko, ed. *Abe Kaoru 1949–1978*. Tokyo: Bun'yûsha, 1994.

Mortier, Paul. 1955. *Art: Its Origins and Social Function*. Sydney, Current Book Distributors (October).

Mu, Shiying. 1933. *Gongmu*. Shanghai: Xiandai shuju.

———. 1988. "Luotuo, Nicai zhuyizhe yu nüren." In Li Oufan, ed., *Xin ganjue pai xiaoshuo xuan*. Taipei: Yunchen wenhua. 191–97.

Mushiake, Aromu. 1976. "Kyōki o sasō, hakuya no kisetsu." In Bungei Shunjū, eds., *Itsuki Hiroyuki no sekai*. Tokyo: Bungei Shunjūsha. 21–37.

Nettl, Bruno. 1974. "Thoughts on Improvisation: A Comparative Approach." *Musical Quarterly* 60.1: 1–19.

———. 1985. *The Western Impact on World Music: Change, Adaptation, and Survival*. New York: Schirmer Books.

Nabe, Marc-Edouard. 1993. *Nuage*. Paris: Le Dilettante.

Neves, José Maria. 1981. *Música Contemporânea Brasileira*. São Paulo: Ricordi Brasileira.

Nichols, H. Minor. 1955. *Manual of Hand Injuries*. Chicago: The Year Book Publishers.

Nketia, Kwabena. 1974. *The Music of Africa*. New York: W.W. Norton.

Noglik, Bert. 1981. *Jazzwerkstatt international*. Berlin: Verlag Neue Musik Berlin.

Obrecht, Jas, ed. 2000. *Rollin' and Tumblin': The Postwar Blues Guitarists*. San Francisco: Miller Freeman.

Odell, Jay Scott and Robert B. Winans. 2001. "Banjo." In Stanley Sadie, ed., *The New Grove Dictionary of Music and Musicians* (2nd edition), 2: 660–65. London: Macmillan.

Ogren, Kathy J. 1989. *The Jazz Revolution*. New York: Oxford University Press.

Oliver, Paul. 1975. "Jazz is Where You Find It: The European Experience of Jazz." In C.W.E. Bigsby, ed., *Superculture: American Popular Culture and Europe.* London: Paul Elek. 140–51.

———. 1988. "Introduction: Aspects of the South Asia/Western Cross-over." *Popular Music* 6: 119–22.

Ou, Manlang. 1934. "Kelian de jueshi." *Guangzhou yinyue* 3.12 (December): 1–2.

Panish, Jon. 1997. *The Color of Jazz: Race and Representation in Postwar American Culture.* Jackson: University Press of Mississippi.

Paulot, Bruno. 1993. *Albert Mangelsdorff: Gesprache.* Waakirchen: Oreos Verlag.

Pender, Graeme. 1995. "The Eureka Youth League and Its Influence on Melbourne Jazz." *Jazzline: Official Publication of the Victorian Jazz Club Inc.* 18.4 (Summer): 11–27.

Peretti, Burton W. 1997. *Jazz in American Culture.* Chicago: Ivan R. Dee.

Peters, Mike. 1982. "Teach-in: Django Reinhardt." *Sing Out!* 29.1: 12.

Peterson, Richard. 1992. "La fabrication de l'authenticité: la country music." *Actes de la recherche* 93 (juin): 3–19.

Piedade, Acácio Tadeu de C. 1999a. "Música Instrumental Brasileira e Fricção de Musicalidades." In Rodrigo Torres, ed., *Música Popular en América Latina: Actas del Ilo.* Congresso Latinoamericano del IASPM. Santiago de Chile: FONDART. 383–98.

———. 1999b. "São Paulo." In John Shepherd, ed., *The Encyclopedia of Popular Music of the World,* Vol. II. Canada/United Kingdom: Cassell, in press.

Pinckney, Warren R., Jr. 2000. "American Musics: Toward a History of Jazz in Bermuda." *The Musical Quarterly* 84.3 (Fall): 333–71.

Pinheiro, Luiz Roberto M. 1992. "Ruptura e Continuidade na MPB: A Questão da Linha Evolutiva." Dissertação de Mestrado em Antropologia Social, UFSC.

Piras, Marcello. 1992. Liner notes to Gianluigi Trovesi Octet, *From G to G.* Soul Note 121 231.

———. 1994. "Libri & riviste." *Il simosgrafo: Bollettino della S.IS.M.A.* 3.11: 39.

———. 1997. "Africa: il battito cardiaco del mondo." *daQui* (March): 181–94.

———. Forthcoming. *That Old Black Magic: The Worldwide Dissemination of Black Musical Influence.* Boston: Northeastern University Press.

Poiger, Uta G. 2000. "American Music, Cold War Liberalism, and German Identities." In Fehrenbach and Poiger 2000. 127–47.

Pope, Edgar. 1998. "Signifying China: The Exotic in Pre-war Japanese Popular Music." In Tōru Mitsui, ed., *Popular Music: Intercultural Interpretations.* Kanazawa (Japan): Graduate Program in Music, Kanazawa University. 111–20.

Preitano, Massimo. 1994. "Gli albori della concezione tonale: aria, ritornello strumentale e chitarra spagnola nel primo Seicento." *Rivista Italiana di Musicologia* 29.1: 27–88.

Quintero-Rivera, Mareia. 2000. *A cor e o som da nação: a idéia de mestiçagem na crítica musical do Caribe hispânico e do Brasil (1928–1948).* São Paulo: Annablume/FAPESP.

Radano, Ronald M. 1993. *New Musical Figurations: Anthony Braxton's Cultural Crititque.* Chicago: University of Chicago Press.

———. 2000. "Hot Fantasies: American Modernism and the Idea of Black Rhythm." In Ronald Radano and Philip V. Bohlman, eds., *Music and the Racial Imagination.* Chicago: University of Chicago. 459–80.

Ratliff, Ben. 2000. "A Delirium of Gypsy Music Barrels Along in Overdrive." *The New York Times* December 4: E5.

Reily, Suzel Ana. 2000. "Introduction: Brazilian Musics, Brazilian Identities." *British Journal of Ethnomusicology* 9.1: 1–10.

Richardson, Jerry. 1999. "B. B. King: Analysis of the Artist's Evolving Guitar Technique." In Steven C. Tracy, ed., *Write Me a Few of Your Lines: A Blues Reader.* Amherst, MA: University of Massachusetts Press. 282–307.

Rippin, John. 1946. "Editorial." *Jazz Notes* 69 (December): 3.

Roberts, John Storm. 1999. *Latin Jazz: The First of the Fusions, 1880s to Today.* New York: Schirmer Books.

Robertson, Roland. 1992. *Globalization: Social Theory and Global Culture.* London: Sage.

Rogers, J. A. 1997. "Jazz at Home." In Alain Locke, ed., *The New Negro.* New York: Touchstone. 216–24.

Rosen, Steve. 1975. "Mahavishnu John McLaughlin." In *Jazz Guitarists: Collected Interviews From Guitar Player Magazine.* Saratoga, CA: Guitar Player Productions. 72–74.

Rosenberg, Joe. 1993. "Anthony Braxton." *Windplayer* 10.5: 50.

Rycroft, David. 1977. "Evidence of Stylistic Continuity in Zulu 'Town' Music." In *Essays for a Humanist: An Offering to Klaus Wachsman.* New York: Town House Press.

Sachs, Curt. 1933. *Eine Weltgeschichte des Tanzes.* Berlin: Dietrich Reimer A.G.

Saitō, Shinya. 1982. "Kaisetsu." In Itsuki Hiroyuki, *Saraba Mosukuwa gurentai.* Tokyo: Shinchō Bunko. 258–65.

Salazar, Max. 1993. "Alberto Socarás." *Latin Beat* 2.10 (December/January): 26–30.

Sales, Grover. 1984. *Jazz: America's Classical Music.* Englewood Cliffs: Prentice-Hall.

Sanches, Pedro Alexandre. 2000. *Tropicalismo: decadência bonita do samba.* São Paulo: Bomtempo editorial.

Sandroni, Carlos. 2001. *Feitiço decente: transformações do samba no Rio de Janeiro (1917–1933).* Rio de Janeiro: Jorge Zahar.

Sargeant, Winthrop. 1946 [1938]. *Jazz: Hot and Hybrid.* New York: E.P. Dutton.

Schaefer, William. 2003. "Shanghai Savage." In Andrew F. Jones and Nikhil P. Singh, eds., "The Afro-Asian Century," *positions: east asia cultures critique* 11.1 (Spring): 91–133.

Schmitz, Alexander. 1997. "Stilprägende Elemente in der Musik von Django Reinhardt." In *Awosusi 1997,* 29–45.

Schmitz, Alexander, and Peter Maier. 1985. *Django Reinhardt: Sein Leben, Seine Musik, Seine Schallplatten.* Buchendorf: Oreos Verlag.

Schulze, Laurie, Anne Barton White, and Jane D. Brown. 1993. "A Sacred Monster in her Prime: Audience Construction of Madonna as Low-Other." *The Madonna Connection: Representational Politics, Subcultural Identities, and Cultural Theory.* Ed. Cathy Schwichtenberg. Boulder: Westview Press. 15–38.

Schuller, Gunther. 1989. *The Swing Era: The Development of Jazz, 1930–1945.* New York: Oxford University Press.

Shack, William A. 2001. *Harlem in Montmartre: A Paris Jazz Story Between the Great Wars.* Music of the African Diaspora 4. Berkeley: University of California Press.

Shami, Seteney. "Prehistories of Globalization: Circassian Identity in Motion." *Public Culture* 12.1 (2000): 177–204.

Shaughnessy, Mary Alice. 1993. *Les Paul: An American Original.* New York: William Morrow.

Shih, Shu-mei. 2001. *The Lure of the Modern: Writing Modernism in Semicolonial China, 1917–1937.* Berkeley: University of California Press.

Silverman, Carol. 2000. "Rom (Gypsy) Music." In Timothy Rice, James Porter, and Chris Goertzen, ed., *The Garland Encyclopedia of World Music,* Vol. 8: New York: Garland Publishing. 270–93.

Škvorecky, Josef. 1988. "Red Music." In *Talkin' Moscow Blues.* Ed. Sam Solecki. New York: The Ecco Press. 83–97.

Smith, Geoffrey. 1987. *Stéphane Grappelli.* London: Pavillion.

Spence, Jonathan. 1990. *The Search for Modern China.* New York: W.W. Norton.

Staley, S. James. 1936. "Is It True What They Say About China?" *Metronome* (December): 17, 47–48.

Starr, S. Frederick. 1994. *Red & Hot: The Fate of Jazz in the Soviet Union.* Rev. ed. New York: Limelight.

———. 1995. *Bamboula! The Life and Times of Louis Moreau Gottschalk.* New York: Oxford University Press.

Steele, Tom. 1997. *The Emergence of Cultural Studies 1945–65: Cultural Politics, Adult Education and the English Question.* London: Lawrence and Wishart.

Stein, Harry. 1985. "If These Walls Could Only Speak." *Jazz: The Australasian Contemporary Music Magazine* (Winter/Spring): 22–26.

———. 1994. *A Glance Over an Old Left Shoulder.* Sydney: Hale & Iremonger.

Stewart, Rex. 1991. *Boy Meets Horn.* Ed. Claire P. Gordon. Ann Arbor: University of Michigan Press.

Stokes, Martin. 1994. *Ethnicity, Identity and Music: The Musical Construction of Place.* Oxford & Providence USA: Berg.

Stovall, Tyler. 1996. *Paris Noir: African Americans in the City of Light.* Boston: Houghton Mifflin.

Sudhalter, Richard M. 1999. *Lost Chords: White Musicians and Their Contribution to Jazz, 1915–1945.* New York: Oxford University Press.

Tang, Yating. 1998. "Shanghai youtai nanmin shequ de yinyue shenghuo." *Yinyue yishu: Shanghai yinyue xueyuan xuebao* 4: 7–13, 28.

Taylor, William "Billy." 1999 [1986]. "Jazz: America's Classical Music." Reprinted in Robert Walser, ed., *Keeping Time: Readings in Jazz History.* New York: Oxford University Press. 327–32.

Taylor, Timothy D. 1997. *Global Pop: World Musics, World Markets.* New York: Routledge.

Tinhorão, José Ramos. 1974. *Pequena História da Música Popular: da modinha à canção de protesto.* Petrópolis: Vozes.

———. 1998. *História social da música popular brasileira.* São Paulo: Editora 34.

Tra, Gijs. 1978a. "Instant Composers Pool: A Decade of Musical and Political Innovation." *Key Notes: Musical Life in the Netherlands* 7.1: 7–9.

————. 1978b. "De Voldharding, an Offbeat Jazz Group or a Crazy Band of Windplayers." *Key Notes: Musical Life in the Netherlands* 7.1: 10–12.

————. 1978c. "Herman de Wit's Workshops." *Key Notes: Musical Life in the Netherlands.* Donemus Foundation 7.1: 13–14.

Tubiana, Raoul. 1988. "Movements of the Fingers." *Medical Problems of Performing Artists* 3.4 (December): 123–28.

————. 2000. "Anatomy of the Hand and Upper Limb." In *Medical Problems of the Instrumentalist Musician.* Ed. Raoul Tubiana and Peter C. Amadio. London: Martin Dunitz. 5–53.

Tubiana, Raoul, and Philippe Chamagne. 1988. "Functional Anatomy of the Hand." *Medical Problems of Performing Artists* 3.3 (September): 83–87.

Tucker, Sherrie B. 2001 *Swing Shift: "All-Girl" Bands of the 1940s.* Durham: Duke University Press.

Turner, C. Ian. 1946. "Editorial." *Jazz Notes* 65 (June): 3.

Turner, Ian. 1982. *Room to Manoeuvre: Writings on History, Politics, Ideas and Play.* Victoria: Drummond Publishing.

Uekusa, Jin'ichi. 1976. "Yoku suingu suru naa, kore wa." In Bungei Shunjū, eds., *Itsuki Hiroyuki no sekai.* Tokyo: Bungei Shunjūsha. 38–52.

van der Bliek, Rob. 1991. "Wes Montgomery: A Study of Coherence in Jazz Improvisation." *Jazzforschung* 23: 117–78.

van Eyle, William, ed. 1981. *The Dutch Jazz and Blues Discography, 1916–80.* Het Spectrum B.V.

Veloso, Caetano. 1997. *Verdade Tropical.* São Paulo: Companhia das Letras. Published in English: *Tropical Truth.* New York: Knopf, 2002.

Vianna, Hermano. 1995. *O mistério do samba.* Rio de Janeiro: Jorge Zahar/Editora da UFRJ.

Walser, Robert. 1993. *Running with the Devil: Power, Gender and Madness in Heavy Metal Music.* Hanover: University Press of New England.

————, ed. 1999. *Keeping Time: Readings in Jazz History.* New York: Oxford University Press.

Ward, Geoffrey C., and Ken Burns. 2000. *Jazz: A History of America's Music.* New York: Alfred Knopff.

Weinstein, Norman C. 1992. *A Night in Tunisia: Imaginings of Africa in Jazz.* Metuchen, NJ, and London: The Scarecrow Press.

Whitehead, Kevin. 1998. *New Dutch Swing.* New York: Billboard Books.

Whiteoak, John. 1993. "From Jim Crow to Jazz: Imitation African-American Improvisatory Musical Practices in Pre-Jazz Australia." *Perfect Beat* 1.3 (July): 50–74.

Wilkinson, Irén Kertész. 2001. " 'Gypsy' Music." In Stanley Sadie, ed., *The New Grove Dictionary of Music and Musicians,* 2nd ed., Vol. 10. London: MacMillan. 613–20.

Williams, Linda F. 1997. " 'Straight-Fashioned Melodies': The Transatlantic Interplay of American Music in Zimbabwe." *American Music* 15.3: 285–304.

Williams, Martin. 1993. *The Jazz Tradition.* 2nd rev. ed. New York: Oxford University Press.

Williams, Michael. 1981. *The Australian Jazz Explosion.* Sydney: Angus & Robertson.

Williams, Patrick. 1991. *Django Reinhardt.* Paris: Éditions du Limon.

Wilmer, Valerie. 1970. *Jazz People*. London: Allison & Busby.

Wilson, John S. 1966. *Jazz: The Transition Years, 1940–1960*. New York: Appleton-Century-Crofts.

Wilson, Rob, and Wimal Dissanayake, eds. 1996. *Global/Local: Cultural Production & the Transnational Imaginary*. Durham: Duke University Press.

Wisnik, José Miguel. 1977. *O coro dos contrários: a música em torno da semana de 22*. São Paulo: Duas cidades.

Wong, K.C. 2000. *Shidai qu de liuguang suiyue*. Hong Kong: Joint Publishing.

Xiao, Youmei. 1934. "Yinyue de shili." *Yinyue jiaoyu* 3 (March): 9–13.

Zenni, Stefano. 1996. "George Russell e la 'Follia' rivisitata." *Musica Jazz* 11: 50–52.

Zhdanov, Andrei. [1934] 1992. "Speech to the Congress of Soviet Writers." Sections reprinted in Charles Harrison and Paul Wood, eds., *Art in Theory 1900–1990: An Anthology of Changing Ideas*. Oxford: Blackwell. 409–12.

Zwerin, Mike. 1985. *La Tristesse de Saint Louis: Swing Under the Nazis*. London: Quartet.

———. 2000. "Jazz in Europe." In Bill Kirchner, ed., *The Oxford Companion to Jazz*. New York: Oxford University Press. 534–47.

Internet Sites

Ornette Coleman website <www.harmolodic.com>.

Europe Jazz Network <http://www.ejn.it/>.

European Free Improvisation Pages <www.shef.ac.uk/misc/rec/ps/efi/index.html>.

Reinhardt, Django. 1938. <http://www.lobsterfilms.com/loax04.htm> (July 5, 2001).

Rumos Itaú cultural Música Project <http://www.itaucultural.org.br>.

Discography

Brown, Marion. 1968. *Gesprachsfetzen*. Calig-Verlag CAL 30601, 1968.

———. 1970. *Afternoon of a Georgia Faun*. ECM 1004 ST.

Carter, James. 2000. *Chasin' the Gypsy*. Atlantic 83304.

Cherry, Don, and Jon Appleton. 1970. *Human Music*. Flying Dutchman FDS 121.

¡Cubanismo!. 2000. *Mardi Gras Mambo*. Hannibal 1441.

De Voldharding. 1992. *Orkest deVoldharding, 1972–1992*. NM Classics 92021.

Divya. 1987. *Madras Café*. CBS Gramophone Records and Tapes (India) Ltd.

Dixon, Bill. 1980. *Bill Dixon in Italy, Volume One*. Soul Note 121008.

Dolphy, Eric. 1960. *Far Cry*. Prestige NJLP 8270.

———. 1964a. *Eric Dolphy in Holland*. ICP 015.

———. 1964b. *Last Date*. Limelight 86013; Fontana 822226; and EmArcy 510124.

Gabrieli, Giovanni, Andrea Gabrieli, and Giuseppe Guami. 1979. *Canzoni da Sonare*. EMI 63141.

Gordon, Dexter. 1969. *Live at Amsterdam Paradiso*. Catfish 5C199–24336t; Affinity AFFD 27.

Harper, Billy. 1971. *On Tour in Europe*. Black Saint BSR 0001.

Instant Composers Pool. 1984, 1986. *Two Programs: The ICP Orchestra Performs Nichols-Monk.* ICP 026.

Jaikishan, Shankar. 1968. *Raga-Jazz Style.* Gramophone Company of India, Ltd., ECSD 2377.

Jazz Yatra Sextet. 1981. *Sangam.* Elgeistein Musikproduktion, ES 2016.

Jazz Workshop. 1962. *Jazz Workshop Concert, Ruhrfestspiele 1962.* Columbia C83342.

Jazz Workshop Ensemble. 1966. *Jazz Workshop Ensemble.* NDR 629904.

Jost, Ekkehard. *Weimar Ballads.* Fish Music FM 005.

Lagréne, Biréli. 2001. *Gypsy Project.* Dreyfus Jazz FDM 36626.

Lang, Eddie. 1927. "A Little Love, A Little Kiss" (Matrix W 80941-D). *Eddie Lang: Guitar Virtuoso.* Yazoo 1059.

Li, Jinhui. 1928. "Tebie kuaiche." Shanghai dazhong shuju.

McLaughlin, John. 1975. *Shakti.* Columbia, PC 34162; CK 467095.

McPhee, Joe. 1970. *Underground Railroad.* Hat hut hat A.

Mengelberg, Misha. 1966. *The Misja Mengelbert Quintet as heard at the Newport Jazz Festival.* Artone M GOS 9467.

Murray, Sunny. 1966. *Sunny Murray, Hommage to Africa.* BYG-Actuel France 529303.

Nelson, Willie. 1999. *Night and Day.* Free Falls Entertainment FF 7002.

New York Art Quartet. 1964. *New York Art Quartet.* ESP Disk 1004–2.

Reinhardt, Django. 1928a. "Miss Columbia" (Matrix H 966-B). *Intégrale Django Reinhardt: The Complete Django Reinhardt Volume 1 (1928–34).* Frémaux & Associés FA 301.

———. 1928b. "Moi Aussi" (Matrix H 968-A). *Intégrale Django Reinhardt: The Complete Django Reinhardt Volume 1 (1928–34).* Frémaux & Associés FA 301.

———. 1937a. "A Little Love, A Little Kiss" (Matrix OLA 1716–1). *The Complete Django Reinhardt and Quintet of the Hot Club of France Swing/HMV Sessions 1936–1948.* Mosaic MD6-190.

———. 1937b. "Sweet Georgia Brown" (Matrix OLA 2220–1). *The Complete Django Reinhardt and Quintet of the Hot Club of France Swing/HMV Sessions 1936–1948.* Mosaic MD6-190.

———. 1938. "It Had To Be You" (Matrix DTB 3533–1). *Parisian Swing: Django Reinhardt & Stéphane Grappelli with The Quintet of the Hot Club of France.* Avid AMSC648.

———. 1998. *Django With His American Friends.* DRG 8493.

———. 1999. *The Complete Django Reinhardt and Quintet of the Hot Club of France Swing/HMV Sessions 1936–1948.* Mosaic MD6-190.

Russell, George, and the Living Time Orchestra. 1989. *The London Concert.* Label Bleu LBLC 6527/8.

Trovesi, Gianluigi. 1978. *Baghét.* Dischi dela Quercia Q28008.

———. 1981. *Cinque Piccole Storie.* Dischi dela Quercia Q28010.

———. 1999. *Around Small Fairy Tales.* Soul Note 121341.

Trovesi, Gianluigi, Nontet. 1999. *Round About a Midsummer's Dream.* ENJA 9384.

Trovesi, Gianluigi, Octet. 1992. *From G to G.* Soul Note 121231.

———. 1997. *Les Hommes Armés.* Soul Note 121311.

Trovesi, Gianluigi, and Gianni Coscia. 1995. *Radici.* Egea SCA 050.

van Baaren, Kees. 1972. *Musica per orchestra (1965/66)*. Donemus Audio-Visual Series 7273/2.

van Delden, Ate. 1986. *Jazz and Hot Dance in the Netherlands, 1910–1950*, v. 13. Harlequin Records, HQ 2022.

Various artists. 1994. *Bulgarie—Musique du pays Chope: Anthologie de la musique bulgare vol. 1*. Chant du Monde LDX 274 970.

———. 1984. *Jazz and Hot Dance in India—1926–1944*. Harlequin HQ 2013.

———. 1999a. *The Cuban Danzón: Before There Was Jazz*. Arhoolie Folklyric 7032.

———. 1999b. *Freedom Blues: South African Jazz Under Apartheid*. Music Club 50095.

———. 2000. *Rough Guide to South African Jazz*. World Music Network 1045.

———. 2001. *Django Reinhardt NY Festival: Live At Birdland*. Division One/Atlantic 83498.

Vignola, Frank. 2001. *Blues for a Gypsy*. Acoustic Disc 43.

Waldron, Mal. 1969. *Free at Last*. ECM 1001.

———. 1971. *Black Glory*. ENJA 2004 ST.

Filmography

Brown, Sidney, and Eugene Enrico. 1999. *Jazz in Japan*. Early Music Television.

Burns, Ken. 2000. *Jazz*. Florentine Films.

France, Chuck. 1986. *Jazz in Exile*. Rhapsody Films.

Hylkema, Hans. 1992. *Last Date: Eric Dolphy*. Netherlands Production Rhapsody Films.

McTurk, Craig. 1999. *Tokyo Blues: Jazz and Blues in Japan*.

Interviews

Christopher Bakriges:
Bennink, Han. July 1997, Toronto, Ontario.
Szwed, John. April 1995, Middletown, Connecticut.
Tchicai, John. April 1999, Brattleboro, Vermont.

Christopher Ballantine:
Beusen, Tommy. April 28, 1986, London.
Bikitsha, Doc. November 24, 1986, Johannesburg.
Makanya, Lindi. February 13, 1987, Soweto.
Mocumi, Ernest. June 2, 1984, Soweto.
Oliphant, Babsy. May 13, 1987, Johannesburg.
Petersen, Louis Radebe. February 2, 1984, Johannesburg.
Phillips, James. April 8, 1986, London.
Pretorius, Marjorie. October 18, 1987, Johannesburg.
Rezant, Peter. June 3, 1984, Riverlea.

Raúl A. Fernández:
del Puerto, Carlos. May 29, 1999.
López, Israel "Cachao." January 24–25, 1994, Miami (with Anthony Brown).

Flynn, Frank Emilio. December 18, 1999, Havana, Cuba.

Valdés, Bebo. September 20–21, 2000, Stockholm, Sweden.

Bruce Johnson:

Audio and videotapes and transcripts (except Blake 8/14/89; and notes of conversations with Roger Bell 2/11/02; Blake 9/11/01; and Haesler 2/15/02) are available in the Australian Jazz Archive (AJA). A complete list of its oral history holdings can be accessed through www.screensound.gov.au.

Bell, Graeme. February 16, 1989, Sydney.

Bell, Roger. December 28, 1988, Sydney; February 11, 2002, Sydney/Melbourne (telephone).

Blake, Audrey. August 14, 1989, Sydney; September 11, 2001, Sydney.

Dallwitz, Dave. January 25, 1982, Adelaide; December 28, 1988, Sydney.

Gray, Bruce. January 27, 1982, Adelaide.

Haesler, Bill. February 15, 2002, Sydney; February 18, 2002 (correspondence).

Johnson, Frank. December 28, 1988, Sydney.

Pearce, Ian. May 15, 1984, Hobart; December 28, 1988, Sydney.

Pickering, Tom. May 16, 1984, Hobart.

Polites, Nick. December 28, 1988, Sydney.

Roberts, Don "Pixie." December 28, 1988, Sydney.

Stein, Harry. February 15, 1989, Sydney.

Wright, Bob. January 24, 1982, Adelaide.

Warren R. Pinckney, Jr.

Banks, Louis. March 3, 1988.

Fernandes, Tony. February 25, 1988

Gonsalves, Braz. March 5, 1988.

Jhaveri, Niranjan. March 5, 1988.

Linda Williams:

Unless otherwise noted, all interviews were conducted in Harare, Zimbabwe.

Chabuka, Christopher. March 3, 1992; October 19, 1992 (Kariba); November 20, 1993.

Chakanyuka, Andrew. April 23, 1992; June 2, 1992; September 13, 1992; September 20, 1992.

Chifunyise, Stephen. January 17, 1992; November 2, 1992; December 12, 1993.

Gwanzura, Samuel Banana. May 7, 1992.

Lannas, Michael. February 9, 1992; October 14, 1992; November 6, 1992.

Lunga, Paul. October 29, 1992 (Bulawayo); November 14, 1992; August 2, 1993.

Makaya, Timothy. June 16, 1992; June 23, 1992.

Mandishona, Gibson. March 1, 1992; August 7, 1992; November 14, 1993.

Mapango, Nelson. February 2, 1992; June 14, 1992; August 3, 1992.

Maraire, Dumisani. November 4, 1992.

Marshall, Cleveland. June 10, 1992; September 15, 1992; December 1, 1993.

Marumahoko, Jonah. April 4,1992; May 9, 1992; July 26, 1992.

Mbirimi, Friday. October 9, 1992.

Mhlanga, Louis. January 26, 1992.

Mhungu, Jacob. April 9, 1992; June 23, 1992; September 4, 1992; December 9, 1993.

Mlonyeni, Max. February 11, 1992; May 10, 1992.

Papas, Johnny. February 26, 1992; August 6, 1992.

Paul, Bryan. March 30, 1992; May 1, 1992; November 16, 1993.

Shasha, Jethro. January 30, 1992; April 8, 1992; April 22, 1992; July 19, 1992.

Tutani, Kookie. March 5, 1992.

Tutani, Simangaliso. January 30, 1992; March 5, 1992; March 12, 1992.

CONTRIBUTORS

E. TAYLOR ATKINS is Associate Professor of History at Northern Illinois University, and has held visiting appointments at the University of California-Berkeley, the University of Iowa, and the University of Arkansas. His publications include *Blue Nippon: Authenticating Jazz in Japan* (Duke University Press, 2001), and (with Katharine C. Purcell) "Korean *P'ansori* and the Blues: Art for Communal Healing" (*East-West Connections: Review of Asian Studies*, 2002).

CHRISTOPHER G. BAKRIGES received the Ph.D. in ethnomusicology from York University in Toronto, with a dissertation on African American musical avant-gardism, and teaches at Elms College. He has conducted fieldwork on the cultural role of improvisation in the Republic of China, Turkey, Pakistan, and India. He is also a pianist and composer performing with his own groups Ensemble and Quarter 'Til the End of Time (Q'TET).

CHRISTOPHER BALLANTINE is the L. G. Joel Professor of Music at the University of Natal, in Durban, South Africa, and a Fellow of the University of Natal. His publications explore issues in the fields of popular music studies, musicology, and ethnomusicology. His books include *Music and Its Social Meanings* (Gordon & Breach), and *Marabi Nights: Early South African Jazz and Vaudeville* (Ravan Press and Ohio University Press). Recent journal articles have appeared in *Popular Music* and *Ethnomusicology*.

RAÚL A. FERNÁNDEZ is Professor in the School of Social Sciences at the University of California, Irvine. His research has focused on economic and cultural transactions between the United States and Latin America. A Fulbright Fellow, Dr. Fernández serves as Curator for an exhibit-in-progress at the Smithsonian Institution on Latin music, and has published essays on Celia Cruz, Cachao, and Mongo Santamaría.

JOHAN FORNÄS is Professor at the Department of Culture Studies and Director of the Advanced Cultural Studies Institute (ACSIS) at Linköping University in Norrköping, Sweden. As a musicologist and media researcher, he has done research on popular music, youth culture, media consumption and the Internet. His publications include *Cultural Theory and Late Modernity* (Sage, 1995), *In Garageland: Rock, Youth and Modernity* (Routledge, 1995), and *Digital Borderlands: Cultural Studies of Identity and Interactivity on the Internet* (Peter Lang, 2002).

BENJAMIN GIVAN is a doctoral candidate in music theory at Yale University. His dissertation is on the music of Django Reinhardt. He has published articles in *Current Musicology* and *Annual Review of Jazz Studies*.

BRUCE JOHNSON is Associate Professor in the School of English, University of New South Wales, Sydney, where he lectures on popular cultures from the Renaissance to the present day. He has written on popular music, cultural politics, and Australian studies, including

277

The Oxford Companion to Australian Jazz, and *The Inaudible Music,* a study of the connections between jazz, gender, and Australian modernity. He is active in music and record production, has worked in arts administration, research and policy formation, and was the prime mover in the establishment of the government funded Australian Jazz Archives. He is also an award-winning radio broadcaster and producer, and performs regularly as a jazz musician.

ANDREW F. JONES is Associate Professor of Chinese in the Department of East Asian Languages and Cultures at the University of California, Berkeley. He is the author of *Yellow Music: Media Culture and Colonial Modernity in the Chinese Jazz Age* (Duke University Press, 2001) and *Like a Knife: Ideology and Genre in Contemporary Chinese Popular Music* (Cornell East Asia Series, 1992, 1997); and co-editor (with Nikhil P. Singh) of "The Afro-Asian Century," *positions: east asia cultures critique* 11.1 (Spring 2003).

MICHAEL MOLASKY is Associate Professor and Graduate Studies Director in the Department of Asian Languages and Literatures at the University of Minnesota. He is author of *The American Occupation of Japan and Okinawa: Literature and Memory* (Routledge, 1999), and co-editor (with Steve Rabson) of *Southern Exposure: Modern Japanese Literature from Okinawa* (University of Hawai'i Press, 2000). He is currently conducting research for a book on representations of jazz in postwar Japanese culture.

ACÁCIO TADEU DE CAMARGO PIEDADE is professor of music at the State University of Santa Catarina, Brazil, a Ph.D. student in social anthropology at the Federal University of Santa Catarina, and also a jazz pianist/composer. His principal fields of research are Brazilian music, and the musics of Amazonian indigenous societies. His essays have appeared in *Horizontes Antropológicos, Musica Popular en America Latina* (ed. Rodrigo Torres), *Música, Cultura e Sociedade: Investigações Recentes em Estudos Musicais no Mercusul* (eds. Maria Elisabeth Lucas and Rafael José de Menezes Bastos), and *The Encyclopedia of Popular Music of the World* (ed. John Shepherd).

WARREN R. PINCKNEY, Jr., teaches African American music, the history of jazz, theory, and composition at California State University, Chico. He has also directed a Latin jazz and salsa band. Dr. Pinckney has conducted field research in the Anglophone and Hispanic Caribbean regions as well as in Asia. His recent publications include "Toward a History of Jazz in Bermuda," *The Musical Quarterly* 84.3 (Fall 2000): 333–71.

S. FREDERICK STARR is Senior Research Fellow at the Foreign Policy Institute of the Paul H. Nitze School of Advanced International Studies, Chairman of the Central Asia-Caucasus Institute, and pro-tem Rector of the University of Central Asia. He is a leading specialist on the society and politics of Central Asia, including Afghanistan, as well as Russian politics and foreign policy, U.S. policy in Eurasia, and the regional politics of oil. Professor Starr also leads the Louisiana Repertory Jazz Ensemble, which performs New Orleans jazz from the 1920s and 1930s on period instruments.

LINDA F. WILLIAMS received her Ph.D. in Ethnomusicology with major concentrations in Jazz and African music from Indiana University, and is currently Associate

Professor of Music and African American Studies at Bates College in Lewiston, Maine, where she teaches courses on Black Women Musicians and Hip Hop Feminism, Music of the African Diaspora, and Ethnomusicology Research Methods, and conducts the Bates College Steel Pan Ensemble. She serves on the National Endowment of the Humanities Panel, the International Jazz Resource Institute, and the Lionel Hampton Scholarship Adjudicators' Advisory Board. As recipient of a Fulbright Scholar Grant (2003–04), she will research the impact of jazz on musical cultures in Harare and Cape Town. Her anthology *African American Women Musicians and Black Feminism* will be published by University of Illinois Press in 2003, and her articles appear in *American Music, International Jazz Archives Journal,* and *Readings in African Diaspora Music.*

STEFANO ZENNI, Italian musicologist, is President of the Società Italiana di Musicologia Afroamericana, and artistic director of Metastasio Jazz in Prato and a classical concert series in Pescara. He teaches jazz history at Bologna Conservatory and Analysis at Siena Jazz Workshops. He has written books on Louis Armstrong, Herbie Hancock, and Charles Mingus, and edited books on Miles Davis and Louis Armstrong. Zenni's essays on jazz history have also appeared in several music magazines and *The New Grove Dictionary of Jazz* (2nd edition). He was nominated for a Grammy award for liner notes on Mingus.

INDEX